PUBLISHMENTS, MARRIAGES, BIRTHS AND DEATHS

— FROM THE —

EARLIER RECORDS

— OF —

GORHAM, MAINE

Compiled by

Marquis F. King
President of the Maine Genealogical Society

HERITAGE BOOKS
2013

HERITAGE BOOKS
AN IMPRINT OF HERITAGE BOOKS, INC.

Books, CDs, and more—Worldwide

For our listing of thousands of titles see our website
at
www.HeritageBooks.com

A Facsimile Reprint
Published 2013 by
HERITAGE BOOKS, INC.
Publishing Division
100 Railroad Ave. #104
Westminster, Maryland 21157

Copyright © 1897 Maine Genealogical Society

— Publisher's Notice —
In reprints such as this, it is often not possible to remove blemishes from the original. We feel the contents of this book warrant its reissue despite these blemishes and hope you will agree and read it with pleasure.

International Standard Book Numbers
Paperbound: 978-0-7884-1815-0
Clothbound: 978-0-7884-6965-7

Inscriptions on Monument:

South Side.

This town was incorporated by the name of Gorham Oct. 30, 1764.

Captain John Gorham for whom town was named was born in Benefield Northamptonshire Eng. where he was baptised Jan. 28, 1621. He died at Swansea, Mass. Feb. 5, 1676 of disease resulting from exposure in the expeditions against the Narragansett Indians in December 1675.

The following is an extract from a letter written by him October 1 1675 to Much honored Gov. Winslow: "For my own part, I shall be ready to serve God and the country so long as I have life and health."

West Side.

Gorham is one of the seven townships granted by Gen. Court, in the year 1732 to the Narragansett Soldiers on a division of the property, among the original Grantees, this town was assigned to Capt. John Gorham & 119 others and was then called Narragansett No. 7.

INTRODUCTORY.

IN the autumn of 1895 Col. Fred^k N. Dow representing the publishers of the Portland *Evening Express*, recognizing a growing interest in Historical and Genealogical research, concluded to devote a column or two each week to "Notes and Queries" on these subjects, and invited the compiler to edit the same. To insure a continuity of interest, the vital statistics were carefully copied from the early records of the town of Gorham, Me., arranged in alphabetical order and made a part of each issue.

Linotype machines are used in the composition of the *Express*, and by the courtesy of the publishers we were permitted to make use of the setting after it had been stereotyped for the paper. As often as a signature of eight pages was complete, one hundred impressions were taken and the type returned to the melting pot. This volume, somewhat an oddity in book typography, is the result.

The proprietors' records of Narragansett No. 7, or Gorhamtown as it was often called, are not now in the possession of the officers of Gorham, and one or more volumes of the town records, covering the years 1770 to 1803 inclusive are also missing.

It is evident that Judge Pierce in writing his admirable history of Gorham had access to both proprietors' and town records for he makes no mention of their loss, although he regrets that "this interest had not been earlier excited, while fuller records and the actors themselves in these proceedings were accessible."

We therefore conclude that subsequent to 1862 — the date of Judge Pierce's publication—there was a wholesale removal of books from the town clerk's office, and the town left for several years with few records bearing dates prior to the present century. The loss was unaccountable and the mystery not lessened by the return, four or five years ago, of the two oldest volumes of town records express from Boston, consignor unknown.

These old books are in good condition, bound in untanned leather and the writing for the most part perfectly legible. The oldest book commences with the record of the first town meeting. It contains a few records of intentions of marriage and marriages but is mostly records of the transactions of the town. The second volume was opened by Capt. Wentworth Stuart, town clerk, with his own family record, and our compilation is largely from this book, but including all of the vital statistics in both volumes. The next oldest book now at the clerk's office, was opened in 1804, evidently taking up the vital statistics where Volume II leaves off; we conclude, therefore, that the missing books contain few family records.

ABSTRACTS FROM VOLUME I.

On the seventh day of February, 1765, by warrant from Stephen Longfellow, Esq., John Phinney summoned the qualified voters of the town of Gorham to appear at the meeting house on Monday, the eighteenth day of February, at ten o'clock in the forenoon, to choose all such officers as are required by law to manage the affairs of the town.

GORHAM, February 18, 1765.

At a Town meeting Leagually warnd met at time & place & past the following Votes: —

1st Voted Captn John Phinney, Moderator.

2dly Voted Amos Whitney, Town Clerk.

3dly Voted to Choose three Selectmen.

4thly Voted Mr. Benjn Skillings, Amos Whitney & Joseph Weston, Selectmen for said Town.

5thly Voted Benjn Stevens, Constable.

6thly Voted Hart Williams & William Cotten, Tythingmen.

Amos Whitney, Town Clerk.

At the annual town meeting held March 12th, 1765, officers were elected as follows: —

Capt. Briant Morton, Moderator.
Amos Whitney, Town Clerk.
Benj. Skillings, Capt. Briant Morton and Amos Whitney, Selectmen.
Elder Edmund Phinney, Treasurer.
Saml Crocket, Constable and Collector.
Edmund Phinney and Hart Williams, Wardens.
James Gilkey & William Cotton, Tythingmen.
Edmund Phinney, John Barnal, Joseph Brown and William Haskell, Surveyors of Highways. Wentworth Stuart's name added at an adjourned meeting.
William McLallen, Eliphlet Watson, John Phinney, Jr. and Benjn Stevens, Fence Viewers.
James McLallen, James Mosher, James Irish and James Phinney, Field Drivers.
James Mosher and Nathaniel Whitney, Hog Reeves. The hogs to run at large being yoked and ringed.
Capt. Briant Morton, Wentworth Stuart and Ebenezer Murch, Surveyors of Lumber.
Joseph Weston and Solomon Lombard Esq. Lot Layors.
Seth Harding, Culler of Staves.
Johnathan Freeman, Preserver of Moose and Deer.
Jacob Hamblen, Pound Keeper.

At a meeting nine days later the following votes were passed:
For the support of the gospel, sixty-six pounds, thirteen shillings and four pence.
For schools, forty pounds.
To clear and repair the roads, one hundred and eighty pounds.
That each man have four shillings per day, and three and four pence for each yoke of oxen per day. Boys from 12 to 16 one and a penny and three farthings per day. Carts and plows one shilling per day.

It was at the same time voted to build a pound forty feet square and five pounds six shillings and eight pence was appropriated for that purpose.

It was also voted to give six pence per pound for gathering the taxes.

At a subsequent meeting it was voted to accept the high ways laid out by the Proprietors for town roads.

Voted to and concurred with the Church in their sending out for a minister.

Voted Solomon Lombard Esq. to serve for and represent this town at a great and General Court, convened at Boston.

Voted February 10, 1766 "to concur with the Church to give Mr.

Pelatiah Tingley a Call to Settle with us in the work of the ministry as a Congregational Minister."

At the Annual Meeting 1766 no change was made in the principal officers, except that Edmund Phinney was elected Selectman in place of Capt. Morton.

July 17, 1766, the town voted to send Deacon Eliphalet Watson after a learned "Orthodox Congregational Minister" and that he shall engage him for eight Sabbaths, and that Elder Edm^d Phinney, Solomon Lombard and Amos Whitney be a committee to give instructions to the town messenger to introduce a candidate for settlement in the work of the gospel among us.

Sept. 27, 1766, a call with twelve articles, for a meeting on the 29th, was convened, the third article being to see if the town will send a messenger for a learned orthodox Presbyterian minister to preach the gospel to us on probation for eight Sabbaths. The 12th article being to see if the town will vote that the "Quakers & Anabaptists & Antipedobaptists shall be excused from ministerial Taxes". Both of the above named articles and nearly all of the others named in the call were dismissed.

Nov. 3, 1766, the town voted to employ Mr. Josiah Thacher to preach the gospel to us as a probationer for three months if he engages to return to us, and thirty pounds was voted for the support of the gospel for the ensuing year.

March 2, 1767, it was again voted to send out after a minister to preach the gospel to us, and Elder Phinney was chosen as a messenger.

At the annual meeting the officers of last year were re-elected.

June 1 the town voted to concur with the church in giving Mr. Josiah Thacher a call, that his salary be eighty pounds yearly while he remains our minister and that he have one hundred pounds lawful money, settlement. At same meeting it was voted not to remit Mr. Rich's ministerial taxes.

At the annual meeting in 1768, Solomon Lombard was chosen Moderator; Amos Whitney, Town Clerk; Jacob Hamblen, Treasurer and Hugh McLallen, Edmund Phinney and Joseph Cates, Selectmen.

The Selectmen to direct where the school shall be kept and to employ Mr. John Green for Schoolmaster.

At a meeting in May it was at first voted not to send a representative, but that was reconsidered and it was "voted and agreed on that the Representative Solomon Lombard, Esq. shall be paid the customary wages allowed in this government to Representative for the service for and during the May Sessions, be it longer or shorter, and for the remainder of his service to have the one half of what shall be obtained by the Petition now Lying at the General Court to be acted on at the May Session next and the other half to be for the use of the town of Gorham."

"Consented to, Solomon Lombard."

May 9 it was voted to concur with the neighboring towns in a petition to the General Court to let the fish up Presumpscot River.

Sept. 21 a meeting was held in response to "a brief from the Selectmen of Boston requiring that the Town of Gorham would send their agent to Boston as soon as may be to join in the convention of the agents of said Boston and of the rest of the agents from the several towns within the Province to consult and resolve upon as may most conduce to the safety and welfare of the inhabitants of said Province in this alarming and critical conjuncture."

It was voted to chose Esqr Lombard a committee man to consult with the Congress at Boston and to allow eight days for going and coming while attending the Congress.

At the annual meeting in 1769, Capt. Edmund Phinney was chosen Moderator.

Amos Whitney, Town Clerk.
Edmund Phinney, Treasurer.
Edmund Phinney, Amos Whitney and James Gilky, Selectmen.

THE GORHAMS.

The name of the town symbolizes the patriotism of the early settlers, also an appreciation of personal favors. It not only perpetuates the name of a brave captain who gave his life to his country, but will forever keep in the minds of their children the remembrance of the service of Col. Shubael Gorham, in securing from the General Court of Massachusetts an acknowledgment of their obligations to Capt. John Gorham and his self-sacrificing neighbors, by granting to their heirs the fertile township on the bank of the Presumpscot.

Very few bearing the name of Gorham have had settlement in the town, but in the long roll of great and good men who have been proud of their connection with this ancient town none were more beloved and respected in life or regretted in death than William Gorham, a grandson of Col. Shubael and a great-great-grandson of the famous Narragansett captain.

Judge Gorham was born in Barnstable, July 12, 1743,

and settled in Gorham about 1770. He was much in public service and during the war of the Revolution was active on committees of safety and with tongue and pen advocated the cause of the colonies.

He was appointed Judge of Probate in 1782 and Judge of the Court of C. P. in 1787, holding both offices until his death. His first wife was widow Temperance White of Scituate, who died April 1788, aged 43 years. He married the next year, Temperance, daughter of Richard Garrett of Barnstable, who surviving him became the second wife of Dr. Jeremiah Barker of Falmouth, whose first wife was Judge Gorham's sister Abigail.

The following is copied from the *Portland Gazette*, of Monday, July 30, 1804:

FUNERAL OF THE LATE JUDGE GORHAM.

On Wednesday last, the remains of the Hon. William Gorham were committed to the grave. A number of citizens of the town of Portland and of other towns, joined those of the town of Gorham, to manifest their last token of respect for their departed friend. The procession was extensive. Besides those who followed the corpse on horseback and on foot, there were upwards of seventy carriages. The order of the procession was as follows:

The Clergy.
Justices of the County.
Gentlemen of the Bar.
The Sheriff.

Pall bearers.		Pall bearers.
Stephen Longfellow, Esq.,		John Frothingham, Esq.,
John Deane, Esq.,	The Corpse	George Lewis, Esq.,
Robert Southgate, Esq.,		Wm. Thompson, Esq.

Relatives.
Citizens of the town of Gorham.
Citizens of Portland and other towns.

The procession moved from the mansion of the deceased (that place which once knew him, but will hereafter know him no more) about half after three.

The corpse was carried to the meeting house, about two miles distant, where the following services were well performed, viz:

A Funeral Hymn, by a choir belonging to the Parish.
A prayer by the Rev. Mr. Noyes.
An Eulogy by the Rev. Mr. Hilliard.

The corpse was thence borne to the Grave, followed by the mourners in the same order, and was deposited about half past six o'clock. There it must rest until the voice of the archangel and the trump of God shall at his command call it forth at the general resurrection.

CHARACTER.

"When a Righteous man dies, the people have cause to mourn."

Died on Sunday, the 22d inst., and on Wednesday last was decently interred, the Hon. William Gorham, Esq., Judge of Probate and Chief Justice of the Court of Common Pleas for the County of Cumberland, aged sixty-one years.

By this event a tender woman is deprived of a kind husband, his acquaintance of an agreeable companion, the widowed and fatherless of a good friend, the town of Gorham of a useful citizen, the people of the county of an upright judge, and the public at large of a valuable member of society.

The important affairs he sustained, afforded evidence of the confidence which was placed in his discretion, learning and fidelity.

He was born at Barnstable the 12th of July, 1748, and was descended of respectable parents and grandparents, from whom the town where he has resided upwards of thirty years, had its name. He received his first commission as a justice of the peace from the governor of Nova Scotia, at the age of twenty-four years. His first commission under the Massachusetts government is of an older date than that of any justice in the county, one only excepted. He sustained the office of Judge of Probate about twenty-two and that of Judge of the Court of Common Pleas about twenty-one years.

In his public character he was honored, in his private esteemed. He possessed a benevolent mind, a calm temper, a hospitable disposition, and a truly christian spirit. Without ostentation, he was in the various situations of his life an amiable man, sincere in friendship, just in his dealings, agreeable in his conversation, modest in his manner, inoffensive in his conduct, true to his country, and if we may judge from his outward actions, faithful to his God.

But what affords perhaps the best evidence of his virtues, and of his having "a conscience void of offence towards God and man," was the temper and situation of his mind at life's closing scene. When about four months before his death he was attacked by an alarming disorder, he was not terrified at his expected dissolution, but calmly settled his worldly concerns and gave himself up to the will of God. Altho' after his disorder abated he had hopes of recovery, he was prepared for what might be the event, and when it was intimated to him by a friend that it was not probable he would recover, he received the opinion with unconcern; and while his flesh was consuming and his bodily strength failing, his mind was tranquil and composed. Comforted by the blessed hope of a true believer in Christ, of his faith in whom he had long ago made a public profession, he waited with great patience until his change came, and with the glorious prospect of future happiness through the merits of his Savior, manifested that " Peace in which a christian can die."

A few days before his death he said to two of his friends that he had never been elated with the honors, nor attached to the pleasures of the world, but had been an honest man : and added "I never was in the upper world, but I have heard that there are many mansions of bliss prepared there for those who are righteous here, and I believe there is one prepared for me." While these sentiments, and the patience and resignation with which he met death, afford consolation to his friends, they justify the declaration that

"Faith hath an overcoming power
And triumphs in a dying hour."

Trusting Christ, death was disarmed of terror. May all by his example be excited to live the life of the righteous, that our latter end may be like his; and while we mourn that we are deprived of the private conversation and public services of this man, we cannot but rejoice in the thought that he will be forever happy in a better world, for

"*Blessed are the dead that die in the Lord, for they rest from their labor, and their works follow them.*"

PUBLISHMENTS.

Intentions of Marriage from Books 1 and 2 Records of Gorham, Me.

The first publishment is that of Ebenezer Murch of Gorham, with Margaret Philips of Pepperelborough, Dec. 8, 1763, attested by Amos Whitney, town clerk. His successors in office appear to have been Wentworth Stuart in 1770, Amos Whitney, again in 1772, William Gorham in 1773, Caleb Chase in 1776, Austin Alden in 1778, and Josiah Alden in 1804, completing the second book. These records are plainly written and in fair condition. Our copy retains original spelling, but superfluous words are omitted; the residence of contracting parties when of Gorham is left out.

Adam, a negro man with Dinah, a negro woman, both of Pearsontown, July 26, 1785.

Adams, Benjamin, of Falmouth, with Elizabeth Frost, Nov. 7, 1778.

—Joseph with Mercy Elwell, April 4, 1802.
—Joshua, with Hannah Foot, Dec. 3, 1774.
—Joshua, with Hannah Brown, July 26, 1777.
—Joshua, with Sally Plummer, May 26, 1792.
—Stephen, with Sarah Elwell, Dec. 8, 1781.

INTENTIONS OF MARRIAGE.

—William, of Buxton, with Rebecca Elwell, Oct. 21, 1786.

Akers, Jenny, with Thomas Bracket, Mar. 20, 1784.

—John, with Eunice Newbegin, Oct. 14, 1783.

—Moses, with Mary Clark, Oct. 21, 1780.

—Rbecca with Aaron Hanscome Aug. 14, 1799.

Alden, Anner with Warren Nickerson of Penobscot, Nov. 5, 1785.

—Austin, with Hannah Battle of Cape Elizabeth, Sept. 27, 1781.

—Elizabeth, with Jesse Harding, March 8, 1777.

—Josiah, with Sarah Robinson of Cape Elizabeth, Oct. 12, 1782.

Ashley, Hannah, of Windham, Conn., with Joseph Cresey, Aug. 28, 1776.

Atkinson, Betty, of Buxton, with Nathaniel Dunn, Jr., April 7, 1787.

Ayer, Benjamin, of Buxton, with Rachel Sanborn of Pearsontown, April 2, 1785.

Babb, John, with Betsey Murray, May 15, 1795.

Baron, Josiah, with Lucy Hopkins of Standish, Feb. 28, 1788.

—Martha, with Charles Hopkins, Nov. 17, 1792.

—Miriam, with Nicholas Harding, Mar. 28, 1789.

—Nathaniel, with Betty Dyer of Cape Elizabeth, Dec. 13, 1781.

—Polly, with Joseph Hanscome, May 12, 1798.

—Susanna, of Barnstable, with John Gilkey, Mar. 14, 1789.

—Thomas, with Sally Burton, Sept. 17, 1803.

Bachelor, Samuel, with Anna Richardson, both of Pearsontown, Nov. 5, 1783.

Bailey, Jenny, of Falmouth, with James Murch, Nov. 5, 1785.

Baker, Moses, of Summersworth, with Sarah Thomas, Jan. 31, 1800.

Bangs, Anna, with Stephen Irish, Dec. 26, 1778.

INTENTIONS OF MARRIAGE.

—Barnabas, Jr., with Catherine Stevens, Oct. 27, 1777.
—Barnabas, Jr., with Betty Cloutman, Oct. 10, 1789.
—Benjamin, with Elizabeth Rand, Dec. 21, 1793.
—Ebenezer, with Polly Cobb, Sept. 29, 1787.
—Hannah, with William Whitney, of Limington, Aug. 18, 1792.
—Hannah, with John Hamblen, Jr., Jan. 12, 1804.
—James, with Deborah Cates, July 23, 1774.
—James, with Elizabeth Easters of Windham, Nov. 4, 1789.
—Joseph, with Polly Bangs, Dec. 28, 1794.
—Mary, with Nathaniel Phinney, Nov. 5, 1791.
—Mehitable, with Jonathan Parsons, Jan. 16, 1790.
—Nathan, with Sarah Bangs, Apr. 2, 1798.
—Polly, with Joseph Bangs, Dec. 28, 1794.
—Rebecca, of Buxton, with John Haskel, Mar. 28, 1801.
—Sarah, with Joseph Brackett, Mar. 30, 1781.
—Sarah, with Nathan Bangs, April 2, 1798.
—Thomas, with Hannah Lakeman, Sept. 20, 1777.
Barker, David, of Windham, with Rhoda Millet, Sept. 8, 1781.
—Hannah of Windham, with William Murch, Aug. 31, 1782.
—Doct. Jeremiah, of Falmouth, with Susanna Garrett, Oct. 23, 1790.
—Doct. Jeremiah, of Falmouth, with Mary Williams, July 2, 1802.
—Samuel, of Windham, with Jenny McLellan, Oct. 10, 1798.
Bartlett, Jonathan, of Sudbury, Canada, with Mary Shaw, of Pearsontown, Nov. 20, 1784.
—Samuel, with Sarah Coleman Jenkins, May 19, 1804.
Battle, Hannah, of Cape Elizabeth, with Austin Alden, Sept. 27, 1781.

INTENTIONS OF MARRIAGE.

Beal, Elizabeth, of New Town, with John Cookson, of Pearsontown July 30, 1785.

Bean, Anna, of Pearsontown, with Ithiel Smith of Limington, July 17, 1779.

—Daniel, with Margaret Shaw, both of Pearsontown, Dec. 30, 1780.

—Eunice, with Joseph Shaw, both of Pearsontown, May 12, 1780.

—Jonathan, with Abigail York, both of Pearsontown, Oct. 22, 1774.

—Lois with John Marcan, both of Pearsontown, Nov. 10, 1781.

—Mercy, with William Wood, Dec. 7, 1796.

Beard, Abigail, of Buxton, with John Rand, April 25, 1800.

Berry, Polly, of Falmouth, with Nathaniel Frost, June 3, 1780.

—Sarah, of Falmouth, with Benj. Haskell, July 24, 1784.

Beverly, Varnum, with Lucy Peabody, Jan. 1, 1791.

Bickford, James, with Betsy Wentworth, of Buxton, May 31, 1793.

Black, Josiah, with Mary Cookson, Nov. 6, 1773.

Blake, Affia, with Thomas Thomes, of Buxton, Dec. 26, 1789.

—Benj., Jr., with Phebe Lombard, Aug. 21, 1785.

—Betty, with Caleb Pike Philbrick, of Standish, Mar. 26, 1794.

—Freeman, with Mary Whitney, Aug. 12, 1803.

—Ithiel, with Apphia Higgins, June 29, 1769.

—Ithiel, with Eunice Phinney, July 31, 1802.

—Joseph, with Hannah Hopkins, of Pearsontown, Jany. 6, 1781.

—Lydia, with Samuel Bryant, of Pepperellboro, Apr. 27, 1800.

—Martha, with Samuel Irish, Mar. 27, 1792.

—Mary with Jonathan Shaw of Standish, Jan. 1, 1800.

—Mehitable, with Benj. Elwell of Buxton, Dec. 27, 1788.

INTENTIONS OF MARRIAGE.

—Nathaniel, with Mary Fogg of Scarboro, Aug. 23, 1777.

—Nathaniel, with Hannah Wood, Feb. 8, 1793.

Blake, Nathaniel, Jr., with Rebecca Higgins of Standish, Nov. 7, 1801.

—Phebe, with Samuel Boynton of Buxton, Mar. 2, 1804.

—Polly, with Jonathan Whitney of Buxton, Nov. 24, 1781.

—Ruth, with John Blake Rand, June 22, 1799.

—Sally, with Nathan Hanson of Buxton, Mar. 2, 1804.

—Seth, with Abigail Larrabee, Aug. 2, 1799.

—Thomas, of Falmouth, with Sarah Libby, June 20, 1790.

Blanchard, John, with Dorcas Carsley, Mar. 14, 1792.

—Polly, with Daniel Gammon, Mar. 14, 1781.

Bodge, Benjamin, of Windham, with Betsey Gammon, Nov. 1, 1788.

Bohonon, John, with Mary Roff, (Ross), June 16, 1765.

Bolton, Anna, with William Libby, Jr., Mar. 8, 1797.

—Benjamin, with Sarah Brown, Nov. 1, 1788.

—Hannah, with Joseph Lombard, July 11, 1795.

—Mary, of Windham, with Daniel Haskel, Mar. 30, 1794.

—Sarah, of Windham, with Edward Webb, April 7, 1787.

—Thomas, of Windham, with Hannah Crocket, Oct. 27, 1781.

—William, with Eunice Nason, Aug. 20, 1803.

—William, Jr., of Windham, with Anna Webb, Dec. 3, 1785.

Boothby, Elias, with Abigail Murch, April 6, 1793.

—Rachel, of Scarboro, with George McLellan, Feb. 18, 1801.

INTENTIONS OF MARRIAGE.

Boston, Susanna, with Joshua Duker, Mar. 13, 1773.

Bowman, Doct. Nathaniel, with Miss Sally Johnson of Andover, July 10, 1789.

Boynton, Samuel, of Buxton, with Phebe Blake, Mar. 2, 1804.

Brackett, Dorcas of Falmouth, with James McCorson, Jr., Jan. 31, 1801.

—Joseph, with Sarah Bangs, Mar. 30, 1781.

—Mary, with Pelatiah March, Aug. 31, 1776.

—Thomas, of Falmouth, with Jenny Akers, Mar. 20, 1784.

Bradbury, Joseph, of Buxton, with Susanna Crokit, June 10, 1798.

Bradley, David Lothrop, with Eliza McDonald, April 28, 1804.

Bragdon, Jenny, with John Edwards, Aug. 2, 1801.

—Jonathan, with Lucy Libby, Oct. 31, 1777.

Bramhall, Betty, with James Goodwin, Sept. 27, 1794.

—Cornelius, with Meribah McDonald, Jan. 13, 1788.

Briant, Rebecca, of Scarboro, with John Collins, Aug. 5, 1769.

Bridges, Dorcas, of Andover with James Tyler, Jan. 11, 1800.

Briggs, Abiel, with Lucy Perkins, Aug. 26, 1786.

—Abiel, with Polly Dunn, Dec. 25, 1790.

Brooks, Francis of N. Yarmouth, with Susanna Stuart, Sept. 29, 1785.

Brossard, Priscilla, with James Cobb, Oct. 13, 1803.

Brown, Abel, with Abigail Crockit, July 7, 1799.

—Amos, with Sarah Cilley, Jan. 25, 1777.

—Asaph, of Waterford, with Hannah Shaw of Pearsontown, April 27, 1785.

—Benjamin, Tertius, of Georgetown, with Sarah McLellan, Jan. 3, 1776.

—Benjamin, with Betsy Hamblen, Nov. 27, 1803.

INTENTIONS OF MARRIAGE.

—Betty, with Simon Davis McDonald, June 27, 1800.
—Daniel, with Sarah Libby, Dec. 1, 1802.
—Edmund, with Elizabeth Skillings, July 2, 1797.
—Elizabeth, with John McQuillan, Sept. 24, 1796.
—Fear, with John Poland, Jan. 30, 1790.
—Hannah, with Joshua Adams, July 26, 1777.
—Hannah with Elkanah Harding, Feb. 20, 1802.
—Herman Merrick, of Freeport, with Elizabeth Hicks, Sept. 13, 1802.
—Hezekiah, with Abiah Moody of Standish, Mar. 22, 1794.
—Jesse, with Alice Strout, Nov. 4, 1786.
—John, with Mary Gammon, Nov. 14, 1801.
—Jonathan, formerly of Wellfleet, with Deborah Eldridge, July 22, 1779.
—Joseph, with Hannah Whitney, Dec. 15, 1768.
—Joseph, with Hannah Elder, Oct. 4, 1798.
—Joseph, of Windham, with Betty Thomes, June 13, 1801.
—Lydia, with Barnabas Rich, April 18, 1779.
—Lydia, with George Thomas, Feb. 26, 1780.
—Mary, with Daniel Cobb, Oct. 5th, 1776.
—Mary of Windham, with Ephraim Smith, Oct. 7, 1796.
—Mercy, with David Emerson of Ossapee, Sept. 10, 1803.
—Rachel, with Chipman Cobb, Jr., Feb. 25, 1797.
—Sarah of Falmouth, with Capt. Nathaniel Frost, June 16, 1787.
—Sarah, with Benjamin Bolter, Nov. 1, 1788.
—Silvanus, with Hannah Harding, Nov. 21, 1801.
—Simeon, with Elizabeth Emery, June 22, 1776.
—Susanna, with John Hodsdon, both of Gorham, April 6, 1770.

INTENTIONS OF MARRIAGE.

—Timothy, with Mary Irish, Jan. 10, 1789.
Burnell, Benjamin, with Dorcas Carsley, Oct. 18, 1788.
Brunel, Betsey, with William Nason, July 2, 1791.
Burnell, John 3d, with Patty Libby of Scarboro, March 15, 1788.
—Joseph, with Mary Weeks, Sept. 26, 1789.
—Mary, with Thomas Skilling, Nov. 24, 1781.
—Mehitable, with Amos Thomes of Pearsontown, Dec. 5, 1781.
—Owen, with Susanna Whitney, July 23, 1774.
—Polly, with William Riggs, Mar. 22, 1794.
—Samuel, with Amy Irish, Aug. 20, 1791.
Bryan, Martin, with Joanna Penfield, both of Pearsontown, Jan. 16, 1786.
Bryant, Samuel, of Pepperellboro, with Lydia Blake, Apr. 27, 1800.
Buck, John, of New Gloucester, with Abigail Irish, Feb. 8, 1777.
Burnam, Jeremiah, with Molly Burnham, both of Bridgton, Nov. 4, 1783.
—Molly, with Jeremiah Burnam, both of Bridgton, Nov. 4, 1783.
—Phebe, with Benjamin Kimball, Jr., both of Bridgton, Nov. 7, 1782.
Burton, Sally, with Thomas Bacon, Sept. 17, 1803.
—William, with Mary Ross, July 29, 1780.
Butler, John, with Jane Holbrook, Jan. 13, 1787.
Butterfield, Joseph, of Pearsontown, with Mary Harding, Sept. 2, 1773.
Byanton, Polly, of Buxton, with John Murch, Jr., Mar. 24, 1801.
Cahoon, Betsy, with Prince Davis, Sept. 3, 1796.
Cain, Mehitable, of Buxton, with George Elwell, Aug. 5, 1798.
Cammel, Thomas, of Standish, with Margaret Nason, June 30, 1797.
Carlton, Lydia, with Theodore Emerson, both of Bridgton, Dec. 13, 1781.
Carpenter, Molly, with Joseph Richardson, both of Pearsontown, Jan. 12, 1782.

INTENTIONS OF MARRIAGE.

Carsley, Benjamin, with Eunice Moody, Aug. 25, 1799.
—Dorcas, with Benjamin Burnell, Oct. 18, 1788.
—Dorcas, with John Blanchard, Mar. 14, 1792.
—Isaac, with Jenny Mosher, May 7, 1797.
—John, Jr., with Martha Crocket, March 20, 1790.
—Mary, with Joshua Moody, Dec. 13, 1769.
—Mary, with James Watson of Philips Gore, Jan. 21, 1792.
—Nathan, with Susanna Cotton, Jan. 17, 1792.
—Patience, with Philemon Rand of Scarboro, May 28, 1795.
Cates, Abigail, with Ephraim Hunt, Sept. 2, 1769.
—Andrew with Comfort Thomes, Sept. 10, 1785.
—Benjamin, with Anne Skillings, July 23, 1774.
—Deborah with James Bangs, July 23, 1774.
—Ebenezer, with Anna Cobb, Dec. 21, 1793.
—Elizabeth, with Joel Rich, April 17, 1779.
—James, with Esther Perkins, Sept. 20, 1768.
—James, with Betsy Whitney, Nov. 11, 1797.
—Joseph, Jr., with Mary Sinclair, Dec. 25, 1773.
—Lydia, with William Cobb, Nov. 6, 1791.
—Sarah, with Philip Horr of Waterford, Sept. 25, 1786.
Cato, negro man with Clarace, negro woman, Nov. 22, 1783.
Cavans, Charles, with Sally Holbrook, Feb. 12, 1790.
Chadbourn, James, with Dorcas Whitmore, Dec. 6, 1788.
—Silas, with Abigail Crockett, April 1, 1775.
—Rebecca, with James Irish, Jr., July 22, 1798.
Chamberlain, Lydia, with John Merrill, Feb. 23, 1799.

INTENTIONS OF MARRIAGE.

Chandler, Benj., of Pepperrellborough, with Martha Gilkey, Sept. 6, 1799.
Chase, Betty, with Ebenezer Cotton, Nov. 25, 1788.
—Caleb, with Joanna Whitney, Dec. 31, 1769.
—Hezekiah, of Sandy Stream, with Sally Gilkey, June 17, 1803.
—Isaac, of Pearsontown, with Lois Smith, Sept. 13, 1783.
—Mary, with Nathaniel Freeman, Dec. 31, 1774
Chesley, Isaac, with Fanny Hamblen, April 24, 1803.
Chick, Ephraim, of Ossapee, with Phebe Cobb, Mar. 16, 1782.
—Nathan of Falmouth, with Abigail Crockett, July 8, 1789.
—Sally, of Berwick, with Ebenezer Cresey, Aug. 6, 1803.
Choate, Elizabeth, with Capt. Abner McDonald, June 21, 1801.
Cilley, Sarah, with Amos Brown, Jan. 25, 1777.
Clarace, negro woman, with Cato, Jan. 25, man, Nov. 22, 1783.
Clark, Betsy, with Joseph Young, July 9, 1803.
—Jacob, with Elizabeth Fly, Aug. 4, 1792.
—Josiah, with Mitty Kemp, Sept. 30, 1797.
—Mary, with Moses Akers, Oct. 21, 1780.
—Sally, with Almary Hamblen, Sept. 15, 1797.
Clay, Benjamin, of Buxton, with Jane Hunnewell, of Pearsontown, Oct. 2, 1779.
—Jemima, with Butler Lombard, May 25, 1787.
—Mary, with Samuel Hamblen, Jr., Nov. 29, 1777.
—Rachel, with James Rounds, Sept 8, 1781.
—Thomas, of Buxton, with Ruth Gammon, Oct. 15, 1781.
Clements, Polly, with Seth Webb, Oct. 23, 1800.
Clemmons, Jacob, with Phebe Coffin, April 5, 1790.
—John with Mary McLellan, Dec. 18, 1788.

INTENTIONS OF MARRIAGE.

Cloe, the negro woman, with Prince, the negro man, Aug. 18, 1798.

Cloutman, Betty, with Barnabas Bangs, Jr., Oct. 10, 1789.
—Jesse, with Hannah Swett, Mar. 9, 1799.
—John, with Lydia Freeman, Jan. 9, 1802.
—John, with Sarah Cobb, July 17, 1802.
—Nathan, with Eunice Swett, Nov. 12, 1802.
—William, with Sarah Hamblen, Jan. 12, 1804.

Cobb, Andrew, Jr., with Betty Irish, Dec. 14, 1782.
—Dea. Andrew with Hannah Fowler, Apr. 21, 1804.
—Anna, with Ebenezer Cates, Dec. 21, 1793.
—Chipman, Jr., with Rachel Brown, Feb. 25, 1797.
—Daniel, with Mary Brown. Oct. 5, 1776.
—David, with Sally Watson, Oct. 23, 1802.
—Ebenezer, with Sarah Hanscom, Dec. 17, 1791.
—Elisha, Jr., with Molly Murch of Biddeford, Sept. 4, 1790.
—Esther, with Josiah Lakeman, June 28, 1783.
—Hannah, with Micah Whitney, Nov. 13, 1779.
—James, with Priscilla Brossard, Oct. 13, 1803.
—Mary, with William Leavit of Buxton, Nov. 23, 1795.
—Phebe, with Ephraim Chick of Ossapee, Mar. 16, 1782.
—Phebe, with Daniel Eldridge, March 5, 1785.
—Polly, with Ebenezer Bangs, Sept. 29, 1787.
—Reuben, with Betsy Hatch, Mar. 14, 1801.
—Samuel, with Tabitha Elwell, of Buxton, Nov. 6, 1802.
—Sarah, with John Cloutman, July 17, 1802.
—William, with Lydia Cates, Nov. 6, 1791.

INTENTIONS OF MARRIAGE.

—William, with Nancy Poak, Mar. 10, 1798.

Coffin, Betsy, of Buxton, with Nathaniel Gould, Nov. 2, 1793.

—John, with Loruhama Cotton, Oct. 29, 1791.

—Phebe, with Jacob Clemmons, April 5, 1790.

—Tristram, with Joanna Moulton of Standish, Jan. 9, 1802.

Collins, John, with Rebecco Briant, of Scarboro, Aug. 5, 1769.

Cook, Abigail, with John McQuillan, April 17, 1784.

—Mercy, with Simeon Tryon, Dec. 12, 1801.

—Rebecca, with Samuel Prentiss, Nov. 10, 1787.

—Sarah, of Windham, with John Gammon, Mar. 19, 1797.

—Solomon, with Elizabeth Snow, Dec. 22, 1780.

Cookson, John, of Pearsontown, with Elizabeth Beal, of New Town, July 30, 1785.

—Joseph, of Buxton, with Jenny Lagben, Dec. 5, 1795.

—Mary, with Josiah Black, Nov. 6, 1773.

—Reuben, with Mary York, both of Pearsontown, Jan.— 1769.

Cotton, Ebenezer, with Betty Chase, Nov. 25, 1788.

—Loruhama, with John Coffin, Oct. 29, 1791.

—Sarah, with Jonathan Elwell, Jan. 11, 1794.

—Susanna, with Nathan Carsley, Jan. 17, 1792.

Cram, Daniel, Jr., of Pearsontown, with Chloe Stevens of Bridgton, August 26, 1780.

Cresy, Betsy, of Buxton, with Edmund Watson, April 15, 1797.

—Daniel, with Eliza Harding of Flintstown, June 14, 1799.

—Ebenezer, with Sally Chick, of Berwick, **Aug. 6, 1803.**

INTENTIONS OF MARRIAGE.

—Elizabeth, with Simon Harding, Dec. 17, 1774.
—Hannah, of Buxton, with William Paine, Jr., Dec. 9, 1797.
—John, with Susanna McDonall, Dec. 1, 1770.
—Joseph, with Hannah Ashley of Windham, Conn., Aug. 28,, 1776.
—Mary, with David Watts, Sept. 4, 1784.
—Miriam, of Buxton, with Samuel Watts, July 16, 1803.
Crocker, Luther, with Hannah Paine, June 6, 1801.
—Mehitable, with Wingate Snell of Buxton, May 24, 1788.
Crockett, Abigail, with Silas Chadbourne, April 1, 1775.
—Abigail, with Nathan Chick, of Falmouth, July 8, 1789.
—Abigail, with Abel Brown, July 7, 1799.
—Andrew, with Abigail Wallis, of Cape Elizabeth, Oct. 27, 1781.
—Betty, with Benjamin Gammon, Sept. 10, 1787.
—Content, with Joseph Moody, of Buxton, April, 11, 1802.
—Dorcas, with Daniel Merrill, of Falmouth, Dec. 3, 1774.
—Enoch, with Drusilla Sanborn, Mar. 29, 1801.
—Ephraim, with Martha Gray, Nov. 19, 1791.
—Hannah, with Thomas Boulton, of Windham, Oct. 27, 1781.
—James, with Sarah Sanborn, Dec. 3, 1796.
—Johathan, with Ruth Foss, of Stratham, N. H., April, 25, 1792.
—John, with Betty Hunt, Aug. 20, 1796.
—Joshua, Jr., with Sarah Hamblen, May 19, 1787.
—Martha, with Nathaniel Hill, Nov. 24, 1773.
—Martha, with John Carsley, Jr., Mar. 20, 1790.
—Mary with Isaac Whitney, April 7, 1772.
Crockit, Miriam, with John Thomas, Dec. 19, 1795.

INTENTIONS OF MARRIAGE.

—Nancy with Caleb Page, of Conway, June 30, 1797.
—Pelatiah, with Lucy Seeiver, July 2, 1802.
—Peter, with Mary Warren of Falmouth, Oct. 12, 1782.
—Phebe, with Moses Hanscom, April 7, 1781.
—Rebecca, with Asa Hatch, April 19, 1783.
—Rebecca, with Isaac Libby, Nov. 28, 1798.
—Sally with Mathew Tobin, of Windham, Oct. 13, 1799.
—Samuel, with Tabitha Hamlen, February 2, 1771.
—Samuel, Jr., with Elizabeth Pickit, of Buxton, April 5, 1783.
—Sarah, with Philip Gammon, Feb. 1, 1777.
—Susanna, with Joseph Bradbury, of Buxton, June 10, 1798.
—Susanna, with Joseph Phinney, May 13, 1780.
—William, with Sally Thomson, Oct. 17, 1802.
Cross, Daniel Emerson, of Fryeburg, with Sarah Haywood, of Brownfield, Feb. 10, 1776.
—Eliza, with Jonathan Stevens, of Portland, Sept. 13, 1794.
—Joseph, with Betsy Duston, of Haverhill, March 30, 1793.
—Sally with Enoch Preble, of Portland, Aug. 22, 1800.
Dam, John, of Freeport, with Mary Webb, April 16, 1792.
Darker, Mary, with Malachi Waterman, Dec. 21, 1776.
Darling, John, with Annah Lewis, July 30, 1785.
Dauset, Salome, with Sargeant Shaw, of Pearsontown, July 12, 1777.
Davis, Alice, with Enoch Frost, April 15, 1780.
—Allen, with Martha Morris, of Scarboro, May 19, 1792.

INTENTIONS OF MARRIAGE.

—Chloe, with Alexander McLellan, Dec. 12, 1802.
—David, with Martha Watson, May 17, 1788.
—Ebenezer, with Mary Paine, Jan. 23, 1790.
—Elijah, with Phebe Hopkins, April 8, 1780.
—Gershom, with Elizabeth McCullister, Nov. 13, 1779.
—James, with Thankful Paine, Feb. 12, 1793.
—John, with Molly Har'er, of Falmouth, Feb. 14, 1784.
—John, with Patience Irish, Mar. 14, 1789.
—Jonathan, with Molly Murch, of Buxton, Aug. 10, 1796.
—Joseph, with Abigail Whitney, Dec. 14, 1794.
—Josiah, with Martha Hill, of Buxton, Nov. 7, 1802.
—Mary, with James Watson, April 30,
—Phebe, with Asa Whitney, May 28, 1785. 1785.
—Prince, with Betsy Cahoon, Sept. 3, 1796.
—Prudence, with Josiah Jenkins, June 15, 1776.
—Rebecca, with George Knight, of Windham, Nov. 27, 1786.
—Samuel, Jr., with Mary Skilling, Oct. 9, 1784.
—Sarah, with David Watts, Sept. 11 1779.
—Sarah, with Charles Wood, July 23, 1786.
—Sarah, with Benj. Emory of Buxton, June 19, 1801.
—Silvanus, with Hannah Gorham, Nov. 7, 1789.
—Temperance, with David Harding, June 23, 1781.
—William, with Martha Kimbal, May 11, 1796.
Day, Dorothy, with Jesse Walker, both of Fryeburg, Jan. 23, 1776.
Dean, Mary, with Obediah Irish, of Little Ossapee, Oct. 29, 1789.

INTENTIONS OF MARRIAGE.

—Rachel, with James Hasty, both of Pearsontown, May 17, 1783.
Decker, Joshua, with Susanna Boston, Mar. 13, 1773.
Deacker, John, with Catherine Hall, both of Pearsontown, September 14, 1771.
Derburn, Mary, with John Dyer, Jr., Jan. 9, 1790.
Dickey, Nathaniel, with Hannah Hez..i-tine, of Concord, N. H., Dec. 29, 1802.
Dinah, a negro woman, with Adam, a negro man, both of Pearsontown, July 26, 1785.
Dinnes, Melroy of Limington, with Katy McIntosh, Sept. 10, 1796.
Doane, Mary, of Cape Elizabeth, with David Gammon, May 3, 1777.
—Lydia, of Derham, with Nathan Freeman, July 1, 1775.
Dosset, Jedediah, with Susanna Libby, June 25, 1796.
Douty, Priscilla, with Samuel Pote, Oct. 2, 1779.
Dow, Abner, with Martha Hinkley, both of Pearsontown, July 27, 1782.
—Joseph, with Lucy Sanborn, both of Pearsontown, April 26, 1782.
Drake, Robert, of Cape Elizabeth, with Mary Whitney, Aug. 19, 1786.
Dresser, Mark, of Scarboro, with Nancy Holbrook, July 4, 1789.
—Richard, with Temperance Hamblen, Feb. 20, 1796.
—Sarah, with Job Eastman, both of Fryeburg, Jan. 23, 1776.
Duguit, Mary, with John Tyng Smith, Mar. 24, 1798.
Dunn, Christopher, with Susanna Lombard, Jan. 19, 1782.
—Christopher, with Betty Fogg, Mar. 1, 1794.
—Deborah, with Joshua Harmon, of Scarboro, Aug. 22, 1789.
—Capt. Joshua, with Rebecca Jones, of Cape Elizabeth, Aug. 27, 1791.
—Mercy, with James Emory, June 14, 1783.

INTENTIONS OF MARRIAGE.

Dunn, Nathaniel, Jr., with Betty Atkinson of Buxton, April 7, 1787.
—Polly, with Abiel Briggs, Dec. 25, 1790. ~~April 21, 1792.~~
Durgin, Mary, of Scarboro, with Thomas Green, Aug. 18, 1787.
Durrel, Anna, with William Thomson,
Duston, Betsey, with Joseph Cross, March 30, 1793.
Dyer, Betty, of Cape Elizabeth, with Nathaniel Baron, Dec. 13, 1781.
—Deborah, with Daniel Moulton, Jr., of Scarboro, Oct. 30, 1790.
—Isabelle, of Cape Elizabeth, with Nathaniel Freeman, Jr., Aug. 10, 1792.
—John, Jr., with Mary Derburn, Jan 9, 1790.
—Levi, with Elizabeth Starbird of Cape Elizabeth, Oct. 9, 1791.
—Lydia, with Samuel Jenkins, Jr., April 15, 1780.
—Mary, with Daniel Davis Lewis, Mar. 31, 1798.
—Mary, with Jacob Morse, July 26, 1800.
—Mercy, of Cape Elizabeth, with Reuben Morton, Dec. 25, 1792.
—Moses, of Falmouth, with Polly Patrick, Nov. 20, 1797.
—Paul, with Mary Edwards, Nov. 13, 1802.
—Polly, with William Wood, Jr., Nov. 14, 1790.
—Rebecca, of Cape Elizabeth, with Benjamin Roberts, Aug. 18, 1794.
—Sarah, of Cape Elizabeth, with Hugh McKinze, Oct. 29, 1767.
—Sheba, with Sarah Whitney, May 28, 1797.
—Susanna, of Cape Elizabeth, with James Morton, July 12, 1777.
—William, with Rebecca Huston, Aug. 18, 1792.
Easters, Elizabeth, of Windham, with James Bangs, Nov. 4, 1789.
Eastman, Job, with Sarah Dresser, both of Fryeburg, Jan. 23, 1776.

INTENTIONS OF MARRIAGE.

Edgecomb, William Nason, of Limington, with Eunice Strout, Aug. 20, 1892.

Edmunds, Jonathan, with Alley Libbee, Dec. 17, 1774.

Edwards, Abigail with Joseph Wise, of Falmouth, Feb. 20, 1801.

—Dorcas, of Wells, with Samuel Rounds, of Narraganset, No. 1, Feb. 15, 1768.

—Enoch, with Abigail McLellan, May 4, 1799.

—Hannah, with John Sawyer, of Philips Gore, April 21, 1792.

—Joanna, with Gideon. Snow, Dec. 1, 1788.

—John, with Jenny Bragdon, Aug. 2, 1801.

—Mary, with Paul Dyer, Nov. 13, 1802.

—Nathaniel, with Sarah Hunt, Sept. 16, 1775.

—Nathaniel, with Bathsheba Snow, Aug. 26, 1786.

—Olive, of Buxton, with John McQuillian, Aug. 11, 1798.

—Richard, with Hannah Lothrop, July 2, 1765.

—Samuel, with Martha McLellan, May 19, 1792.

—Stevens, with Dilla Hamblen, Sept. 1, 1798.

—Susanna, with Thomas Wooster, Aug. 23, 1800.

—William, with Dorcas Morrill, Nov. 5, 1803.

Elder, Anna, with David McDugle, Oct. 21, 1786.

—Betty, with John Wright Morris, of Scarboro, Oct. 4, 1798.

—Damask, of Falmouth, with Jonathan Stone, Nov. 16, 1782.

—Elijah, with Eleanor McLellan, July 28, 1798.

—Eunice, with Nathaniel Mosher, May 9, 1795.

—Eunice, with Cary McLellan, Jan. 3, 1767.

—Hannah, with Joseph Brown, Oct. 4, 1798.

INTENTIONS OF MARRIAGE.

—Lydia, of Windham, with Ebenezezr Kemp, Nov. 7, 1800.
—Margaret, with Samuel Lurnmus, May, 23, 1801.
—Mary, with Ebenezer File, April 8, 1780.
—Matilda, with William Hanson of Windham, Oct. 28, 1785.
—Polly, with Daniel Gammon, Dec. 9, 1786.
—Reuben, with Elizabeth Huston, Nov. 6, 1786.
—Samuel, with Hannah Freeman, Jan. 29, 1774.
—Samuel, with Mary Graffam, of Windham, Oct. 23, 1786.
—William, of Cape Elizabeth, with Mary Thombs, Feb. 8, 1777.
Eldridge, Elizabeth, with Benjamin Woodman, of Buxton, May 2, 1778.
—Daniel, with Phebe Cobb, March 5. 1785.
—Deborah, with Jonathan Brown, formerly of Wellfleet, July 26, 1779.
Elwell, Benjamin, of Buxton, with Mehitable Blake, Dec. 27, 1788.
—George, with Mehitable Cain, of Buxton, Aug. 5, 1798.
—Jonathan, with Sarah Cotton, Jan. 11, 1794.
—Jonathan, with Sarah Whitney, June 5, 1802.
Mercy, with Joseph Adams, April 4, 1802.
—Rebecca, with William Adams, of Buxton, Oct. 21, 1786.
—Sarah, with Stephen Adams, Dec. 2, 1781.
—Tabitha, of Buxton, with Samuel Cobb, Nov. 6, 1802.
—William, with Mary Thompson, of Windham, April 23, 1803.
Emerson, David, of Ossapee, with Mercy Brown, Sept. 10, 1803.
—Theodore, with Lydia Carlton, both of Bridgton, Dec. 13, 1781.
Emory, Benjamin, of Buxton, with Sarah Davis, June 19, 1861.

INTENTIONS OF MARRIAGE.

—Comfort, of Buxton, with George Strout, Jr., May 19, 1804.
—Elizabeth, with Simeon Brown, June 22, 1776.
Emory, James, with Mercy Dunn, June 14, 1783.
—James, with Sarah Fogg, June 22, 1796.
—Jerusha of Buxton, with Samuel Strout, April 28, 1787.
—John, with Sarah Phinney, Dec. 21, 1776.
—Jonathan, of Buxton, with Jenny Stevens, Nov. 29, 1801.
Farnum, Simeon, with Elizabeth Johnson, of Andover, May 26, 1787.
Farrington, William, with Hannah Freeman, both of Pearsontown, Sept. 16, 1780.
Ficket, Benjamin, with Hannah Parker. Dec. 24, 1803.
—Ezra, with Sally Penfield, Oct. 19, 1796.
—Molly, of Falmouth, with Jeremy Fogg, May 29, 1801.
—Samuel, of Cape Elizabeth, with Sally Parker, June 21, 1794.
Filbrick, John, with Sarah Ross, April 1769.
File, Ebenezer, with Mary Elder, April 8, 1780.
—Elizabeth, with Joseph Higgins, Joseph of Lincoln, Aug. 23, 1803.
—George, with Temperance Sturges, Aug. 1, 1789.
—Joseph, with Anna Haskel, Dec. 22, 1798.
—Samuel, with Esther Thomes, April 29, 1780.
—William Jr., with Hannah Sturges, Oct. 9, 1784.
—William Elder, with Abigail Shaw, of Standish, Feb. 11, 1803.
Flood, Anna, with Isaac Irish, July 27. 1786.
—Edmund, with Martha Lombard, Jan. 27, 1788.
—Henry, with Sarah Irish, March 1, 1777.
—Mary, with James McCollister, Dec. 22, 1781.

INTENTIONS OF MARRIAGE.

—Morrison, with Lydia, Roberts, May 19, 1793.
Fly, Elizabeth, with Jacob Clark, Aug 4, 1792.
—Isaac, with Joanna Libby of Scarboro, June 10, 1786.
—Lucy, with Rufus Kimball, of Scarboro, Mar. 23, 1787.
Fogg, Betty, with Christopher Fogg, Mar. 1, 1794.
—Elias, of Buxton, with Lucy Harding, Sept. 14, 1799.
—Esther, with Joseph Waterhouse, of Falmouth, Aug. 8, 1795.
—Jeremiah, Jr., with Dorcas Lombard, Sept. 8, 1794.
—Jeremy, with Molly Ficket, of Falmouth, May 29, 1801.
—Leah, with Jonathan Martin, of Buxton, Jan. 1, 1793.
—Louisa, with James McLellan, July 11, 1802.
—Mary, of Scarboro, with Nathaniel Blake, Aug. 23, 1777.
—Nelson, of Scarboro, with Polly Lombard, Mar. 7, 1790.
—Sarah, of Machias, with Samuel Rich, Mar. 9, 1767.
—Sarah, with James Emory, June 22, 1796.
Foard, Anna, with George Knight, June 26, 1798.
—Olly, with Joseph Roberts, 3d, Sept. 5, 1793.
Foot, Hannah, with Joshua Adams, Dec. 3, 1774.
Foss, Joseph with Nancy McDonald, Oct. 22, 1792.
—Ruth of Stratham, N. H., with Jonathan Crockit, April 25, 1792.
—Wallis, of Rochester, N. H., with Mary Libby, June 11, 1799.
Foster, William H., with Betsy Harding, Apr. 21, 1804.
Foy, John, with Ruth Higgins, Dec. 15, 1781.
—John, with Hannah Wood, Dec. 5, 1778.

INTENTIONS OF MARRIAGE.

Fowler, Hannah with Deacon Andrew Cobb, April 21, 1804.
—Moses, of Falmouth, with Hannah Hamblen, June 27, 1765.
—Polly, with Elias Whitney, Oct. 10, 1788.
Francis, Thomas, (a molatto man) with Lucy Ludlow, (a negro woman,) July 15, 1792.
Freeman, Benjamin, with Eunice Sevey of Scarboro, Dec. 15, 1787.
—Ebenezer, with Polly Prentiss, Oct. 14, 1798.
—Hannah, with Samuel Freeman, Jan. 29, 1774.
—Hannah, with William Farrington, both of Pearsontown, Sept. 16, 1780.
—Jenny, with Ebenezer Lombard, Aug. 16, 1794.
—Jonathan, Jr., with Hannah Thomson, of Falmouth, Aug. 23, 1794.
—Lydia, with John Cloutman, Jan. 9, 1802.
—Lydia, with Gersham Hamblen, Aug. 28, 1802.
—Mary, with Joseph Whitney, Jr., May 16, 1801.
—Nathan, with Hepsabah Whitney, Oct. 13, 1766.
—Nathan, with Lydia Doane, of Derham, July 1, 1775.
—Nathaniel, with Mary Chase, Dec. 31, 1774.
—Nathaniel, Jun., with Isabella Dyer, of Cape Elizabeth, Aug. 10, 1792.
—Phebe, of Pearsontown, with Richard Lamb, of Buxton, Dec. 14, 1782.
—Rebecca, with Josiah Harmon, of Scarboro, Sept. 3, 1785.
—Sally, with Isaac Larrabee, of Scarboro, April 19, 1781.
—Susanna with Samuel Harding, May 2, 1781.
—Susanna, with Dominicus Harmon, of Scarboro, Mar. 22, 1788.
Frost, Benj., with Susanna Frost, June 24, 1765.

INTENTIONS OF MARRIAGE.

Frost, Elizabeth, with Benjamin Adams, of Falmouth, Nov. 7, 1778.
—Benjamin, with Pelina Rackley, Aug. 11, 1792.
—Betsy, of Summerworth, with James Mosher, Jr., Oct. 5, 1793.
—Betty, with Thomas Morton, Feb. 9, 1787.
—David, with Mary Johnson, of Falmouth, April 10, 1766.
—Elizabeth, with Coleman Phinney Watson, Mar. 20, 1802.
—Enoch, with Alice Davis, April 15, 1780.
—Jenny, with Nathaniel Webster, Aug. 3, 1799.
—Jeremiah, with Hannah Atkins Higgins, May 5, 1804.
—Love, with Nathan Wing of Limerick, Oct. 17, 1791.
—Lovey, of Berwick, with Briant Morton Dec. 29, 1766.
—Nathaniel, with Polly Berry of Falmouth, June 3, 1780.
—Capt. Nathaniel with Sarah Brown, of Falmouth, June 16, 1787.
—Nathaniel, Jr., with Esther Hamblen, Jan. 17, 1796.
—Col. Nathaniel, with Rebecca Higgins, of Standish, Oct. 3, 1801.
—Nathaniel, Jr., with Content Hamblen, Mar. 20, 1802.
—Polly, with Joseph Hamblen, Nov. 8, 1788.
—Rebecca with Silas White July 10, 1804.
—Samuel, with Rebecca Hamblen, June 11, 1791.
—Susanna, with Benj. Frost, June 24, 1765.
—Susanna, with Lemuel Hicks, Oct. 17, 1778.
Gammon, Benjamin, with Betty Crockit, Sept. 10, 1787.
—Betsey with Benjamin Bodge, of Windham, Nov. 1, 1788.
—Christian, with Robert Knight, of Otisfield, Nov. 27, 1796.
—Daniel, with Polly Blancher, March 14, 1781.

INTENTIONS OF MARRIAGE.

—Daniel, with Polly Elder, Dec. 9, 1786.
—David, with Mary Doane, of Cape Elizabeth, May 3, 1777.
—John, with Sarah Cook of Windham, Mar. 19, 1797.
—Jona., with Lydia Millet, of Cape Elizabeth, Dec. 31, 1785.
—Jonathan with Nabby Gammon, of Cape Elizabeth, Mar. 3, 1796.
—Joseph Jr., with Polly Patrick, Mar. 1, 1795.
—Mary, with John Brown, Nov. 14, 1801.
—Nabby, of Cape Elizabeth, with Jonathan Gammon, Mar. 3, 1796.
—Nathaniel, with Mary Lowell, July 5, 1777.
—Philip, with Sarah Crockett, Feb. 1, 1777.
—Ruth, with Thomas Clay, of Buxton, Oct. 15, 1781.
—Samuel with Susannah Perkins, Oct. 5, 1776.
—William, with Polly Hasty, of Scarboro, Dec. 8, 1798.
Garrett, Miss Temperance, with Hon. William Gorham, Esq., Feb. 28, 1789.
—Susanna, with Doct. Jeremiah Barker, of Falmouth, Oct. 23, 1790.
Gates, Timothy, with Susanna Marsters, both of Bridgton, Oct. 16, 1777.
Gibbs, Alice, with James Mains, April 23, 1795.
Gilkey Betty, with Frederick Stevens of 25 Mile Pond, Sept. 23, 1800.
—Isaac, with Caty Staples, of Scarboro, June 2, 1792.
—James, Jun., with Polly Marr, May 17, 1782.
—John, with Susanna Bacon, of Barnstable, March 14, 1789.
—Joseph, with Phebe Larrabee of Scarboro, July 16, 1774.
—Martha with Benjamin Chandler, of Pepperrellborough, Sept. 6, 1799.
—Rebecca, with James Small, of Gray, Mar. 9, 1787.
—Sally, with Hezekiah Chase, of Sandy Stream, June 17, 1803.

INTENTIONS OF MARRIAGE.

Golt, Alice, of Allenstown, with Samuel Stevens, Mar. 12, 1791.

Goodwin, James, with Betty, Bramhall, Sept. 27, 1794.

—Mary, with Alexander Stimpson, April 4, 1792.

Gordon, Hugh, with Elizabeth Lindsey, both of Fryeburg, July 8, 1775.

—Zebulon, of Little Falls, with Sarah Hatch, April 7, 1781.

Gorham, Eunice, with William Shaw, of Falmouth, March, 16, 1799.

—Hannah, with Silvanus Davis, Nov. 7, 1787.

—Frances, with James Tyler, Nov. 26, 1796.

—Hon. William Esq., with Miss Temperance Garrett, Feb. 28, 1789.

Gould, Nathaniel, with Betsy Coffin of Buxton, Nov. 2d, 1793.

—Nathaniel, with Elizabeth McLellan, April, 8, 1798.

Graffam, Elizabeth, of Windham, with Samuel Swett,, Dec. 3, 1785.

—Mary, of Windham, with Samuel Elder, Oct. 23, 1786.

Gragg, Marcey, with John Knight, June 5, 1784.

Grant, Daniel, with Susanna Strout, Mar. 23, 1787.

—David, of Falmouth, with Rachel Haskel, Oct. 14, 1802.

—James, with Lois Harding, July 16, 1784.

—Lucy, with William Pride, of Falmouth, Mar. 30, 1782.

Gray, Anna, with Charles Thomes, June 22, 1782.

—James, with Susanna Thomes, Oct. 2, 1790.

—Martha, with Ephraim Crockit, Nov. 19, 1791.

Greele, John, with Elizabeth Thompson, Aug. 14, 1773.

Green, Benjamin, with Sarah Lombard, July 23, 1774.

—Isaac, with Susanna Rowe, June 13, 1801.

INTENTIONS OF MARRIAGE.

—John, with Mary Stuart, both of Gorham, April 17, 1770.
Green, John, with Elizabeth Rand, of Scarboro, Nov. 7, 1802.
—Jonathan, with Rebecca, Young, Sept. 3, 1796.
—Josiah, with Eunice Newcomb, Sept. 19, 1789.
—Molly, of Standish, with Nathan Cook Penfield, Aug. 25, 1800.
—Salome, with Ebenezer Shaw, of Standish, Feb. 16, 1793.
—Thomas, with Mary Durgin, of Scarboro, Aug. 18, 1787.
Greenlaw, John, with Lucy Whitney, Feb. 23, 1788.
Hadaway, Louis, with John Perkins, May 18, 1769.
Hall, Abraham, with Elizabeth Sanborn, Feb. 6, 1790.
—Catherine, with John Dracker, both of Pearsontown, September 14, 1771.
—Charles, with Lydia Noble, both of Pearsontown, July 28, 1781.
—Dorothy, with John Woodward, Sept. 10, 1791.
—Ebenezer, Jr., with Susanna Honeywell, of Windham, Dec. 1, 1799.
—Isaac, with Anna Whitney, April 20, 1793.
—Israel, with Abigail Hutchinson, Sept. 11, 1795.
—John, with Naoma York, both of Pearsontown, Feb. 2, 1769.
—Rebecca, with Thomas Thompson, both of Pearsontown, Mar. 31, 1778.
—Sally, of Standish, with Jonathan Ward, Dec. 21, 1793.
—Sarah, with David Sanborn, both of Pearsontown, Dec. 7, 1765.
—William, of Standish, with Mary Ward, July 14, 1800.
Hamblen, Abigail, with Stephen Lary, Nov. 29, 1788.
—Almary, with Sally Clark, Sept. 15, 1797.
—Anna, with Benj. Skillings, Dec. 24, 1803.
—Betsy, with Benjamin Brown, Nov. 27, 1803.

INTENTIONS OF MARRIAGE.

—Content, with James Miller, of Cape Elizabeth, Feb. 12, 1780.
—Content, with Nathaniel Frost, Jr., Mar. 20, 1802.
—Dilla, with Stevens Edwards, Sept. 1, 1798.
—Dorcas, with Nathaniel Rand, Feb. 14, 1798.
—Ebenezer, with Betty McCorson, Jan. 5, 1799.
—Elijah, with Jenny Murch of Buxton, Aug. 22, 1801.
—Enoch, with Happy Whitney, April 7, 1802.
—Esther, with Nathaniel Frost, Jr., Jan. 17, 1796.
—Fanny, with Isaac Chesley, April 24, 1803.
—George, with Sarah Rich, Nov. 4, 1773.
—Gershom, with Deborah Jenkins, Dec. 17, 1774.
—Gershom, with Lydia Freeman, Aug. 28, 1802.
—Hannah, with Moses Fowler, of Falmouth, June 27, 1765.
—Hannah, with Decker Phinney, Nov. 27, 1773.
—Hannah, with Jeremiah Jones, Aug. 1, 1798.
—Jacob, with Elizabeth Watson, Oct. 4, 1777.
—John, Jr., with Hannah Bangs, Jan. 12, 1804.
—Joseph, with Polly Frost, Nov. 8, 1788.
—Rachel, with Tappin Sawyer, Mar. 27, 1801.
—Rebecca, with Samuel Frost, June 11, 1791.
—Ruth, with Nathaniel Lombard, Jr., June 7, 1783.
—Samuel Jr., with Mary Clay, Nov. 29, 1777.
—Sarah, with Edmund Phinney, Jr., March 11, 1780.
—Sarah, with Joshua Crockit, Jr., May 19, 1787.
—Sarah, with Robert Mayo, May 27, 1795.

INTENTIONS OF MARRIAGE.

—Sarah, with William Cloutman, Jan. 12, 1804.
—Seth, with Jerusha Sawyer of Standish, June 11, 1791.
—Susanna, with John Sawyer, of Standish, Jan. 1, 1797.
—Tabitha, with Samuel Crockett, February, 2, 1771.
—Temperance, with Richard Dresser, Feb. 20, 1796.
—Timothy with Anna Harding, Aug. 12, 1769.
—Prince, with Bethiah Webb, of Falmouth, Feb. 17, 1781.
Hammon, William, with Abigail Moulton, both of Pearsontown, Aug. 17, 1782.
Hanscome, Aaron, with Rebecca Akers, Aug. 14, 1799.
—Deborah, of Cape Elizabeth, with Joseph Jones, Dec. 25, 1784.
—Eunice, with Elisha Sanborn, Oct. 27, 1799.
—George, Jr., with Eunice Whitney, Jan. 27, 1776.
—Hannah, with Josiah Swett, Mar. 22, 1783.
—John, with Polly Hanscom, of Kittery, June 2, 1792.
—Joseph, with Polly Bacon, May 12, 1798.
—Katherine, with Ezra Hanson, of Windham, June 7, 1788.
—Moses, with Phebe Crockett, April 7, 1781.
—Nathan, with Abigail Moody, of Scarboro, Oct. 12, 1776.
—Polly, of Kittery, with John Hanscom, June 2, 1792.
—Polly, with Daniel Watson, May 2, 1803.
—Sarah, with Ebenezer Cobb, Dec. 17, 1791.
Hanson, Ezra, of Windham, with Katherine Hanscom, June 7, 1788.
—Moses, of Windham, with Sally Lowell, May 28, 1801.
Hanson, Nathan of Buxton, and Sally Blake, Mar. 2, 1804.
—William, of Windham, with Matilda Elder, Oct. 28, 1785.

INTENTIONS OF MARRIAGE.

Harding, Abigail, with John Harding, Jr., Sept. 13, 1777.

—Anna, with Timothy Hamblen, Aug. 12, 1769.

—Barnabas, with Mehitable Jordan, Mar. 31, 1798.

—Betsy, with William H. Foster, April April 21, 1804.

—Content, with Daniel Meserve, of Scarboro, Nov. 11, 1796.

—David, with Temperance Davis, June 23, 1781

—Eliza, of Flintstown, with Daniel Cresy, June 14, 1799.

—Elizabeth, with Josiah Whitney, Sept. 16, 1775.

—Elkanah, with Martha Knight, of Windham, Nov. 29, 1788.

—Elkanah, with Hannah Brown, Feb. 20, 1802.

—Hannah, with James Lewis, Sept. 7, 1793.

—Hannah, with Silvanus Brown, Nov. 14, 1801.

—Jenny, with William McLellan, July 27, 1782.

—Jesse, with Elizabeth Alden, March 8, 1777.

—John, Jr., with Abigail Harding, Sept. 13, 1777.

—Lois, with James Grant, July 16, 1784.

—Lucy, with Zephaniah Harding, Dec. 12, 1772.

—Lucy, with Elias Fogg, of Buxton, Sept. 14, 1799.

—Martha, with Jeremiah Tole, Dec. 27, 1790.

—Mary, with Joseph Butterfield, of Pearsontown, Sept. 2, 1773.

—Nicholas, with Miriam Bacon, Mar. 28, 1789.

—Phebe, with Thomas Hogin, April 26, 1800.

—Priscilla, with John Lombard, Jr., May 6, 1780.

—Samuel, with Susanna Freeman, May 2, 1781.

INTENTIONS OF MARRIAGE.

—Samuel, of Buxton, with Eunice Huston, July 2, 1790.
—Simon, with Elizabeth Creasy, Dec. 17, 1774.
—Thankful with William Murch, Dec. 4, 1773.
—Zephaniah, with Lucy Harding, Dec. 12, 1772.
Harmon, Dominicus, of Scarboro, with Susanna Freeman, Mar. 22, 1788.
—Joshua, of Scarboro, and Deborah Dunn, Aug. 22, 1789.
—Josiah, of Scarboro, with Rebecca Freeman, Sept. 3, 1785.
—Josiah, with Anna Moulton, both of Pearsontown, Sept. 27, 1785.
—Rufus, of Standish, with Eunice Sawyer, Nov. 21, 1797.
Harper Molly, of Falmouth, with John Davis, Feb. 14, 1784.
Haskell, Abigail, with David Plummer, May 6, 1799.
—Anna, with Thomas Paine, Sept. 8, 1781.
—Anna, with Joseph File, Dec. 22, 1798.
—Benj., with Sarah Berry, of Falmouth, July 24, 1784.
—Daniel, with Mary Bolton, of Windham, Mar. 30, 1794.
—Jacob, with Mary Whitmore, Nov. 19, 1785.
—John, with Rebecca Bangs, of Buxton, Mar. 28, 1801.
—John, Jr., with Mary Paine, Feb. 10, 1781.
—Jonathan, of Standish, with Martha Phinney, Aug. 12, 1792.
—Josiah, with Abigail Wallace, May 14, 1786.
—Rachel, with David Grant of Falmouth, Oct. 14, 1802.
—Samuel, with Lydia Plummer, Jan. 14, 1799.
—Stephen, with Rebecca Marston, of N. Yarmouth, Mar. 5, 1791.
—William, with Katharine Weston, Jan. 23, 1773.
Hasty, James, with Rachel Dean, both of Pearsontown, May 17, 1783.

INTENTIONS OF MARRIAGE.

—Nancy Warren, with Nimrod Libby, of Scarboro, Dec. 3, 1796.
—Polly, of Scarboro, with William Gammon, Dec. 8, 1798.
Hardy, William, of Falmouth, with Hannah Parker, Sept. 10, 1791.
Harrison Hannah, with Joseph Libby, Mar. 21, 1782.
Hatch, Asa, with Rebecca, Crockit, April 19, 1783.
—Asa, with Jane McIntosh, Nov. 17, 1792.
—Betty, with Reuben Cobb, Mar. 14, 1801.
—Capt. Ebenezer, with Elizabeth McLellan, Feb. 6, 1802.
—Elizabeth, of Cape Elizabeth, with Nathaniel Hatch, Dec. 14, 1776.
—Nathaniel, with Elizabeth Hatch, of Cape Elizabeth, Dec. 14. 1776.
—Sarah, with Zebulon Gordan, of Little Falls, April 7, 1781.
Haynes, Jerusha, of Buxton, with John Lamb, July 7, 1786.
—Hannah, with John Stuart, 3d, of Scarboro, Jan. 9, 1796.
Haywood, Sarah, of Brownfield, with Daniel Emerson Cross, of Fryeburg, Feb. 10, 1776.
Hazeltine, Hannah, of Concord, N. H., with Nathaniel Dickey, Dec. 29, 1802.
Heddle, Eliza, with Timothy Hilliard, July, 2, 1801.
Hicks, Elizabeth, with Heman Merrick Brown, of Freeport, Sept. 13, 1802.
—Ephraim, with Rachel Morton, of Standish, June 2, 1804.
—Lemuel, with Mary Rich, April 20, 1771.
—Lemuel, with Susanna Frost, Oct. 17, 1778.
Higgins, Apphia, with Ithiel Blake, June 29, 1769.
Higgins, Hannah Atkins, with Jeremiah Frost, May 5, 1804.
—Isaac, with Esther Parker, Sept. 27, 1800.
—Joseph, of Lincoln, with Elizabeth File, Aug. 23, 1803.
—Knowles, of Standish, with Mary Rand, Dec. 20, 1794.

INTENTIONS OF MARRIAGE.

—Mathew, of Scarboro, with Dorcas Plummer, May 10, 1797.
—Mercy, with Daniel Lowell, Jr., of Standish, Jan. 14, 1799.
—Rebecca, of Standish, with Col. Nathaniel Frost, Oct. 3, 1801.
—Rebecca, of Standish, with Nathaniel Blake, Jr., Nov. 7, 1801.
—Robert, of Standish, with Sarah Whitney, Sept. 19, 1789.
—Ruth, with John Foy, Dec. 15, 1781.
Hill, Anna of Buxton, with Daniel Whitmore, March 23, 1782.
—Hannah, of Wells, with Samuel Lewis, July 14, 1799.
—Martha, of Buxton, with Josiah Davis, Nov. 7, 1802.
—Nathaniel, with Martha Crockett, Nov. 24, 1773.
—Sarah, of Buxton, with Thomas Paine, Oct. 9, 1802.
Hilliard, Timothy, with Eliza Heddle, July 2, 1801.
Hine, Richard, with Abiah Perkins, Feb. 11, 1775.
Hinkley, Martha, with Abner Dow, both of Pearsontown, July 27, 1782.
Hobart, Rebecca, with Archelaus Lewis of Falmouth, May 16, 1777.
Hodsdon, John, with Susanna Brown, both of Gorham, April 6, 1770.
Hodgdon, Joseph, with Mary Snow, Jan. 24, 1789.
Hogin, Thomas, with Phebe Harding, April 26, 1800.
Holbrook, Jane, with John Butler, Jan. 13, 1787.
—Lucy, with James Ross, Jan. 2, 1789.
—Nancy, with Mark Dresser of Scarboro, July 4, 1789.
—Sally, with Charles Cavans, Feb. 12, 1790.
Holmes, William, with Emme Mariner, Oct. 22, 1791.
Honeyford, Mehitable, with Charles Lord, March 12, 1796.
Hopkins, Benjamin, with Hannah Jordan, May 22, 1789.

INTENTIONS OF MARRIAGE.

—Charles, with Martha Bacon, Nov. 17, 1792.
—Hannah, of Pearsontown, with Joseph Blake, Jan. 6, 1781.
—Lucy, of Standish, with Josiah Bacon, Feb. 28, 1788.
—Phebe, with Elijah Davis, April 8, 1780.
Horr, Philip, of Waterford, with Sarah Cates, Sept. 25, 1786.
Hunewell, Jane, of Pearsontown, with Benjamin Clay of Buxton, Oct. 2, 1779.
—Lydia, of Windham, with Edward Webb, Dec. 11, 1784.
—Susanna, of Windham, with Ebenezer Hall, Jr., Dec. 1, 1799.
Hunt, Abigail, with James Lord, Feb. 18, 1804.
—Betty, with John Crockit, Aug. 20, 1796.
—Ephraim, with Abigail Cates, Sept. 2, 1769.
—Francis, with Nancy Merrill, Jan. 16, 1796.
—Ichabod, with Mary Stone, July 9, 1780.
—Ichabod, with Eunice Stone, March 3, 1801.
—Joseph, with Polly McLellan, Oct. 20, 1803.
—Sarah, with Nathaniel Edwards, Sept. 16, 1775.
—Susanna, with Solomon Lombard, Jr., June 26, 1796.
Huston, Ann, with Stephen Phinney, May 9, 1788.
—Elizabeth, with Reuben Elder, Nov. 6, 1786.
—Eunice, with Samuel Harding of Buxton, July 2, 1790.
—Mary, with Richard Mabury, Sept. 15, 1798.
—Rebecca, with William Dyer. Aug. 18, 1792.
—Simon, with Elizabeth Ross Whitmore, Jan. 24, 1801.
Hutchinson, Abigail, with Israel Hall, Sept. 11, 1795.
Huzzey, Fanny, with Jeremiah Rolf of Buxton, May 14, 1785.

INTENTIONS OF MARRIAGE.

Ingals, Isaiah, with Esther Stevens, both of Bridgton. Feb. 28, 1778.
Irish, Abigail, with John Buck of New Gloucester, Feb. 8, 1777.
—Abigail, with Reuben Libby, Jr., Aug. 30, 1794.
—Amy, with Samuel Brunel, Aug. 20, 1791.
—Benjamin, with Jenny Libby of Scarboro, Sept. 2, 1791.
—Betty, with Andrew Cobb, Jr., Dec. 14, 1782.
—Betsy, with John Skillings, Sept. 16, 1802.
—Ebenezer, with Martha Morton, Jan. 1, 1785.
—Isaac, with Anna Flood, July 27, 1786.
—James, Jr., with Mary Jenking, Dec. 13, 1777.
—James, Jr., with Rebecca Chadbourn, July 22, 1798.
—John, Jr., with Eleanor Moffat, April 18, 1775.
Martha, with Stephen Whitney, Oct. 28, 1780.
—Martha, with Samuel Larrabee of Limington, June 5, 1802.
—Mary, with Timothy Brown, Jan. 10, 1789.
—Mehitable, with Joseph Smith, July 23, 1796.
—Obediah, of Little Ossapee, with Mary Dean, Oct. 29, 1789.
—Patience, with John Davis, March 14, 1789.
—Samuel, with Martha Blake, March 27, 1792.
Irish, Sarah, with Henry Flood, March 1, 1777.
—Sarah, with Joshua Young, May 29, 1779.
—Stephen, with Anna Bangs, Dec. 26, 1778.
—Susanna, with Ebenezer Morton, Jr., Oct. 28, 1789.
—William, with Mary McCollister, July 9, 1765.

INTENTIONS OF MARRIAGE.

—William, with Sarah Murch, Sept. 29, 1781.

Jacobs, Lois, with George Scott, March 19, 1774.

Jenkins, Deborah, with Gershom Hamblen, Dec. 17, 774.

—Josiah, with Prudence Davis, June 15, 1776.

—Mary, with James Irish, Jr., Dec. 13, 1777.

—Samuel, Jr., with Lydia Dyer, April 15, 1780.

—Samuel, Jr., with Thankful Snow, Dec. 7, 1793.

Johnson, David, with Jenny Whitney, March 5, 1785.

—Elizabeth, of Andover, with Simeon Farnum, May 26, 1787.

—Ephraim, with Sally Titcomb, Nov. 12, 1791.

—Hannah, of Falmouth, with Amos Whitney, Aug. 14, 1773.

—Jasper, with Rebecca Ross, Nov. 13, 1784.

—Margaret, of Falmouth, with Alexander McLellan, Oct. 12, 1765.

—Mary, of Falmouth, with David Frost, April 10, 1766.

—Nancy, with Nathaniel Knight of Windham, Dec. 20, 1800.

—Oliver, with Betsy Quinby of Falmouth, April 25, 1801.

—Miss Sally, of Andover, with Doct. Nathaniel Bowman, July 10, 1789.

—Stephen, of Bridgton, with Susanna Parker, June 8 ,1775.

Jones, Abigail, with John Sanborn, Jr., both of Pearsontown, Sept. 17, 1782.

—Ephraim, with Mercy Phinney, Dec. 26, 1778.

—Ephraim, Jr., with Judah Philbrick, both of Pearsontown, Jan. 31, 1780.

—Jeremiah, with Hannah Hamblen, Aug. 1, 1798.

—Joseph, with Deborah Hanscom of Cape Elizabeth, Dec. 25, 1784.

INTENTIONS OF MARRIAGE.

—Lydia, with Jeremiah Rand, Jr., April 2, 1791.
—Rebecca, of Cape Elizabeth, with Capt. Joshua Dunn, Aug. 27, 1791.
—Stephen, with Sarah Paine, April 17, 1802.
Jordan, Achsah, with Thomas Paine of Standish, Nov. 29, 1801.
—Betsy, of Buxton, with David Patrick, Oct. 29, 1803.
—Elizabeth, with Walter Libby of Scarboro, March 29, 1800.
—Hannah, with Benjamin Hopkins, May 1781.
—Jonathan, with Lydia Knight, Oct. 13,
—Mehitable, with Barnabas Harding, March 31, 1798.
—Phebe, of Cape Elizabeth, with Daniel Ward, Nov. 22, 1783.
—Polly, with Daniel Tyler, Sept. 24, 1803.
—Sally, with James Tyler of Scarboro, June 13, 1804.
Junkins, Lucy, of Buxton, with Samuel Paine, Oct. 22, 1803.
—Sarah Coleman, with Samuel Bartlett, May 19, 1804.
Kemp, Ebenezer, with Lydia Elder of Windham, Nov. 7, 1800.
—Mary, with Levi Knight of Windham, June 11, 1804.
—Mitty, with Josiah Clark, Sept. 30, 1797.
Kendrick, Mary, of Pepperellborough, with Robert McDonald of Gorham, April 4, 1770.
—Sabrina, with Robert Walker, Aug. 14, 1802.
Kimball, Abigail, with Enoch Stiles, both of Bridgton, Oct. 2, 1776.
—Abigail, with Moses Whitney, Dec. 30, 1791.
—Benjamin, Jr., with Phebe Burnum, both of Bridgton, Nov. 7, 1782.
—Caleb, with Abigail Skillings, Jan. 15, 1774.
—Martha, with William Davis, May 11, 1796.

INTENTIONS OF MARRIAGE.

—Nathan, of Buxton, with Rebecca Parker, Oct. 18, 1788.
—Polly, with Solomon Young, Oct. 2, 1796.
—Rufus, of Scarboro, with Lucy Fly, March 23, 1787.
—Isabella, of Cape Elizabeth, with Nathan Ward, Sept. 30, 1797.
Kirk-Patrick, James, with Sarah Phinney, Oct. 1, 1769.
Kneeland, Elizabeth, with Joseph Stone, March 30, 1781.
—David, with Joanna March, both of Bridgton, May 18, 1776.
Knight, George, of Windham, with Rebecca Davis, Nov. 27, 1786.
—George, of Falmouth, with Anna Foard, June 26, 1798.
—John, with Marcey Gragg, June 5, 1784.
—Joseph, with Mary Lavit of Windham, July 28, 1798.
—Levi, of Windham, with Mary Kemp, June 11, 1804.
—Lydia, with Jonathan Jordan, Oct. 13, 1781.
—Martha, of Windham, with Elkanah Harding, Nov. 29, 1788.
—Nabby, with Joseph Lakin, Oct. 26, 1798.
—Nathaniel, of Falmouth, with Hannah McKenney, Aug. 27, 1782.
—Nathaniel, with Sarah Webb, Dec. 25, 1786.
—Nathaniel, of Falmouth, with Susanna Roberts, Oct. 27, 1798.
—Nathaniel, of Windham, with Nancy Johnson, Dec. 20, 1800.
—Phebe, with John Libby, Jan. 10, 1789.
—Robert, of Otisfield, with Christian Gammon, Nov. 27, 1796.
—Sarah, of Gorham, with Sargent Shaw of Pearsontown, April 17, 1770.
Lagben, Jenny, with Joseph Cookson of Buxton, Dec. 5, 1795.
Laha, Mercy, with Simeon Strout, May 10, 1783.

INTENTIONS OF MARRIAGE.

Lakeman, Josiah, with Esther Cobb, June 28, 1783.

—Hannah, with Thomas Bangs, Sept. 20, 1777.

Lakin, Joseph, with Nabby Knight, Oct. 26, 1798.

Lamb, John, with Jerusha Haynes of Buxton, July 7, 1786.

—Richard, of Buxton, with Phebe Freeman of Pearsontown, Dec. 14, 1782.

Larrabee, Abigail, with Seth Blake, Aug. 2, 1799.

—Isaac, of Scarboro, with Sally Freeman, April 19, 1781.

—Phebe, of Scarboro, with Joseph Gilkey, July 16, 1774.

—Samuel, of Limington, with Martha Irish, June 5, 1802.

—Thomas, of Durham, with Anna Parker, Nov. 7, 1797.

—William, of Scarboro, with Tabitha Whitmore, July 4, 1802.

Lary, Samuel, of Falmouth, with Elizabeth Wise, Dec. 3, 1796.

—Stephen, with Abigail Hamblen, Nov. 29, 1788.

Lathrop, Hannah, with Richard Edwards, July 2, 1765.

Lavit, Mary, of Windham, with Joseph Knight, July 28, 1798.

Leavitt, William, of Buxton, with Mary Cobb, Nov. 23, 1795.

Lewis, Annah, with John Darling, July 30, 1785.

—Archelaus, of Falmouth, with Rebecca Hobart, May 16, 1777.

—Daniel Davis, with Mary Dyer, March 31, 1798.

—George, of Bridgton, with Ruth Lincoln, Dec. 14, 1799.

—James, with Hannah Harding, Sept. 7, 1793.

—Lothrop, with Tabitha Longfellow, Aug. 17, 1793.

—Sally, with Ebenezer Peabody, Jan. 7, 1792.

INTENTIONS OF MARRIAGE.

—Samuel, with Hannah Hill of Wells, July 14, 1799.

Libby, Abigail, with Enos Newcomb, Jan. 27, 1797.

—Alley, with Jonathan Edmunds, Dec. 17, 1774.

—Betty, of Scarboro, with Paul Lombard, April 23, 1791.

—Betty, of Scarboro, with Edward Libby, Aug. 13, 1791.

—Charlotte, with James Thomas, Aug. 25, 1795.

—Dorcas, with George Waterhouse, Oct. 28, 1775.

—Dorcas, with Daniel Maxey, Nov. 22, 1775.

—Edward, with Betty Libby of Scarboro, Aug. 13, 1791.

—Isaac, with Rebecca Crockit, Nov. 28, 1798.

—Jenny, of Scarboro, with Benjamin Irish, Sept. 2, 1791.

—Joab, with Susanna Lombard, April —, 1769.

—Joanna, of Scarboro, with Isaac Fly, June 10, 1786.

—John, with Phebe Knight, Jan. 10, 1789.

—John, of Scarboro, with Dorcas Roberts, April 16, 1802.

—Joseph, with Mercy Whitney, June 6, 1801.

—Joseph, with Hannah Harrison, March 21, 1782.

—Lemuel, of Scarboro, with Patience Whitmore, Feb. 22, 1795.

—Lucy, with Jonathan Bragdon, Oct. 31, 1777.

—Lucy, of Scarboro, with John Roberts, Feb. 21, 1794.

—Mary, with Wallis Foss of Rochester, N. H., June 11, 1799.

—Mary with Greenleaf Rand of Windham, Nov. 12, 1802.

—Mehitable, with Timothy Plummer, Jan. 22, 1800.

—Nimrod, of Scarboro, with Nancy Warren Hasty, Dec .3, 1796.

INTENTIONS OF MARRIAGE.

—Patty, of Scarboro, with John Burnell, 3d, March 15, 1788.
—Polly, with Mathias Murch, March 14, 1781.
—Reuben, Jr., with Abigail Irish, Aug. 30, 1794.
—Richard, with Sarah Ross, Oct. 18, 1788.
—Sarah, of Scarboro, with Benjamin Weeks, June 3, 1790.
—Sarah, with Thomas Blake of Falmouth, June 20, 1790.
—Sarah, with Daniel Brown, Dec. 1, 1802.
—Susanna, with Zedekiah Lombard, Sept. 4, 1784.
—Susanna, with Jedediah Dosset, June 25, 1796.
—Walter, of Scarboro, with Elizabeth Jordan, March 29, 1800.
—William, Jr., with Anna Bolton, March 8, 1797.
Lincoln, Elizabeth, with Nathal Stevens, Dec. 7, 1765.
—Ruth, with George Lewis of Bridgton, Dec. 14, 1799.
Lindsey, Elizabeth, with Hugh Gordon, both of Fryeburg, July 8, 1775.
Linnel, Samuel, with Anna York, both of Pearsontown, June 15, 1782.
Linnet, Hannah, of Pearsontown, with Thomas Lombard, Oct. 15, 1785.
Lombard, Bethshuah, with Elisha Morton of Standish, Jan. 25, 1796.
—Butler, with Jemima Clay, May 25, 1787.
—Dorcas, with Jeremiah Fogg, Jr., Sept. 8, 1794.
—Ebenezer, with Jenny Freeman, Aug. 16, 1794.
—Ephraim, with Polly Perkins, Aug. 7, 1794.
—Hannah, with Ebenezer Murch, Jr., Sept. 9, 1786.
—James, with Bethiah Smith, Nov. 18, 1792.
—Jedediah, Jr., with Lydia Ran, April 23, 1785.
—John, Jr., with Priscilla Harding, May 6, 1780.

INTENTIONS OF MARRIAGE.

—John, with Elizabeth Sawyer, Oct. 2, 1784.
—Joseph, with Fanny Silley, April 11, 1788.
—Joseph, with Hannah Bolton, July 11, 1795.
—Luther, with Mary Plummer, Oct. 20, 1792.
—Lydia, with Joseph Morton, Aug. 22, 1789.
Lombard, Lydia, with Abraham Nason, Oct. 20, 1792.
—Martha, with Edmund Flood, Jan. 27, 1788.
—Nathaniel, Jr., with Ruth Hamblen, June 7, 1783.
—Paul, with Betty Libby of Scarboro, April 23, 1791.
—Phebe, with Benj. Blake, Jr., Aug. 21, 1785.
—Polly, with Nelson Fogg of Scarboro, March 7, 1790.
Lombard, Sarah, with Benjamin Green, July 23, 1774.
—Sarath, with Samuel Thomas, Nov. 6, 1779.
—Solomon, Jr., with Susanna Hunt, June 26, 1796.
—Susanna, with Joab Libby, April, 1769.
—Susanna, with Christopher Dunn, Jan. 19, 1782.
—Thomas, with Hannah Linnet of Pearsontown, Oct. 15, 1785.
—Zedekiah, with Susanna Libbe, Sept. 4, 1784.
Longfellow, Abigail, with Capt. Samuel Stephenson, Oct. 3, 1801.
—Tabitha, with Lathrop Lewis, Aug. 17, 1793.
Lord, Betsy, of North Yarmouth, with Lot Nason, June 30, 1797.
—Charles, with Mehitable Honeyford, March 12, 1796.
—James, with Abigail Hunt, Feb. 18, 1804.
—Nahum, with Charlotte Waterhouse, May 8, 1802.
Lothrop, Thomas, with Betsy Mosher, Jan. 26, 1799.

INTENTIONS OF MARRIAGE.

Lowell, Daniel, Jr., of Standish, with Mercy Higgins, Jan. 14, 1799.

—Jonathan, with Mary Pierce, both of Pearsontown, July 18, 1779.

—Jonathan Moulton, of Flintstown, with Rachel Morton, Nov. 4, 1783.

—Mary, with Nathaniel Gammon, July 5, 1777.

—Sally, with Moses Hanson, May 28, 1801.

Ludlow, Lucy, (a negro woman), with Thomas Francis, (a mulatto man), July 15, 1792.

Lurnmus, Hannah, of Hamilton, with Joseph Ward, Jr., July 12, 1800.

—Samuel, with Margaret Elder, May 23, 1801.

Macy, Susanna, with Joseph McLellan, Oct. 6, 1774.

Maines, Patty, with Samuel Nason, May 19, 1793.

—Benjamin, of Windham, with Abigail Nason, May 30, 1799.

—James, with Alice Gibbs, April 23, 1795.

Mann, Daniel, with Hannah Phinney, Aug. 11, 1792.

—Mercy, with Eli Phinney, Jan. 6, 1799.

March, Deborah, with James Whitney, March 26, 1785.

—Elizabeth, with Samuel March, Jr., April 19, 1798.

—Joanna, with David Kneeland, both of Bridgton, May 18, 1776.

—Pelatiah, with Mary Brackett, Aug. 31, 1776.

—Samuel, Jr., with Elizabeth March, April 19, 1798.

Marean, John, with Lois Bean, both of Pearsontown, Nov. 10, 1781.

Mariner, Emme, with William Holmes, Oct. 22, 1791.

—John, with Betsy Millet, March 5, 1796.

Marr, Polly, with James Gilkey, Jr., May 17, 1782.

Marston, Daniel, of North Yarmouth, with Deborah Young, Jan. 3, 1789.

—John, of North Yarmouth, with Olly Ross, July 19, 1795.

INTENTIONS OF MARRIAGE.

—Rebecca, of North Yarmouth, with Stephen Haskel, March 5, 1791.
Marsters, Susanna, with Timothy Gates, both of Bridgton, Oct. 16, 1777.
Martin, Bryan, with Anna Morton, Jan. 3, 1798.
—Jonathan, of Buxton, with Leah Fogg, Jan. 1, 1793.
—John, with Hannah Swett, Oct. 22, 1794.
Maxey, Daniel, with Dorcas Libbee, Nov. 22, 1775.
Maxfield, Anna, with Daniel Watson, Oct. 3, 1789.
Maxwell, Mary, with Luke Hovey Worster of Falmouth, Nov. 9, 1776.
May, Joshua, with Catharine Weymouth, Feb. 27, 1798.
Mayberry, Richard, of Windham, with Elizabeth Sanborn, July 21, 1787.
—Richard, with Mary Huston, Sept. 15, 1798.
Mayo, Apphia, of Falmouth, with Rev. Josiah Thacher, June 12, 1768.
—Robert, with Sarah Hamblen, May 27, 1795.
McCollif, Polly, with Samuel Snow, March 3, 1798.
McCorson, Betty, with Ebenezer Hamblen, Jan. 5, 1799.
—James, Jr., with Dorcas Brackett of Falmouth, Jan. 31, 1801.
McCullister, Elizabeth, with Gershom Davis, Nov. 13, 1779.
McCollister, James, with Deliverance Pich, Sept. 18, 1765.
—James, with Mary Flood, Dec. 22, 1781.
—Lemuel, with Mehitable Richardson of Standish, Oct. 17, 1792.
—Mary, with William Irish, July 9, 1765.
McDonald, Abner, with Polly Wiswell of Falmouth, July 21, 1781.
—Capt. Abner, with Elizabeth Choat,
—Eliza, with David Lothrop Bradley, April 28, 1804.
—Hannah, with John Paine, Jr., June 20, 1798.

INTENTIONS OF MARRIAGE.

—Jacob, with Betsy Morse of Gray, Sept. 17, 1799.
—James, with Rachel Webb, Jan. 7, 1803.
—Joseph, with Sarah Towell, Nov. 16, 1776.
—Meribah, with Cornelius Bramhall, Jan. 13, 1788.
—Nancy, with Joseph Foss, Oct. 22, 1792.
—Pelatiah, with Dorcas Stuart, June 24, 1787.
—Robert, of Gorham, with Mary Kendrick of Pepperillborough, April 4, 1770.
—Samuel Mosher, of Standish, with Anna Whitten, Oct. 5, 1794.
—Sarah, with Ezekiel Webb, March 17, 1797.
—Simon Davis, with Betty Brown, June 27, 1800.
—Susanna, with John Cresey, Dec. 1, 1770.
McDugle, David, with Anna Elder, Oct. 21, 1786.
—David, with Phebe Paine of Buxton, Jan. 11, 1794.
McGill, Mary, with Brice McLellan of Falmouth, June 5, 1773.
McIntosh, James, with Pegge Patrick, Feb. 10, 1798.
McIntosh, Jane, with Asa Hatch, Nov. 17, 1792.
—Katy, with Dinnes Meloy, Sept. 10, 1796.
—Polly, with Benjamin Patrick, Aug. 16, 1795.
—Sophia, with Perly Whitmore, Nov. 5, 1796.
McKencee, Hugh, with Sarah Dyer of Cape Elizabeth, Oct. 28, 1767.
McKenney, Hannah, with Nathaniel Knight of Falmouth, Aug. 27, 1782.
—Joseph, of Scarboro, with Elizabeth Wiswell, Dec. 21, 1776.
McKinze, Hugh, with Sarah Dyer of Cape Elizabeth, Oct. 29, 1767.
McLellan, Abigail, with Enoch Edwards, May 4, 1799.
—Alexander, with Margaret Johnson of Falmouth, Oct. 12, 1765.

INTENTIONS OF MARRIAGE.

—Alexander, with Chloe Davis, Dec. 12, 1802.
—Brice, of Falmouth, with Mary McGill of Gorham, June 5, 1773.
—Cary, with Eunice Elder, Jan. 3, 1767.
—Carey, with Mary Parker of Cape Elizabeth, Jan. 1, 1785.
—Eleanor, with Elijah Elder, July 28, 1798.
—Elizabeth, with John Smith, May 11, 1782.
—Elizabeth, with Nathaniel Gould, April 8, 1798.
—Elizabeth, with Capt. Ebenezer Hatch, Feb. 6, 1802.
—Eunice, with Ai Staples of Scarboro, Nov. 1, 1800.
—George, with Rachel Boothby of Scarboro, Feb. 18, 1801.
—Hugh, with Rhoda Morris of Scarboro, June 19, 1802.
—James, of Pepperelboro, with Rebecca McLellan, June 8, 1786.
—James, with Louisa Fogg, July 11, 1802.
—Jane, (daughter of Brice) of Falmouth, with Aaron Whitney, Sept. 12, 1765.
—Jenny, with Samuel Barker of Windham, Oct. 10, 1798.
—Joseph, with Susanna Macy, Oct. 6, 1774.
—Margaret, with John Miller of Cape Elizabeth, March 20, 1781.
—Martha, with James Warren, Nov. 20, 1773.
—Martha, with Samuel Edwards, May 19, 1792.
—Mary, with John Clemmons, Dec. 18, 1788.
—Nancy, with Samuel Staples, March 29, 1794.
—Polly, with Joseph Hunt, Oct. 20, 1803.
—Rebecca, with James McLellan of Pepperelboro, June 8, 1786.
—Sarah, with Benjamin Brown Tertius of Georgetown, Jan. 3, 1776.
—Thomas, with Jane Patterson of Pepperelboro, Sept. 20, 1777.

INTENTIONS OF MARRIAGE.

—William, with Jenny Harding, July 27, 1782.
—William, 3d, with Sally Preble of York, March 8, 1795.
McQuillan, John, with Abigail Cook, April 17, 1784.
—John, with Elizabeth Brown, Sept. 24, 1796.
—John, with Olive Edwards of Buxton, Aug. 11, 1798.
Melvins, John, with Abigail Sawyer, Dec. 1772.
Merrill, Daniel, of Falmouth, with Dorcas Crockett, Dec. 3, 1774.
—Daniel, Jr., with Rhoda Roberts, June 5, 1802.
—Dorcas, with William Edwards, Nov. 5, 1803.
—James, of Buxton, with Susanna Whitney, Feb. 18, 1804.
—John, with Lydia Chamberlain, Feb. 23, 1799.
—Nancy, with Francis Hunt, Jan. 16, 1796.
—Priscilla, with Joseph Roberts 3d, March 15, 1804.
Meserve, Daniel, of Scarboro, with Content Harding, Nov. 11, 1796.
—Elizabeth, with Isaac York, both of Pearsontown, May 6, 1780.
—George, of Scarboro, with Dorcas Weeks, Nov. 19, 1791.
—Molly, with Josiah Milliken of Scarboro, Sept. 29, 1781.
—Patty, of Scarboro, with Edmund Whitney, Jan. 28, 1803.
Millet, Betsy, with John Mariner, March 5, 1796.
—Lydia, of Cape Elizabeth, with Jonathan Gammon, Dec. 31, 1785.
—Rhoda, with David Barker of Windham, Sept. 8, 1781.
Miller, James, of Cape Elizabeth, with Content Hamblen, Feb. 12, 1780.
—John, of Cape Elizabeth, with Margaret McLellan, March 20, 1781.
Milliken, Josiah, of Scarboro, with Molly Meserve, Sept. 29, 1781.

INTENTIONS OF MARRIAGE.

Mills, Hannah, of Needham, with David Richardson of Pearsontown, July 24, 1778.

Moffat, Eleanor, with John Irish, Jr., April 18, 1775.

Moody, Abiah, of Standish, with Hezekiah Brown, March 22, 1794.

—Abigail, of Scarboro, with Nathan Hanscom, Oct. 12, 1776.

—Daniel, of Standish, with Polly Sawyer, Sept. 10, 1797.

—Ede, of Cape Elizabeth, with Jacob York of Pearsontown, Sept. 25, 1782.

—Eunice, with Benjamin Carsley, Aug. 25, 1799.

—James, with Elizabeth Shaw of Pearsontown, Sept. 2, 1769.

—Joseph, of Buxton, with Content Crockit, April 11, 1802.

—Joshua, with Mary Carsley, Dec. 13, 1769.

—Joshua, with Zube Nicholson, both of Pearsontown, May 17, 1783.

—Joshua, of Standish, with Rebecca Phinney, Nov. 8, 1788.

—William, of Standish, with Elizabeth Sawyer, Sept. 10, 1803.

Moore, Margaret, of Buxton, with Coleman Phinney, Aug. 11, 1793.

—Lydia, of Buxton, with David Whitney, April 16, 1785.

Morse, Betsy of Gray, with Jacob McDonald, Sept. 17, 1799.

—Jacob, with Mary Dyer, July 26, 1800.

Morton, Abigail, with Ephraim Ryle, Sept. 17, 1792.

—Abraham, with Miriam Roberts, Jan. 1, 1803.

—Anna, with Phinehas Whitney, Aug. 12, 1769.

—Anna, with Bryan Martin, Jan. 3 ,1798.

—Briant, with Lovey Frost of Berwick, Dec. 29, 1766.

Morton, Briant, Jr., with Mary Morton, July 19, 1803.

—Ebenezer, Jr., with Susanna Irish, Oct. 28, 1780.

INTENTIONS OF MARRIAGE.

—Elisha, of Standish, with Bethshuah Lombard, Jan. 25, 1796.
—Hannah, with Edmund Westcot, May 4, 1793.
—Jabez, with Lucy Whitney, October, 1764.
—James, with Susanna Dyer of Cape Elizabeth, July 12, 1777.
—Joseph, with Lydia Lombard, Aug. 22, 1789.
—Martha, with Ebenezer Irish, Jan. 1, 1785.
—Mary, with Briant Morton, Jr., July 19, 1803.
—Rachel, with Jonathan Moulton Lowell of Flints Town, Nov. 4, 1783.
—Rachel, with Thomas Thomes, Nov. 10, 1787.
—Rachel, of Standish, with Ephraim Hicks, June 2, 1804.
—Reuben with Mercy Dyer of Cape Elizabeth Dec. 25, 1792.
—Solomon of Falmouth, with Elizabeth Roberts, Sept. 15, 1798.
—Thankful, with Enos Newcomb, Dec. 27, 1782.
—Thomas, with Betty Frost Feb. 9, 1787.
—Thomas, Jr., with Hannah Wescot, Oct. 23, 1802.
—William with Lydia Strout of Cape Elizabeth, May 26, 1787.
Morris, John Wright, of Scarboro, with Betty Elder, Oct. 4, 1798.
—Martha, of Scarboro, with Allen Davis, May 19, 1792.
—Rhoda, of Scarboro, with Hugh McLellan, June 19, 1802.
Mosher, Abigail, with James Phinney, Jr., Nov. 20, 1790.
—Betsy, with Thomas Lothrop, Jan. 26, 1799.
—James Jr., with Betsy Frost of Summersworth, Oct. 5, 1793.
—Jenny, with Isaac Carsley, May 7, 1797.
—Nathaniel, with Eunice Elder, May 9, 1795.

INTENTIONS OF MARRIAGE.

—Sarah, with William Irish, Sept. 29, 1781.
—Simeon, with Rachel Paine, Dec. 10, 1790.
—Stephen, of Buxton, with Miriam Watson, June 1, 1793.
—Susanna with Joshua Newcomb of Buxton, Oct. 24, 1787.
—Thankful, with Willam Murch of Biddeford, Aug. 28, 1783.
—William, with Thankful Harding, Dec. 4, 1773.
—William with Hannah Barker of Windham, Aug. 31, 1782.
—William, of Biddeford, with Thankful Murch, Aug. 28, 1783.
—Zebulon, with Molly Pennel of Buxton, July 26, 1794.
Murray, Anthony, Jr., with Betsy Preston, March 1, 1788.
—Betsy, with John Babb, May 15, 1795.
—Mary, with Isaac Murch, March 27, 1790.
Myrick, Dorcas, with Myrick Paine of Standish, April 5, 1791.
Nason, Abigail, with Benjamin Mains of Windham, May 30, 1799.
—Abraham, with Lydia Lombard, Oct. 20, 1792.
—David, of Limington, with Martha Vineten, Jan. 21, 1791.
—Eleanor, with Nehemiah Wescot, Feb. 19, 1796.
—Eunice, with William Bolton, Aug. 20, 1803.
—Joseph, with Eliza Waterhouse, March 9, 1804.
—Lot, with Betsy Lord of North Yarmouth June 30, 1797.
—Margaret, with Thomas Cammel of Standish, June 30, 1797.
—Samuel, with Patty Maines May 19, 1793.
—William, with Betsey Brunel, July 2, 1791.
Newbegin, Eunice, with John Akers, Oct. 14, 1783.
—John, of Falmouth, with Molly Thomes, Dec. 10, 1785.
Newcomb, Enos, with Thankful Morton, Dec. 27, 1782.

INTENTIONS OF MARRIAGE.

—Susanna, with Joseph Rounds of Buxton, July 4, 1778.

Moulton, Abigail, with William Hammon, both of Pearsontown, Aug. 17, 1782.

—Anna, with Josiah Harmon, both of Pearsontown, Sept. 27, 1785.

—Daniel, Jr., of Scarboro, with Deborah Dyer, Oct. 30, 1790.

—Joanna, of Standish, with Tristram Coffin, Jan. 9, 1802.

Murch, Abigail, with Elias Boothby, April 6, 1793.

—Ann, with Jeremiah Murch, Sept. 27, 1788.

—Daniel, with Mary Simpson, Jan. 21, 1768.

—Ebenezer, with Margaret Philips of Pepperelboro, Dec. 8, 1763.

—Ebenezer, Jr., with Hannah Lombard, Sept. 9, 1786.

—George, with Hannah Roberts, Jan. 1, 1791.

—Hannah, with Phineas Parker, June 26, 1803.

—Isaac, with Mary Murray, March 27, 1790.

—Isaac, with Charity Smith of Little Falls, Dec. 28, 1794.

—James, with Jenny Bailey of Falmouth, Nov. 5, 1785.

—Jenny, of Buxton, with Elijah Hamblen, Aug. 22, 1801.

—Jeremiah, with Ann Murch, Sept. 27, 1788.

—John, Jr., with Polly Byanton of Buxton, March 24, 1801.

—Martha, with Josedeek Sanborn, Aug. 13, 1796.

—Mary, with Benj. Skillings of North Yarmouth, May 6, 1794.

—Mathias, with Polly Libby, March 14, 1781.

—Molly, with John Silly, July 1, 1786.

—Molly, of Biddeford, with Elisha Cobb, Jr., Sept. 4, 1790.

—Molly, with Jonathan Davis, Aug. 10, 1796.

INTENTIONS OF MARRIAGE.

—Enos with Abigail Libby, Jan. 27, 1797.
—Eunice, with Josiah Green, Sept. 19, 1789.
—Hannah, with Enoch Whitney, June 2, 1792.
—Joshua, of Buxton, with Susanna Murch, Oct. 24, 1789.
—Solomon, with Sarah Whitney, Feb. 1, 1798.
Nickerson, Warren, of Penobscot, with Anner Alden, Nov. 5, 1785.
Nicholson, Martha with William Philbrick, both of Pearsontown, May 31, 1783.
—Zube, with Joshua Moody, both of Pearsontown, May 17, 1783.
Noble, Christopher, with Joanna Rowe, both of Flints Town, Sept. 3 1785.
Noble, Lydia, with Charles Hall, both of Pearsontown, July 28, 1781.
Norton, Joseph, with Anne Whitimore, April 21, 1804.
Ordway, Jonathan Burbank, with Mehitable Rackley, both of Pearsontown, April 23, 1785.
Page, Caleb, of Conway, with Nancy Crockit, June 30, 1797.
Paine, Hannah, with Luther Crocker, June 6, 1801.
—John, Jr., with Hannah McDonald, June 20, 1798.
—Mary, with John Haskell, Jr., Feb. 10, 1780.
—Paine, Mary. with Ebenezer Davis, Jan. 23, 1793.
—Myrick, of Standish, with Dorcas Myrick, April 5, 1791.
—Phebe, of Buxton, with David McDugle, Jan. 11, 1794.
—Rachel, with Simeon Murch, Dec. 10, 1790.
—Richard, with Elizabeth Patrick, Jan. 29, 1774.
—Samuel, with Lucy Junkins of Buxton, Oct. 22, 1803.
—Sarah, with Stephen Jones, April 17, 1802.
—Thankful, with James Davis, Feb. 12, 1793.

INTENTIONS OF MARRIAGE.

—Thomas, with Anna Haskell, Sept. 8, 1781.
—Thomas, of Standish, with Mary Gookins Whitney, March 24, 1792.
—Thomas, of Standish, with Achsah Jordan, Nov. 29, 1801.
—Thomas, with Sarah Hill of Buxton, Oct. 9, 1802.
—William, Jr., with Hannah Cressy of Buxton, Dec. 9, 1797.
Parker, Amos, with Hannah Parker, Dec. 4, 1802.
—Anna, with Thomas Larraby of Durham, Nov. 7, 1797.
—Eleazer Higgins, with Betsy Rand, Aug. 16, 1794.
—Esther, with Isaac Higgins, Sept. 27, 1800.
—Hannah, with William Hardy of Falmouth, Sept. 10, 1791.
—Hannah, with Amos Parker, Dec. 4, 1802.
—Hannah, with Benj. Ficket, Dec. 24, 1803.
—John, with Elizabeth Warren of Scarboro, Jan. 9, 1779.
—Lydia, with Abner Wescot, June 28, 1793.
—Mary, of Cape Elizabeth, with Carey McLellan, Jan. 1, 1785.
—Nathan, of Falmouth, with Zillah Ward, Feb. 14, 1789.
—Phineas, with Hannah Murch, June 26, 1803.
—Polly, with William Riggs of Portland, July 15, 1792.
—Rebecca, with Nathan Kimball of Buxton, Oct. 18, 1788.
—Sally, with Samuel Ficket of Cape Elizabeth, June 21, 1794.
—Susanna, with Stephen Johnson of Bridgton, June 8, 1775.
Parsons, Jonathan, with Mehitable Bangs, Jan. 16, 1790.
Partridge, Zipporah, of Falmouth, with Eliphalet Watson, Jr., July 22, 1780.
Patrick, Benjamin, with Polly McIntosh, Aug. 16, 1795.

INTENTIONS OF MARRIAGE.

—David, with Betsy Jordan of Buxton, Oct. 29, 1803.
—Elizabeth, with Richard Paine, Jan. 29, 1774.
—Pegge, with James McIntosh, Feb. 10, 1798.
—Polly, with Joseph Gammon, Jr., March 1, 1795.
—Polly, with Moses Dyer of Falmouth, Nov. 20, 1797.
Patten, Sarah, of Buxton, with Nathaniel Sturges, Feb. 27, 1802.
Paterson, Jane, of Pepperellboro, with Thomas McLellan, Sept. 20, 1777.
Payne, Mrs. Hannah, with Isaac Whitney, Oct. 12, 1765.
Peabody, Ebenezer, with Sally Lewis, Jan. 7, 1792.
—Lucy, with Varnum Beverly, Jan. 1, 1791.
Peach, Alice, with Jonathan Simpson of Buxton, Dec. 11, 1773.
Pennell, Ephraim, of Buxton, with Lydia Rand, March 3, 1801.
—Molly, of Buxton, with Zebulon Murch, July 26, 1794.
Penfield, Joanna, with Martin Bryan, both of Pearsontown, Jan. 16, 1786.
—Nathan Cook, with Molly Green of Standish, Aug. 25, 1800.
—Sally, with Ezra Ficket, Oct. 19, 1796.
Perkins, Abiah, with Richard Hine, Feb. 11, 1775.
—Esther, with James Cates, Sept. 13, 1768.
—John, with Louis Hadaway, May 18, 1769.
—Lucy, with Abiel Briggs, Aug. 26, 1786.
—Polly, with Ephraim Lombard, Aug. 7, 1794.
—Susannah, with Samuel Gammon, Oct. 5, 1776.
Philbrick, Caleb Pike, of Standish, with Betty Blake, March 26, 1794.
—Elizabeth, with James Thurlo, Nov. 25, 1780.
—Judah, with Ephraim Jones, both of Pearsontown, Jan. 31, 1780.

INTENTIONS OF MARRIAGE.

—Michael, Jr., of Standish, with Jenny Snow, Aug. 7, 1788.
—William, with Martha Nicholson, both of Pearsontown, May 31, 1783.
Philips, Margaret, of Pepperelboro, with Ebenezer Murch, Dec. 8, 1763.
Phinney, Betty, with Joseph Whitney, Sept. 22, 1781.
—Clement, with Joanna Wallace, Jan. 1, 1803.
—Coleman, with Margaret Moore of Buxton, Aug. 11, 1793.
—Decker, with Hannah Hamblen, Nov. 27, 1773.
—Ebenezer, with Sarah Purrington Stuart, May 20, 1781.
—Edmund, Jr., with Sarah Hamblen, March 11, 1780.
—Edmund, Esq., with Mrs. Sarah Stevens, Oct. 15, 1796.
—Eli, with Mercy Mann, Jan. 6, 1799.
—Eunice, with Ithiel Blake, July 31, 1802.
—Hannah, with Daniel Marr, Aug. 11, 1792.
—James, Jr., with Abigail Mosher, Nov. 20, 1790.
—John, Jr., with Susanna Stone, Oct. 20, 1785.
—Joseph, with Susanna Crockett, May 13, 1780.
—Martha, with Jonathan Haskel of Standish, Aug. 18, 1793.
—Mary, with Samuel Shaw of Standish, March 3, 1798.
—Mercy, with Ephraim Jones, Dec. 26, 1778.
—Nathaniel, with Mary Bangs, Nov. 5, 1791.
—Rebecca, with Joshua Moody of Standish, Nov. 8, 1788.
Phinney, Sarah, with James Kirk-Patrick, Oct. 1, 1769.
—Sarah, with John Emery, Dec. 21, 1776.
—Stephen, with Ann Huston, May 9, 1788.
Pickit, Elizabeth, of Buxton, with Samuel Crockit, Jr., April 5, 1783.

INTENTIONS OF MARRIAGE.

Pierce, Elizabeth, with John Sanborn, both of Pearsontown, Sept. 27, 1785.
—Mary, with Jonathan Lowell, both of Pearsontown, July 18, 1779.
Pinkerton, Ann, of Londonderry, with Samuel Warren, Jr., Nov. 28, 1798.
Plummer, David, with Abigail Haskel, May 6, 1799.
—Dorcas, with Mathew Higgins of Scarboro, May 10, 1797.
—Lydia, with Samuel Haskel, Jan. 14, 1799.
—Mary, of Scarboro, with Ebenezer Scott Thomes, Sept. 23, 1780.
—Mary, with Luther Lombard, Oct. 20, 1792.
—Sally, with Joshua Adams, May 26, 1792.
—Timothy, of Scarboro, with Mehitable Libby, Jan. 22, 1800.
Poak, Nancy, with William Cobb, March 10, 1798.
Poland, John, with Fear Brown, Jan. 30, 1790.
Pote, Samuel, with Priscilla Dowty, Oct. 2, 1779.
Pray, James, of Windham, with Loriana Webb, June 27, 1790.
Preble, Enoch, of Portland, with Sally Cross, Aug. 22, 1800.
—Sally, of York, with William McLellan, 3d, March 8, 1795.
Prentiss, Lydia, with Joel Watson of Providence, R. I., Dec. 30, 1797.
—Polly, with Ebenezer Freeman, Oct. 14, 1798.
—Samuel, with Rebecca Cook, Nov. 10, 1787.
Preston, Betsey, with Anthony Murray, Jr., March 1, 1788.
Pride, William, of Falmouth, with Lucy Grant, March 30, 1782.
Prince, the negro man, with Cloe, the negro woman, Aug. 18, 1798.
Purrington, Eleanor, with Walter Ross, Sept. 5, 1800.
Quimby, Betsy, of Falmouth, with Oliver Johnson, April 25, 1801.

INTENTIONS OF MARRIAGE.

Rackley, Joanna, of Pearsontown, with Joseph Stevens, July 10, 1784.
—Mehitable, with Jonathan Burbank Ordway, both of Peasontown, April 23, 1785.
—Pelina, with Benjamin Frost, Aug. 11, 1792.
Rand, Betsy, with Eleazer Higgins Parker, Aug. 16, 1794.
—Elizabeth, with Benjamin Bangs, Dec. 21, 1793.
—Elizabeth, of Scarboro, with John Green, Nov, 7, 1802.
—Greenleaf, of Windham, with Mary Libby, Nov. 12, 1802.
—Jeremiah, Jr., with Lydia Jones, April 2, 1791.
—John Blake, with Ruth Blake, June 22, 1799.
—John, with Abigail Beard of Buxton, April 25, 1800.
—Lydia, with Jedediah Lombard, Jr., April 23, 1785.
—Lydia, with Ephraim Pennell of Buxton, March 3, 1801.
—Mary, with Knowles Higgins of Standish, Dec. 20, 1794.
—Nathaniel, with Dorcas Hamblen. Feb. 14, 1798.
—Philemon, of Scarboro, with Patience Carsley, May 28, 1795.
Rich, Amos, with Eunice Woodman of Gloucester, Feb. 6, 1781.
—Barnabas, with Lydia Brown, April 18, 1779.
—Deliverance, with James McCollister, Sept. 18, 1765.
—Ezekiel, with Sarah Stevens, Oct. 29, 1765.
—James, with Abigail Stevens, May 3, 1775.
—Joel, with Elizabeth Cates, April 17, 1779.
—Mary, with Lemuel Hicks, April 20, 1771.
—Samuel, with Sarah Fogg of Machias, March 9, 1767.
—Sarah, with George Hamblen, Nov. 4, 1773.

INTENTIONS OF MARRIAGE.

Richardson, Anna, with Samuel Bachelor, both of Pearsontown, Nov. 5, 1783.
—David, of Pearsontown, with Hannah Mills of Needham, July 24, 1778.
—David, of Pearsontown, with Sally Wiley of Andover, June 5, 1784.
—Joseph, with Molly Carpenter, both of Pearsontown, Jan. 12, 1782.
—Lydia, with Peter Sanborn, both of Pearsontown, Oct. 23, 1780.
—Mary, of Pearsontown, with Isaac Small of Little Ossipee, Oct. 13, 1777.
—Mehitable, of Standish, with Lemuel McColistor, Oct. 17, 1792.
—Thadeus, with Mary Sanborn, both of Pearsontown, Jan. 16, 1776.
Rideout, William, of North Yarmouth, with Rebecca Thomes, Aug. 29, 1792.
Riggs, William, of Portland, with Polly Parker, July 15, 1792.
—William, with Polly Burnell, March 22, 1794.
Roberts, Benjamin, with Rebecca Dyer of Cape Elizabeth, Aug. 18, 1794.
—Dorcas, with John Libby of Scarboro, April 16, 1802.
—Elizabeth, with Solomon Morton of Falmouth, Sept. 15, 1798.
—Hannah, with George Murch, Jan. 1, 1791.
—Jane, with John Whitmore, June 2, 1792.
—John, with Lucy Libby of Scarboro, Feb. 21, 1794.
—Joseph, 3d, with Olly Foard, Sept. 5, 1793.
—Joseph, Jr., with Sally Strout, Nov. 2, 1801.
—Joseph, 3d, with Priscilla Merrill, March 15, 1804.
—Lydia, with Morrison Flood, May 19, 1793.
—Lucy, with Philip Sceiver of Portland, April 11, 1789.
—Miriam, with Abraham Morton, Jan. 1, 1803.
—Molly, with James Sturges, Oct. 27, 1792.

INTENTIONS OF MARRIAGE.

—Rhoda, with Daniel Merrill, Jr., June 5, 1802.
—Susanna, with Nathaniel Knight of Falmouth, Oct. 27, 1798.
Robinson, John, with Phebe Sanborn, both of Pearsontown, July 30, 1785.
—Sarah, of Cape Elizabeth, with Josiah Alden, Oct. 12, 1782.
Rogers, John, with Hannah Whitney, Oct. 28, 1786.
Rolf, Jeremiah of Buxton, with Fanny Huzzey, May 14, 1785.
—Mary. with John Bohonon, June 16, 1765.
—Molly, with Joseph Weston, Oct. 28, 1786.
Ross, Alexander, with Patience Stowell, Dec. 20, 1788.
—Anne, with William Thomas, Nov. 17, 1798.
—Elizabeth, with Jotham Whitney, Jan. 7, 1792.
Ross, James, with Lucy Holbrook, Jan. 2, 1789.
—Mary, with William Burton, July 29, 1780.
—Sarah, with John Filbrick, April, 1769.
—Olly, with John Marston of North Yarmouth, July 19, 1795.
—Rebecca, with Jasper Johnson, Nov. 13, 1784.
—Sarah, with Richard Libby, Oct. 18, 1788.
—Walter, with Eleanor Purrington, Sept. 5, 1800.
Rounds, Abiel, with Mary Whitney, March 12, 1791.
—James, with Rachel Clay, Sept. 8, 1781.
—Joseph, of Buxton, with Susanna Mosher, July 4, 1778.
—Lemuel, of Buxton, with Molly Whitney, July 14, 1781.
—Samuel, of Narraganset No. 1, with Dorcas Edwards of Wells, Feb. 15, 1768.
Rowe, Affia, with Benjamin Swett, both of Pearsontown, Nov. 18, 1785.
—Joanna, with Christopher Noble, both of Flints Town, Sept. 3, 1785.

INTENTIONS OF MARRIAGE.

—Noah, with Mary Strout, both of Flints Town, March 12, 1785.
—Robert, with Dorcas Thomson, both of Pearsontown, Dec. 27, 1783.
—Susanna, with Isaac Green, June 13, 1801.
Royal, Priscilla, with James Sinclar, March 3, 1793.
Russell, Abraham, with Sarah Swan, both of Fryeburg, Oct. 5, 1775.
Ryle, Ephraim, with Abigail Morton, Sept. 17, 1792.
Ryon, John Butler, with Hannah Wallace of Portland, Aug. 27, 1791.
Sanborn. David, with Sarah Hall, both of Pearsontown, Dec. 7, 1765.
—Drusilla with Enoch Crocket, March 29, 1801.
—Elisha, with Eunice Hanscom, Oct. 27, 1799.
—Elizabeth, with Richard Mayberry of Windham, July 21, 1787.
—Elizabeth, with Abraham Hall, Feb. 6, 1790.
—John, Jr., with Abigail Jones, both of Pearsontown, Sept. 17, 1782.
—John, with Elizabeth Pierce, both of Pearsontown, Sept. 27, 1785.
—Josedeck, with Martha Murch, Aug. 13, 1796.
—Lucy, with Joseph Dow, both of Pearsontown, April 26, 1782.
—Mary, with Thadeus Richardson, both of Pearsontown, Jan. 16, 1776.
—Peter, with Lydia Richardson, both of Pearsontown, Oct. 23, 1780.
—Phebe, with John Robinson, both of Pearsontown, July 30, 1785.
—Rachel, of Pearsontown, with Benjamin Ayer of Buxton, April 2, 1785.
—Sarah, with James Crockit, Dec. 3, 1796.
—Simeon of Pearsontown, with Hannah Ward, Nov. 16, 1782.
—Stephen, with Mary Shaw, both of Pearsontown, Feb. 17, 1774.
Sands, Ephraim, of Buxton, with Elizabeth Stone. March 26, 1774.

INTENTIONS OF MARRIAGE.

Sawyer, Abigail, w'th John Melvins, December, 1772.
—Catharine, with Joseph Weymouth, November, 1768.
—Elizabeth, with John Lombard, Oct. 2, 1784.
—Elizabeth, with William Moody of Standish, Sept. 10, 1803.
—Eunice, with Rufus Harmon of Standish, Nov. 21, 1797.
—Jerusha, of Standish, with Seth Hamblen, June 11, 1791.
—Joel, with Elizabeth Stone of Cape Elizabeth, December, 1772.
—John, of Phillips Gore, with Hannah Edwards, April 21, 1792.
—John, of Standish, with Susanna Hamblen, Jan. 1, 1797.
—Katharine, with James Weymouth, Nov. 3, 1768.
—Nathan, of Falmouth, with Tabitha Skillings, Jan. 30, 1796.
—Polly, with Daniel Moody of Standish, Sept. 10, 1797.
—Sarah, of Phillips, with Benjamin Stevens of Russfield, May 8, 1793.
—Zachariah, of Falmouth, with Susanna Skilling, April 24, 1784.
Sceiver, Lucy, with Pelatiah Crockit, July 2, 1802.
—Philip, of Portland, with Lucy Roberts, April 11, 1789.
Scott, George, with Lois Jacobs, March 19, 1774.
Sevey, Eunice, of Scarboro, with Benjamin Freeman, Dec. 15, 1787.
Shaw, Abigail, of Standish, with William Elder File, Feb. 11, 1803.
—Caleb, of Standish, with Abigail Whitney, Feb. 6, 1796.
—Ebenezer, of Pearsontown, with Sarah Wood of Gorham, Sept. 22, 1771.
—Ebenezer, of Standish, with Salome Green, Feb. 16, 1793.
—Elizabeth, of Pearsontown, with James Moody, Sept. 2, 1769.
—Hannah, of Pearsontown, with Asaph Brown of Waterford, April 27, 1785.

INTENTIONS OF MARRIAGE.

—Hannah, of Standish, with Wentworth Stuart, Sept. 26, 1790.
—Jonathan, of Standish, with Mary Blake, Jan. 1, 1800.
—Joseph, with Eunice Bean, both of Pearsontown, May 12, 1780.
—Josiah, with Tabitha Watson, Nov. 19, 1796.
—Margaret, with Daniel Bean, both of Pearsontown, Dec. 30, 1780.
—Mary, of Pearsontown, with Jonathan Bartlett of Sudbury, Canada, Nov. 20, 1784.
—Mary, with Stephen both of Pearsontown, Feb. 17, 1774.
—Samuel, of Standish, with Mary Phinney, March 3, 1798.
—Sargent, of Pearsontown, with Sarah Knight of Gorham, April 17, 1770.
—Sargent, of Pearsontown, with Salome Dauset, July 12, 1777.
—Thomas of Pearsontown, with Anna Wood, May 2, 1777.
—William, of Falmouth, with Eunice Gorham, March 16, 1799.
Silly, Anna, with Zachariah Weston, Dec. 9, 1786.
—Elizabeth, with Benjamin Skilling, July 10, 1784.
—Fanny, with Joseph Lombard, April 11, 1788.
—John, with Molly Murch, July 1, 1786.
Simpson, Jonathan, of Buxton, with Alice Peach, Dec. 11, 1773.
—Mary, with Daniel Murch, Jan. 21, 1768.
Sinclar, James, with Priscilla Royal, March 3, 1793.
—Mary, with Joseph Cates, Jr., Dec. 25, 1773.
Skillings, Abigail, with Caleb Kimball, Jan. 15, 1774.
—Anne, with Benjamin Cates, July 23, 1774.
—Benjamin, with Elizabeth Silly, July 10, 1784.
—Benjamin, of North Yarmouth, with Mary Murch, May 6, 1794.

INTENTIONS OF MARRIAGE.

—Benjamin, with Anna Hamblen, Dec. 24, 1803.
—Elizabeth, with Edmund Brown, July 2, 1797.
—Isaac, with Susanna Watson, Dec. 7, 1765.
—John, with Betsy Irish, Sept. 16, 1802.
—Mary, with Samuel Davis, Jr., Oct. 9, 1784.
—Susanna, with Zackariah Sawyer of Falmouth, April 24, 1784.
—Tabitha, with Nathan Sawyer of Falmouth, Jan. 30, 1796.
—Thomas, with Mary Burnell, Nov. 24, 1781.
Small, James, of Gray, with Rebecca Gilkey, March 9, 1787.
—Isaac, of Little Ossipee, with Mary Richardson of Pearsontown, Oct. 13, 1777.
Smalley, George, of Raming Town, with Lydia Strout, May 10, 1783.
—Hannah, with Joseph Stuart, June 26, 1779.
Smart, Dorcas, with Pelatiah McDonald, June 24, 1787.
Smith, Bethiah, with James Lombard, Nov. 18, 1792.
—Charity, of Little Falls, with Isaac Murch, Dec 28, 1794.
—Ephraim, Jr., with Mary Brown of Windham, Oct. 7, 1796.
—Hezekiah, with Sally Smith of Windham, Jan. 8, 1797.
—Ithiel, of Limington, with Anna Bean of Pearsontown, July 17, 1779.
—John, with Elizabeth McLellan, May 11, 1782.
—John Tyng, with Mary Duguit, March 24, 1798.
—Joseph, with Mehitable Irish, July 23, 1796.
—Lois, with Isaac Chase of Pearsontown, Sept. 13, 1783.
—Mary, with Amos Whitney, Jr., of Buxton, June 27, 1790.

INTENTIONS OF MARRIAGE.

—Sally, of Windham, with Hezekiah Smith, Jan. 8, 1797.
—Sally, with William H. Waterhouse of Standish, Aug. 4, 1801.
Snell, Wingate, of Buxton, with Mehitable Crocker, May 24, 1788.
Snow, Bathsheba, with Nathaniel Edwards, Aug. 26, 1786.
—Elizabeth, with Solomon Cook, Dec. 22, 1780.
—Gideon, with Joanna Edwards, Dec. 1, 1788.
—Hannah, with Samuel Whitney, July 21, 1798.
—Jenny, with Michael Philbrick, Jr., of Standish, Aug. 7, 1788.
—Lydia, with Joseph Young, 3d, Oct. 5, 1793.
—Mary, with Joseph Hodgdon, Jan. 24, 1789.
—Samuel, with Polly McCollif, March 3, 1798.
—Thankful, with Samuel Jenkins, Jr., Dec. 7, 1793.
Spur, Mary, with David Thurston, both of Otisfield, Nov. 5, 1789.
Staples, Ai, of Scarboro, with Eunice McLellan, Nov. 1, 1800.
—Caty, of Scarboro, with Isaac Gilkey, June 2, 1792.
—Samuel, with Nancy McLellan, March 29, 1794.
Starbird, Elizabeth, of Cape Elizabeth, with Levi Dyer, Oct. 9, 1791.
Sterling, Jane, with Joseph Walker, both of Fryeburg, Nov. 9, 1776.
Stevenson, Catharine, with Ebenezer Storer of Portland, May 26, 1800.
—Capt. Samuel, with Abigail Longfellow, Oct. 3, 1801.
Stevens, Abigail, with James Rich, May 3, 1775.
—Benjamin, Jr., with Amy Webb of Falmouth, May 6, 1784.
—Benjamin, of Russfield, with Sarah Sawyer of Phillips, May 8, 1793.
—Catherine, with Barnabas Stevens, Jr., Oct. 27, 1777.

INTENTIONS OF MARRIAGE.

—Chloe, of Bridgton, with Daniel Cram, Jr., of Pearsontown, Aug. 26, 1780.
—Esther, with Isaiah Ingals, both of Bridgton, Feb. 28, 1778.
—Frederick, of 25 Mile Pond, with Betty Gilkey, Sept. 23, 1800.
—Jenny, with Jonathan Emory of Buxton, Nov. 29, 1801.
—Jonathan, of Portland, with Eliza Cross, Sept. 18, 1794.
—Joseph, with Joanna Rackley of Pearsontown, July 10, 1784.
—Lucy, with Enoch Waite of Falmouth, June 9, 1787.
—Nathal, with Elizabeth Lincoln, Dec. 7, 1765.
—Nathaniel, Jr., with Anna Stuart, Jan. 8, 1791.
—Samuel, with Alice Golt of Allenstown, March 12, 1791.
—Sarah, with Ezekiel Rich, Oct. 29, 1765.
—Mrs. Sarah, with Edmund Phinney, Esq., Oct. 15, 1796.
Stiles, Enoch, with Abigail Kimball, both of Bridgton, Oct. 2, 1776.
Stimpson, Alexander, with Mary Goodwin, April 4, 1792.
Stone, Abigail, with Daniel Whitney, July 9, 1780.
—Elizabeth, of Cape Elizabeth, with Joel Sawyer, December, 1772.
—Elizabeth, with Ephraim Sands of Buxton, March 26, 1774.
—Eunice, with Ichabod Hunt, March 3, 1801.
—Hannah, of Cape Elizabeth, with Zebulon Whitney, May 14, 1774.
—Jonathan, with Damask Elder of Falmouth, Nov. 16, 1782.
—Joseph with Elizabeth Kneeland, March 30, 1781.
—Mary, of Scarboro, with Nephthalim Whitney, March 22, 1777.
—Mary, with Ichabod Hunt, July 9, 1780.
—Susanna, with John Phinney, Jr., Oct. 20, 1785.
Storer, Ebenezer, of Portland, with Catharine Stevenson, May 26, 1800.

INTENTIONS OF MARRIAGE.

Stowell, Patience, with Alexander Ross, Dec. 20, 1788.

Strout, Alice, with Jesse Brown, Nov. 4, 1786.

—Eunice, with William Nason Edgecomb of Limington, Aug. 20, 1792.

—George, Jr., with Comfort Emory of Buxton, May 19, 1804.

—Levi, of Cape Elizabeth, with Rebecca Strout, Oct. 13, 1786.

—Lydia, with George Smalley of Raming Town, May 10, 1783.

—Lydia, of Cape Elizabeth, with William Morton, May 26, 1787.

—Mary, with Noah Rowe, both of Flints Town, March 12, 1785.

—Rebecca, with Levi Strout of Cape Elizabeth, Oct. 13, 1786.

—Sally, with Joseph Roberts, Jr., Nov. 2, 1801.

—Samuel, with Jerusha Emory of Buxton, April 28, 1787.

—Simeon, with Mercy Laha, May 10, 1783.

—Susanna, with Daniel Grant, March 23, 1787.

Stuart, Anna with Nathaniel Stevens, Jr., Jan. 8, 1791.

—John, 3d, of Scarboro, with Hannah Haynes, Jan. 9, 1796.

—Joseph, with Hannah Smally, June 26, 1779.

—Mary, with John Green, both of Gorham, April 17, 1770.

—Sarah Purrington, with Ebenezer Phinney, May 20, 1781.

—Susanna, with William Wood, Feb. 13, 1779.

—Susanna, with Francis Brooks of North Yarmouth, Sept. 29, 1785.

—Wentworth, with Hannah Shaw of Standish, Sept. 26, 1790.

Sturges, Hannah, with William File, Jr., Oct. 9, 1784.

—James, with Molly Roberts, Oct. 27, 1792.

Sturges, Nathaniel, with Sarah Patten cf Buxton, Feb. 27, 1802.

—Temperance, with George File, Aug. 1, 1789.

INTENTIONS OF MARRIAGE.

Swan, Sarah, with Abraham Russell, both of Fryeburg, Oct. 5, 1775.

Swett, Benjamin, with Affia Rowe, both of Pearsontown, Nov. 18, 1785.

—Eunice, with Nathan Cloutman, Nov. 12, 1802.

—Hannah, with John Martin, Oct. 22, 1794.

—Hannah, with Jesse Cloutman, March 9, 1799.

—John, with Betsey Warren of Falmouth, Nov. 20, 1787.

—Josiah, with Hannah Hanscom, March 22, 1783.

—Mehatible, with Jedediah Witham, both of Pearsontown, Oct. 9, 1784.

—Samuel, with Elizabeth Graffam of Windham, Dec. 3, 1785.

—Samuel, of Windham, with Sally Webster, Oct. 1, 1794.

Tappin, Sawyer, with Rachel Hamblen, March 27, 1801.

Thacher, Rev. Josiah, with Apphia Mayo of Falmouth, June 12, 1768.

Thomas, James, with Charlotte Libby, Aug. 25, 1795.

—John, with Miriam Crockit, Dec. 19, 1795.

—William, with Anne Ross, Nov. 17, 1798.

Thombs, Mary, with William Elder of Cape Elizabeth, Feb. 8, 1777.

—Amos, of Pearsontown, with Mehitable Burnell, Dec. 5, 1781.

—Betty, with Joseph Brown of Windham, June 13, 1801.

—Charles with Anna Gray, June 22, 1782.

—Comfort, with Andrew Cates, Sept. 10, 1785.

—Ebenezer Scott, with Mary Plummer of Scarboro, Sept. 23, 1780.

—Esther, with Samuel File, April 29, 1780.

—George, with Lydia Brown, Feb. 26, 1780.

—Joseph, with Abigail Weston of Buxton, June 12, 1781.

—Molly, with John Newbegin of Falmouth, Dec. 10, 1785.

—Patience, widow, with Colman Watson, Aug. 20, 1774.

INTENTIONS OF MARRIAGE.

—Rebecca, with William Rideout of North Yarmouth, Aug 29, 1792.
—Samuel, with Sarah Lombard, Nov. 6, 1779.
—Sarah, with Moses Baker of Summersworth, Jan. 31, 1800.
—Susanna, with James Gray, Oct. 2, 1790.
—Thomas, with Rachel Morton, Nov. 10, 1787.
—Thomas, of Buxton, with Affia Blake, Dec. 26, 1789.
Thompson, Dorcas, with Robert Rowe, both of Pearsontown, Dec. 27, 1783.
—Elizabeth, with John Grcele, Aug 14, 1773.
—Hannah, of Buxton, with Samuel Whitney, March 24, 1781.
—Hannah, of Falmouth, with Jonathan Freeman, Jr., Aug. 23, 1794.
—Mary, of Windham, with William Elwell, April 23, 1803.
—Sally, with William Crockit, Oct. 17, 1802.
—Thomas, with Rebecca Hall, both of Pearsontown, March 31, 1778.
—William, with Anna Durrel, April 21, 1782.
Thorn, Israel, with Sarah York of Pearsontown, no date, probably 1771.
Thurlo, James, with Elizabeth Philbrick, Nov. 25, 1780.
Thurston, David, with Mary Spur, both of Otisfield, Nov. 5, 1789.
—James, of Otisfield, with Sarah West of Raymondtown, July 13, 1796.
Titcomb, Sally, with Ephraim Johnson, Nov. 12, 1791.
Tobin, Mathew, of Windham, with Sally Crockit, Oct. 13, 1799.
Tole, Jeremiah, with Martha Harding, Dec. 27, 1790.
Towell, Sarah, with Joseph McDonald, Nov. 16, 1776.
Tryon, Simeon, with Mercy Cook, Dec. 12, 1801.
Turner, Esther, with Thomas Weston, both of Otisfield, March 5, 1794.

INTENTIONS OF MARRIAGE.

Tyler, Daniel, with Polly Jordan, Sept. 24, 1803.

—James, with Frances Gorham, Nov. 26, 1796.

—James, with Dorcas Bridges of Andover, Jan. 11, 1800.

—James, of Scarboro, with Sally Jordan, June 13, 1804.

Vineten, Martha, with David Nason of Limington, Jan. 21, 1791.

Waite, Enoch, of Falmouth, with Lucy Stevens, June 9, 1787.

Walker, Jesse, with Dorothy Day, both of Fryeburg, Jan. 23, 1776.

—Joseph, with Jane Sterling, both of Fryeburg, Nov. 9, 1776.

—Supply, with Rachel Walker, both of Fryeburg, Dec. 4, 1773.

—Robert, with Sabrina Kendrick, Aug. 14, 1802.

Wallace, Abigail, with Josiah Haskel, May 14, 1786.

—Hannah, of Portland, with John Butler Ryon, Aug. 27, 1791.

—Joanna, with Clement Phinney, Jan. 1, 1803.

—Abigail, of Cape Elizabeth, with Andrew Crocket, Oct. 27, 1781.

Ward, Daniel, with Phebe Jordan of Cape Elizabeth, Nov. 22, 1783.

—Hannah, with Simeon Sanborn of Pearsontown, Nov. 16, 1782.

—Jonathan, with Sally Hall of Standish, Dec. 21, 1793.

—Joseph, Jr., with Hannah Lurnmus of Hamilton, July 12, 1800.

—Mary, with William Hall of Standish, July 14, 1800.

—Nathan, with Isabella Jordan of Cape Elizabeth, Sept. 30, 1797.

—Zillah, with Nathan Parker of Falmouth, Feb. 14, 1789.

Warren, Betsey, of Falmouth, with John Swett, Nov. 20, 1787.

—Elizabeth, of Scarboro, with John Parker, Jan. 9, 1779.

—James, with Martha McLellan, Nov. 20, 1773.

INTENTIONS OF MARRIAGE.

—Mary, of Falmouth, with Peter Crocket, Oct. 12, 1782.
—Samuel, Jr., with Ann Pinkerton of Londonderry, Nov. 28, 1798.
Waterhouse, Charlotte, with Nahum Lord, May 8, 1802.
—Eliza, with Joseph Nason, March 9, 1804.
—George, with Dorcas Libbee, Oct. 28, 1775.
—Joseph, of Falmouth, with Esther Fogg, Aug. 8, 1795.
—Joseph, with Lydia Wescot, April 10, 1802.
—Lydia, of Standish, with Abraham Webb, May 11, 1797.
—William H., of Standish, with Sally Smith, Aug 4, 1801.
Waterman, Malachi, with Mary Darker, Dec. 21, 1776.
—Suky Camel, with Doct. Wm. Whitaker, June 24, 1791.
Watson, Colman, with widow Patience Thoms, Aug. 20, 1774.
—Coleman Phinney, with Elizabeth Frost, March 20, 1802.
—Daniel, with Anna Maxfield, Oct. 3, 1789.
Watson, Daniel, with Polly Hanscom, May 2, 1803.
—Ebenezer, with Anna Whitney, Sept. 22, 1771.
—Edmund, with Betsey Cresy, of Buxton, April 15, 1797.
—Eliphalet, Jr., with Zipporah Partridge, of Falmouth, July 22, 1780.
—Elizabeth, with Jacob Hamblen, Oct. 4, 1777.
—James, with Mary Davis, April 30, 1785.
—James, of Philips Gore, with Mary Carsley, Jan. 21, 1792.
—Joel, of Providence, R. I., with Lydia Prentiss, Dec. 30, 1797.
—John, with Tabitha Whitney, Sept. 18, 1765.
—Martha, with David Davis, May 17, 1788.
—Miriam, with Stephen Murch, of Buxton, June 1, 1793.

INTENTIONS OF MARRIAGE.

—Sally, with David Cobb, Oct. 23, 1802.
—Susanna, with Isaac Skillings, Dec, 7, 1765.
—Tabitha, with Josiah Shaw, Nov. 19, 1796.
Watts, David, with Sarah Davis, Sept. 11, 1779.
—David, with Mary Cresey, Sept. 4, 1784.
—Samuel, with Miriam Cresey, of Buxton, July 16, 1803.
Webb, Abraham, with Lydia Waterhouse, of Standish, May 11, 1797.
—Amy, of Falmouth, with Benjamin Stevens, Jr., May 6, 1784.
—Anna, with William Bolton, Jr., of Windham, Dec. 3, 1785.
—Bethiah of Falmouth, with Prince Hamblen, Feb. 17, 1781.
—Edward, with Lydia Honeywell, of Windham, Dec. 11, 1784.
—Edward, with Sarah Boulton, of Windham, April 7, 1787.
—Ezekiel, with Sarah McDonald, March 17, 1797.
—Loriana, with James Pray, of Windham, June 27, 1790.
—Mary, with John Dam, of Freeport, April 16, 1792.
—Rachel, with James McDonald, Jan. 7, 1803.
—Samuel, of Falmouth, with Polly Wheeler, Oct. 25, 1788.
—Sarah, with Nathaniel Knight, Dec. 25, 1786.
—Seth, with Polly Clements, Oct. 23, 1800.
Webster, Nathaniel, with Jenny Frost, Aug. 3, 1799.
—Sally, with Samuel Swett, of Windham, Oct. 1, 1794.
Weeks, Benjamin, with Sarah Libby, of Scarboro, June 3, 1790.
—Dorcas, with George Meserve, of Scarboro, Nov. 19, 1791.
—Mary, with Joseph Burnell, Sept. 26, 1789.

INTENTIONS OF MARRIAGE.

Wentworth, Betsy, of Buxton, with James Bickford, May 31, 1793.

Wescot, Abner, with Lydia Parker, June 28, 1793.

—Dorcas, with Samuel Whitney, Dec. 25, 1799.

—Edmund, with Hannah Morton, May 4, 1796.

—Hannah, with Thomas Morton, Jr., Oct. 23, 1802.

—Lydia, with Joseph Waterhouse, April 10, 1802.

—Nehemiah, with Eleanor Nason, Feb. 19, 1796.

West, Sarah, of Ramondtown, with James Thurston, of Otisfield, July 13, 1796.

Weston, Abigail, of Buxton, with Joseph Thoms, June 12, 1781.

—Anne, with Amos Whitney, Jr., Oct. 5, 1776.

—Joseph, with Molly Rolf, Oct. 28, 1786.

—Katharine, with William Haskell, Jan. 23, 1773.

—Mary, of Falmouth, with Joel Whitney, Sept. 12, 1765.

—Patience, with Asa Whitney, April 15, 1775.

—Thomas, with Esther Turner, both of Otisfield, Mar. 5, 1794.

—Zackariah, with Anna Silly, Dec. 9, 1786.

Weymouth, Catharine, with Joshua May, Feb. 27, 1798.

—James, with Katharine Sawyer, Nov. 3, 1768.

— Joseph, with Catharine Sawyer, Nov. 1768.

Wheeler, Polly, with Samuel Webb, of Falmouth, Oct. 25, 1788.

Whitaker, Doct. William Smith, with Suky Camel Waterman, June 24, 1791.

White, Silas, with Rebecca Frost, July 10, 1804.

Whitmore, Anne, with Joseph Norton, April 21, 1804.

INTENTIONS OF MARRIAGE.

Whitmore, Daniel, with Anna Hill, of Buxton, Mar. 23, 1782.
—Dorcas, with James Chadbourn, Dec. 6, 1788.
—Elizabeth Ross, with Simon Huston, Jan. 24, 1801.
—John, with Jane Roberts, June 2, 1792.
—Lydia, with Uriel Whitney, Oct. 10, 1784.
—Mary, with Jacob Haskel, Nov. 19. 1785.
—Patience, with Lemuel Libby of Scarboro, Feb. 22, 1795.
—Perly, with Sophia McIntosh, Nov. 5, 1796.
—Tabatha, with William Larrabee of Scarboro, July 4, 1802.
Whitney, Aaron, with Jane McLellan, (daughter of Brice), of Falmouth, Sept. 12, 1765.
—Abigail, with Caleb Shaw of Standish, Feb. 6, 1796.
—Abigail, with Joseph Davis, Dec. 14, 1799.
—Amos, with Hannah Johnson of Falmouth, Aug. 14, 1773.
—Amos, Jr. with Anna Weston, Oct. 5, 1776.
—Amos, Jr., of Buxton, with Mary Smith, June 27, 1790.
—Anna, with Ebenezer Watson, Sept. 22, 1771.
—Anna, with Isaac Hall, April 20, 1793.
—Asa, with Patience Weston, April 15, 1775.
—Asa, with Phebe Davis, May 28, 1785.
—Betsy, with James Cates, Nov. 11, 1797.
—Daniel, with Abigail Stone, July 9, 1780.
—David, with Lydia More of Buxton, April 16, 1785.
—Deborah, with Jeremiah Williams, May 17, 1777.
—Edmund, with Patty Meserve of Scarboro, Jan. 28, 1803.
—Elias, with Polly Fowler, Oct. 10, 1788.

INTENTIONS OF MARRIAGE.

—Enoch, with Hannah Newcomb, June 2, 1792.
—Eunice, with George Hanscom, Jr., Jan. 27, 1776.
—Hannah, with Joseph Brown, Dec. 15, 1768.
—Hannah, with John Rogers, Oct. 28, 1786.
—Happy, with Enoch Hamblen, April 7, 1802.
—Hepsebah, with Nathan Freeman, Oct. 13, 1766.
Whitney, Isaac, with Mrs. Hannah Payne, Oct. 12, 1765.
—Isaac, with Mary Crockett, April 7, 1772.
—James, with Deborah Murch, March 26, 1785.
—Jenny, with David Johnson, March 5, 1785.
—Joanna, with Caleb Chase, Dec. 31, 1769.
—Joel, with Mary Weston of Falmouth, Sept. 12, 1765.
—Jonathan, of Buxton, with Polly Blake, Nov. 24, 1781.
—Joseph, with Betty Phinney, Sept. 22, 1781.
—Joseph, Jr., with Mary Freeman, May 16, 1801.
—Josiah, with Elizabeth Harding, Sept. 16, 1775.
—Jotham, with Elizabeth Ross, Jan. 7, 1792.
—Lucy, with Jabez Morton, October, 1764.
—Lucy, with John Greenlaw, Feb. 23, 1788.
—Mary, with Robert Drake of Cape Elizabeth, Aug. 19, 1786.
—Mary, with Abiel Rounds, March 12, 1791.
—Mary Gookin, with Thomas Paine of Standish, March 24, 1792.
—Mary, with Freeman Blake, Aug. 12, 1803.
—Mercy, with Joseph Libby, June 6, 1801.

INTENTIONS OF MARRIAGE.

—Micah, with Hannah Cobb, Nov. 13, 1779.
—Molly, with Lemuel Rounds of Buxton, July 14, 1781.
—Moses, with Abigail Kimball, Dec. 30, 1791.
—Nephthalim, with Mary Stone of Scarboro, March 22, 1777.
—Phinehas, with Anna Morton, Aug. 12, 1769.
—Priscilla, with David Young, Dec. 3, 1796.
—Samuel, with Hannah Thomson of Buxton, March 24. 1781.
—Samuel, with Hannah Snow, July 21, 1798.
—Samuel, with Dorcas Wescot, Dec. 25, 1799.
—Sarah, with Robert Higgins of Standish, Sept. 19, 1789.
—Sarah, with Sheba Dyer, May 28, 1797.
—Sarah, with Solomon Newcomb, Feb. 1, 1798.
—Sarah, with Jonathan Elwell, June 5, 1802.
—Stephen, with Martha Irish, Oct. 28, 1780.
—Susannah, with Owen Brannels, July 23, 1774.
—Susanna, with James Merrill of Buxton, Feb. 18, 1804.
—Tabitha, with John Watson, Sept. 18, 1765.
—Uriel, with Lydia Whitmore, Oct. 10, 1784.
—William, of Limington, with Hannah Bangs, Aug. 18, 1792.
—Zebulon, with Hannah Stone of Cape Elizabeth, May 14, 1774.
Whitten, Anna, with Samuel Mosher McDonald of Standish, Oct. 5, 1794.
Whittum, Jedediah, with Katharine Wilson, both of Fryeburg, Nov. 30, 1776.
Wiley, Sally, of Andover, with David Richardson of Pearsontown, June 5, 1784.

INTENTIONS OF MARRIAGE.

Williams, Jeremiah, with Deborah Whitney, May 17, 1777.
—Mary, with Doctor Jeremiah Barker of Falmouth, July 2, 1802.
Wilson, Katharine, with Jedediah Whittum, both of Fryeburg, Nov. 30, 1776.
Wing, Nathan of Limerick, with Love Frost, Oct. 17, 1791.
Wise, Elizabeth, with Samuel Lary of Falmouth, Dec. 3, 1796.
—Joseph, of Falmouth, with Abigail Edwards, Feb. 20, 1801.
Wiswell, Elizabeth, with Joseph McKenney of Scarboro, Dec. 21, 1776.
—Polly, of Falmouth, with Abner McDonald, July 21, 1781.
Witham, Jedediah, with Mehitable Swett, both of Pearsontown, Oct. 9, 1784.
Wood, Anna, with Thomas Shaw of Pearsontown, May 2, 1777.
—Charles, with Sarah Davis, July 23, 1786.
—Hannah, with John Foy, Dec. 5, 1778.
Wood, Hannah, with Nathaniel Blake, Feb. 8, 1793.
—Sarah, with Ebenezer Shaw of Pearsontown, September 22, 1771.
—William, with Susanna Stuart, Feb. 13, 1779.
—William, Jr., with Polly Dyer, Nov. 14, 1790.
—William, with Mercy Bean, Dec. 7, 1796.
Woodard, John, with Dorothy Hall, Sept. 10, 1791.
Woodman, Benjamin of Buxton, with Elizabeth Eldridge, May 2, 1778.
—Eunice, of Gloucester, and Amos Rich, Feb. 6, 1781.
—Nathan, with Lydia York, Aug. 5, 1784.
Woods, Joseph, of Bridgton, with Susan York, of Parsontown, Aug. 19, 1776.
Wooster, Thomas, with Susanna Edwards, Aug. 23, 1800.

INTENTIONS OF MARRIAGE.

— Luke Hovey, of Falmouth, with Mary Maxwell, Nov. 9, 1776.

York, Abigail, with Jonathan Beane, both of Pearsontown, Oct. 22, 1774.

—Anna, with Samuel Linnel, both of Pearsontown, June 15, 1782.

—Isaac with Elizabeth Meserve, both of Pearsontown, May 6, 1780.

—Jacob of Pearsontown, with Ede Moody of Cape Elizabeth, Sept. 25, 1782.

—Lydia, with Nathan Woodman, Aug. 5, 1784.

—Mary with Reuben Cookson, both of Pearsontown, Jan., 1769.

—Naoma, with John Hall, both of Pearsontown, Feb. 2, 1769.

—Sarah, of Pearsontown, with Isreal Thorne, no date. probably 1771.

—Susan, of Pearsontown, with Joseph Woods, of Bridgton, Aug. 19, 1776.

Young, David, with Priscilla Whitney, Dec. 3, 1796.

—Deborah, with Daniel Marston, of North Yarmouth, Jan. 3, 1789.

—Joseph 3d, with Lydia Snow, Oct. 5, 1793.

—Joseph, with Betsy Clark, July 9, 1803.

—Joshua, with Sarah Irish, May 29, 1779.

—Rebecca, with Jonathan Green, Sept. 3, 1796.

—Solomon, with Polly Kimball, Oct. 2, 1796.

MARRIAGES.

From the earliest town records of Gorham, Me. These will be followed with births and deaths from the same books. As these latter records are quite deficient, the compiler will be very thankful to those having last century records of any Gorham families to furnish them, also to note errors in these publications.

Abraham, Sarah, and James Sam, July 29, 1749.

—Adam, and Dinah (Negros) of Pearsontown, Aug. 24, 1785.

Adams, Benjamin, and Elizabeth Frost, Nov. 26, 1778.

—Joseph, and Mercy Elwell, April 12, 1802.

—Joshua, and Sally Plummer, June 17, 1792.

—Stephen, and Sarah Elwell, April 14, 1782.

—William, and Susanna Brown, Dec. 3, 1772.

—William, and Rebecca Elwell, Dec. 13, 1786.

Akers, Jenny, and James Bracket of Falmouth, March 17, 1785.

—John, and Eunice Newbegin, Nov. 6, 1783.

—Moses, and Hannah Bracket Mosher, December, 1753.

—Moses, and Mary Clark, Dec. 7, 1780.

—Rebecca, and Aaron Hanscom, May 11, 1780.

MARRIAGES.

Atwood, Sarah, and Jabez Walker, June, 1748.

Alden, Anner, and Warren Nickerson of Penobscot, Nov. 22, 1785.

—Austin, born Marshfield, March 25, 1729, married Nov. 25, 1756, Salome Lombard, born, Truro, June 10, 1736.

—Elizabeth, and Jesse Harding, March 27, 1777.

Babb, William, and Elizabeth Conant, May, 1764.

Bacon, Martha and Charles Hopkins, March 7, 1793.

—Miriam, and Nicholas Harding, June 14, 1789.

—Nathaniel, and Betty Dyer, May 13, 1782.

—Polly, and Joseph Hanscom, June 3, 1798.

—Timothy, and Mary Irish, Feb. 19, 1789.

Baker, Moses, of Summersworth, and Sarah Thomes, Feb. 25, 1800.

Barker, Dr. Jeremiah, of Falmouth, and Susanna Garrett, Dec. 17, 1790.

—Samuel of Windham, and Jenny McLellan, Dec. 16, 1798.

Bangs, Anna, and Stephen Irish, April 1, 1779.

—Barnabas, Jr., and Catharine Stevens, Nov. 20, 1777.

—Barnabas, Jr., and Betty Cloutman, Nov. 1, 1789.

—Ebenezer, and Polly Cobb, Dec. 30, 1787.

—Hannah, and William Whitney, Oct. 11, 1792.

—Heman, and Molly Wood, Jan. 1, 1770.

—James and Elizabeth Easter, Nov. 26, 1789.

—Joseph and Polly Bangs, April 30, 1795.

—Mary and Nathaniel Phinney, April 30, 1792.

—Mehitable and Jonathan Parsons, March, 25, 1790.

—Nathan and Sarah Bangs, July 15, 1798.

MARRIAGES.

—Polly and Joseph Bangs, April 30, 1795.
—Rebecca and John Haskel, April 25, 1801.
—Sarah and Nathan Bangs, July 15, 1798.
Bean, Mercy and William Wood, Dec. 15, 1796.
Beverly, Varnum and Lucy Peabody, Jan. 28, 1791.
Blanchard, John and Dorcas Carsley, June 4, 1792.
—Mary and Daniel Gammon, April 8, 1781.
Blake, Benjamin, Jr., and Phebe Lombard, Oct. 20, 1785.
—Ithiel and Apphia Higgins, July 13, 1769.
—Ithiel and Eunice Phinney, Sept. 9 1802.
—Lydia and Samuel Bryant, of Pepperellboro, May 18, 1800.
—Martha and Samuel Irish, July, 1792.
—Nathaniel and Hannah Wood, Mar. 7, 1793.
—Polly and Jonathan Shaw, 1800.
—Thomas, of Falmouth, and Sarah Libby, Dec. 16, 1790.
Bolton, Anna and William Libby, Jr., March 30, 1797.
—William and Anna Webb, Jan. 5, 1786,
—Thomas and Hannah Crocket, Jan. 24, 1782.
Brackit, James, of Falmouth, and Jenny Akers, March 17, 1785.
Bradbury, Joseph, Jr., of Buxton, and Susanna Crockit, July 22, 1798.
Bragdon, Jenny, and John Edwards, Oct. 1. 1801.
Bramhall, Betty, and James Goodwin, Oct. 23, 1794.
—Cornelius, and Meribah McDonnald, Feb. 28, 1788.
Briggs, Abiel, and Polly Dunn, Jan. 20, 1791.
Brooks, Francis, of North Yarmouth, and Susanna Stuart, Jan. 4, 1786.

MARRIAGES.

Brown, Abiel, and Abigail Crockit, Aug. 15, 1799.
—Betty, and Simon Davis McDonald, July 16, 1800.
—Edmund, and Elizabeth Skillings, Aug. 6, 1797.
—Elizabeth, and John McQuillian, Oct. 13, 1796.
—Fear, and John Poland, April 26, 1791.
—Hannah, and David Whitney, Feb., 1754.
—Hannah, and Elkanah Harding, March 14, 1802.
—Herman Merrick, of Freeport, and Elizabeth Hicks, Dec. 20, 1802.
—Jesse, and Ellis Strout, Dec. 14, 1786.
—Jerusha, and Walter Murch, Nov. —, 1758.
—John, and Mary Gammon, Nov. 29, 1801.
—Jonathan, and Deborah Eldridge, Aug. 1, 1779.
—Joseph, and Hannah Whitney, Dec. 13, 1768.
—Joseph, and Hannah Elder, Oct. 28, 1798.
—Joseph, of Windham, and Betty Thomes, Nov. 5, 1801.
—Lydia, and George Thoms, April 6, 1780.
—Lydia, and Barnabas Rich, June 28, 1779.
—Rachel, and Chipman Cobb, March 12, 1797.
—Susanna, and William Adams, Dec. 3, 1772.
Bryant, Samuel, of Pepperellboro, and Lydia Blake, May 18, 1800.
Butler, John, and Mrs. Jane Holbrook, Jan. 25, 1787.
Burnell, Benjamin, and Dorcas Carsley, Dec. 28, 1788.
—Betsey, and William Nason, Sept. 8, 1791.
—John, and Lydia Whitney, July 3, 1766.
—Joseph, and Mary Weeks, Jan. 7, 1790.

MARRIAGES.

—Polly, and William Riggs, April 13, 1794.
—Samuel, and Amy Irish, Sept. 18, 1791.
Burton, William, and Mary Ross, April 26, 1781.
Cahoon, Betty and Prince Davis, Jr., Jan. 3, 1797.
Carsley, Benjamin, and Eunice Moody, Sept. 23, 1799.
—Dorcas, and Benjamin Burnell, Dec. 28, 1787.
—Dorcas, and John Blanchard, June 4, 1792.
—Ebenezer, and Patience Phinney, Nov. 25, 1766.
—Isaac, and Jenny Mosher, June 18, 1797.
—John, and Marcy Freeman, April 5, 1764.
—John, Jr., and Martha Crockit, April 16, 1790.
—Mary, and James Watson, Feb. 23, 1792.
—Nathan, and Susanna Cotton, March 2, 1792.
—Patience, and Philemon Rand, of Scarboro, March 20, 1796.
Cates, Abigail and Ephraim Hunt, Oct. 6, 1769.
—Andrew and Comfort Thomes, Oct. 6, 1785.
—Benjamin and Anne Skilling, Aug. 18, 1774.
—Betty and Samuel Rich, Jan. 23, 1799.
—Ebenezer and Anne Cobb, Jan. 5, 1794.
Elizabeth and Joel Irish, May 16, 1779.
—James and Esther Perkins, Sept. 20, 1768.
—James and Betty Whitney, Dec. 10, 1797
—Joseph and Mary Sinclear, Jan. 13, 1774.
—Lydia and William Cobb, Jan. 1, 1792.
—Sarah and Philip Horr, of Waterford, Dec. 17, 1786.
Cato and Claracy, (negros,) April 14, 1785.

MARRIAGES.

Chadbourn, James and Dorcas Whitmore, Jan. 4, 1789.

—Rebecca and James Irish, Jr., Sept. 2, 1798.

Chamberlain, Lydia and John Merrill, April 21, 1799.

Chandler, Benjamin of Pepperellboro, and Martha Gilkey, Oct. 20, 1799.

Chase, Betty and Ebenezer Cotton, Mar. 5, 1789.

—Caleb, born in Newbury, Feb. 28, 1746. married Dec. 31, 1679, Joanna Whitney, born in York.

—John of Limington, and Abagail Hooper, Jan. 13, 1797.

Choat, Elizabeth and Abner McDonald, June 28, 1801.

Clark, Jacob and Elizabeth Fly, Oct. 11, 1792.

—Mary and Moses Akers, Dec. 7, 1780.

—Sally and Almory Hamblen, Oct. 8. 1797.

Clay, Jemima and Butler Lombard, Aug. 9, 1787.

Clemons, Jacob and Phebe Coffin, May 11, 1790.

Clemmons, John and Margaret McLellan, Feb. 6, 1789.

Cloe and Prince, negros, Sept. 29, 1799.

Cloutman, Betty and Barnabas Bangs, Jr., Nov. 1, 1789.

—John and Sarah Cobb, Aug. 1, 1802.

Cobb, Anne and Ebenezer Cates, Jan. 5, 1794.

—Chipman and Rachel Brown, Mar. 12, 1797.

—David and Sally Watson, Dec. 9, 1802.

—Ebenezer and Sarah Hanscom, Jan 8, 1792.

—Elisha and Elizabeth Murch, Nov., 1760.

— Esther and Josiah Lakeman, Dec. 24, 1783.

—Hannah, and Micah Whitney, Nov. 29, 1779.

—Mary, and William Leavit, Jan. 10, 1796.

MARRIAGES.

—Phebe, and Daniel Eldridge, Jr., Mar. 17, 1785.
—Polly, and Ebenezer Bangs, Dec. 30, 1787.
—Reuben, and Betsey Hatch, April, 5, 1801.
—Sarah, and John Cloutman, Aug. 1, 1802.
—William, and Lydia Cates, Jan. 1, 1792.
Coffin, John, and Lornhama Cotton, Dec. 11, 1791.
—Phebe, and Jacob Clemons, May 11, 1790.
Conant, Elizabeth, and William Babb, May, 1764.
—Hannah, and Joseph Green, Mar. 8, 1749.
Cook, Abigail, and John McQuilla, May 4, 1784.
—Mercy, and Simeon Tryon, Feb. 16, 1802.
—Rebecca, and Samuel Prentiss, Nov. 29, 1787.
—Sarah, and John Gammon, June 15, 1797.
—Solomon, and Elizabeth Snow, Feb. 23, 1781.
Cookson, Reuben, and Mary York, Feb. 1, 1769.
Coolbroth, John, of Buxton, and Elizabeth Foss, of Scarboro, Nov. 3, 1791.
—Samuel, of Buxton, and Elizabeth Mars, of Scarboro, Sept. 21, 1788.
Cotton, Ebenezer, and Betty Chase, March 5, 1789.
—Lornhama, and John Coffin, Dec. 11, 1791.
—Sarah, and Jonathan Elwell, Feb. 6, 1794.
—Susanna, and Nathan Carsley, March 2, 1792.
Cresy, Mary, and David Watts, Oct. 14, 1784.
Crisp, Margaret, and Roger Jordan, Nov. 25, 1779.
Crocker, Luther, and Hannah Paine, Oct. 1, 1801.

MARRIAGES.

—Mehitable, and Wingate Snell, June 15, 1788.
—Timothy, and Hannah Meserve, Dec., 1754.
Crockit, Abigail, and Abiel Brown, Aug. 15, 1799.
—Betty, and Jonathan Fickit, Dec. 21, 1763.
—Betty, and Benjamin Gammon, Oct. 21, 1787.
—Enoch, and Drusilla Sanborn, Sept. 13, 1801.
—Ephraim, and Martha Gray, Jan. 5, 1792.
—Hannah, and Thomas Bolton, Jan. 24, 1782.
—James, and Sarah Sanborn, Dec. 25, 1796.
—John, and Mary Hunt, Dec. 15, 1796.
—Joshua, and Sarah Hamblen, Nov. 29, 1787.
—Martha, and John Carsley, Jr., April 16, 1790.
—Miriam, and John Thomas, Jan. 17, 1796.
—Nancy, and Caleb Page of Conway, December, 1797.
—Pelatiah, and Lucy Sceiver, July 18, 1802.
—Phebe, and Moses Hanscom, April 23, 1781.
—Rebecca, and Asa Hatch, May 6, 1788.
—Rebecca, and Isaac Silla, Dec. 20 1798.
—Samuel, and Mary Whitney, June 10, 1763.
—Sarah, and Mathew Tobin, Feb. 6, 1780.
—Susanna, and Joseph Phinney, June 18, 1780.
—Susanna, and Joseph Bradbury, Jr., July 22, 1798.
—Tenty, and Joseph Moody of Buxton, Aug. 1, 1802.
—William, and Sally Thompson, Nov. 21, 1802.
Cross, Eliza, and Jonathan Stevens of Portland, Jan. 25, 1795.

MARRIAGES.

Darling, John, and Hannah Lewis, Oct. 14, 1785.
Davis, Alice, and Enoch Frost, April 24, 1780.
—Chloe, and Alexander McLellan, Feb. 9, 1803.
—David, and Martha Watson, June 12, 1788.
—Ebenezer, and Mary Paine, Feb. 18, 1790.
—Gershom, and Elizabeth McCollister, Dec. 26, 1779.
—James, and Thankful Paine, March 21, 1793.
—John, and Patience Irish, April 16, 1789.
—Joseph, and Abigail Whitney, September, 1799.
—Mary, and Zephaniah Harding, November, 1759.
—Mary, and James Watson, June 30, 1785.
—Phebe, and Asa Whitney, July 14, 1785.
—Prince, Jr., and Betty Cahoon, Jan. 3, 1797.
—Priscilla, and Charles McDaniel, January. 1762.
—Rebecca, and George Knight of Windham, March 14, 1787.
—Samuel, Jr., and Mary Skillings, Nov. 11, 1784.
—Sarah, and David Watts, Dec. 9, 1779.
—Sarah, and Charles Wood, Sept. 17, 1786.
—Sarah and Benj. Emory of Buxton, Oct. 4, 1801.
—Silvanus, and Hannah Gorham, Nov. 19, 1789.
Davis, William, and Martha Kimbal, June 5, 1796.
Dean, Mary, and Obediah Irish, Jan. 7, 1790.
Dearing, Samuel, and Nancy Larrabee, both of Scarboro, June 8, 1794.
Derbon, Mary, and John Dyer, Jr., April 1, 1790.

MARRIAGES.

Doane, Hannah, and William Lukeman, December, 1754.

Dole, Samuel, and Mehitable Winship, Nov. 8, 1787, both of Windham.

Donnell, Benjamin, and Elizabeth Hodgdon, October, 1755.

Dorset, Jedediah, and Susanna Libby, May 12, 1797.

Douty, Priscilla, and Samuel Pote, October, 1779.

Dresser, Mark and Nancy Holbrook, Aug. 9, 1789.

—Richard, and Temperance Hamblen, April, 1796.

Dunn, Christopher, and Susanna Lombard, Feb. 3, 1782.

—Christopher, and Betty Fogg, March 30, 1794.

—Deborah, and Joshua Harmon, Jan. 28, 1790.

—Polly, and Abiel Briggs, Jan. 20, 1791.

Dyer, Betty, and Nathaniel Bacon, May 13, 1782.

—Deborah, and Daniel Moulton, Jr., Nov. 25, 1790.

—John, Jr., and Mary Derbon, April 1, 1790.

—Lydia, and Samuel Jenkins, Jr., Oct. 1, 1780.

—Olly, and Daniel Lewis, May 13, 1798.

—Paul, and Mary Edwards, Nov. 25, 1802.

—Polly, and William Wood, Jr., Nov. 25, 1790.

—Sarah, of Cape Elizabeth, and Hugh McKenzie, Oct. 29, 1767.

—Sheba, and Sarah Whitney, July 16, 1797.

—William, and Rebecca Huston, Oct. 11, 1792.

Easter, Elizabeth, and James Bangs, Nov. 26, 1789.

Edgcomb, William Nason, of Limington, and Eunice Strout, Sept. 13, 1792.

Edwards, Abigail. and Joseph Wise, May 21, 1801.

—Dorcas, of Wells, and Samuel Rounds of Narraganset, Feb. 15, 1768.

MARRIAGES.

—Enoch, and Abigail McLillan, June 16, 1799.
—Hannah, and John Sawyer, of Phillips Gore, Oct. 4, 1792.
—Joanna, and Gideon Snow, Dec. 28, 1788.
—John, and Jenny Bragdon, Oct. 1, 1801.
—Mary, and Paul Dyer, Nov. 25, 1802.
—Nathaniel, and Bersheba Snow, Sept. 29, 1786.
—Olive, and John McQuillian, Sept. 20, 1798.
—Richard, and Hannah Lothrop, July 4, 1765.
—Samuel, and Martha McLellan, July 8, 1792.
—Stephen and Dilla Hamblen, Oct. 4, 1798.
—Susanna, and Thomas Wooster, Sept. 11, 1800.

Elder, Anna, and David McDugle, Dec. 20, 1786.
—Betty, and John Wright Morris, Oct. 4, 1798.
—Elijah, and Eleanor McLellan, Aug. 19, 1798.
—Eunice, and Carey McLellan, Jan. 1, 1767.
—Eunice, and Nathaniel Mosher, Nov. 15, 1795.
—Hannah, and Joseph Brown, Oct. 28, 1798.
—Joseph, of Windham, and Anne Morrel, of Falmouth, May 1, 1788.
—Margaret, and Samuel Lummus, May 31, 1801.
—Metilda, and William Hanson, Dec. 8, 1785.
—Polly, and Daniel Gammon, Jan. 4, 1787.
—Rebecca, and Josiah Webb, both of Windham, May 15, 1788.
—Reuben, and Elizabeth Huston, Feb. 4, 1787.
—William and Mary Thoms, February, 1777.
—William and Lydia McCaslin, March 4, 1790.

MARRIAGES.

Eldridge, Daniel, Jr., and Phebe Cobb, March 17, 1785.

—Deborah, and Jonathan Brown, Aug. 1, 1779.

Elwell, Jonathan, and Sarah Cotton, Feb. 6, 1794.

—Mercy, and Joseph Adams, April 12, 1802.

—Rebecca, and William Adams, Dec. 13, 1786.

—Sarah, and Stephen Adams, April 14, 1782.

Emory, Benjamin, of Buxton, and Sarah Davis, Oct. 4, 1801.

—James, and Sarah Fogg, June 14, 1796.

—Jonathan, of Buxton, and Jane Stevens, Dec. 30, 1801.

Evans, Elijah, and Rebecca Green, both of Portland, March 19, 1799.

Ficket, Ezra, and Sally Penfield, Dec. 15, 1796.

—Jonathan, and Betty Crocket, Dec. 21, 1763.

—Samuel, of Cape Elizabeth, and Sarah Parker, July 6, 1794.

Filbrick, Michael, Jr., of Standish, and Jenny Snow, Sept. 4, 1788.

File, George, and Temperance Sturges, Oct. 10, 1789.

—Samuel, and Esther Thomes, Sept. 28, 1780.

—William, Jr., and Hannah Sturges, Dec. 30, 1784.

Flood, Anna, and Isaac Irish, Sept. 28, 1786.

—Edmund, with Martha Lombard, Aug. 10, 1788.

—John, and Katharine Roberts of Falmouth, Jan. 13, 1791.

—Mary, and James McCollister, Jan. 31, 1782.

—Morrison, and Lydia Roberts, June 17, 1793.

Fly, Elizabeth, and Jacob Clark, Oct. 11, 1792.

—Lucy and Rufus Kimball, Jan. 17, 1787.

MARRIAGES.

Fogg, Betty, and Christopher Dunn, March 30, 1794.

—Elias, and Lucy Harding, Sept. 29, 1799.

—Esther, and Joseph Waterhouse of Falmouth, Sept. 13, 1795.

—Jeremiah, and Dorcas Lombard, Dec. 21, 1794.

—Louisa, and James McLellan, Dec. 5, 1802.

—Nelson, of Scarboro, and Polly Lombard, June 3, 1790.

—Sarah, and James Emory, June 14, 1796.

Foot, Martha, and John Murch, Jr., Oct. 8, 1772.

Ford, Olly, and Joseph Roberts, 3d, Oct. 21, 1793.

Foss, Elizabeth, of Scarboro, and John Coolbroth of Buxton, Nov. 3, 1791.

—Joseph, and Nancy McDonald, Nov. 27, 1792.

Fowler, Polly, and Elias Whitney, Dec. 14, 1788.

Francis, Thomas, and Lucy Ludlow,(negroes) Sept. 30, 1792.

Freeman, Ebenezer, and Polly Prentiss, Feb. 3, 1799.

—Eunice, and Elisha Strout, Nov. 27, 1764.

—Jenny, and Ebenezer Lombard, Nov. 12, 1794.

—Lydia, and Gershom Hamblen, Sept. 12, 1802.

—Mary, and Joseph Whitney, Jr., Aug. 2, 1801.

—Nathan, and Hephzibah Whitney, Oct. 15, 1766.

Freeman, Rebecca, and Josiah Harmon of Scarboro, Oct. 27, 1785.

—Susanna, and Dominicus Harmon of Scarboro, April 3, 1788.

Frost, Abigail, and James Mosher, December, 1758.

—Benjamin, and Pelina Rackley, Nov. 27, 1792.

—Betty, and Thomas Morton, Aug. 23, 1787.

—Elizabeth, and Benjamin Adams, Nov. 26, 1778.

MARRIAGES.

—Elizabeth, and Coleman Watson, July 25, 1802.
—Enoch, and Alice Davis, April 24, 1780.
—Jane, and Nathaniel Webster, Oct. 13, 1799.
—Love, and Nathan Wing, of Limington, Dec. 25, 1791.
—Nathaniel, Jr., and Esther Hamblen, Feb. 16, 1796.
—Nathaniel, Jr., and Content Hamblen, April 4, 1802.
—Polly, and Joseph Hamblen, Dec. 18, 1788.
—Samuel, and Rebecca Hamblen, April 5, 1792.
—Susanna, and Lemuel Hicks, Nov. 5, 1778.
Gammon, Benjamin, and Betty Crockit, Oct. 21, 1787.
—Christian, and Robert Knight of Otisfield, Dec. 22, 1796.
—Daniel, and Mary Blanchard, April 8, 1781.
—Daniel, and Polly Elder, Jan. 4, 1787.
—John, and Sarah Cook, June 15, 1797.
—Mary, and John Brown, Nov. 29, 1801.
—Nathaniel, and Mary Lowel, Nov. 20, 1777.
Garrett, Susanna, and Dr. Jeremiah Barker of Falmouth, Dec. 17, 1790.
—Temperance, and Hon. William Gorham, March 8, 1789.
Gates, Timothy, and Susanna Master, both of Bridgton, Dec. 4, 1777.
Gilkey, Betty and Frederic Stevens, Mar. 3, 1801.
—Martha and Benjamin Chandler, of Pepperellboro, Oct. 20, 1799.
—Mary and Daniel Mussey, Dec. 7, 1775.
—Rebecca and James Small, of Gray April 4, 1787.
Goodwin, James and Betty Bramhall, Oct. 23, 1794.
Gorham, Eunice and William Shaw of Falmouth, Mar. 31, 1799.
—Frances and James Tyler, Dec. 11, 1796.
—Hannah and Silvanus Davis, Nov. 19, 1789.

MARRIAGES.

—Hon. William and Temperance Garrett, Mar. 8, 1789.

Gragg, Mercy and John Knight, June 22, 1784.

Grant, Daniel and Susanna Strout, Jan. 11, 1787.

—David of Falmouth and Rachel Haskel, Nov. 14, 1802.

—James and Lois Harding, Nov. 11, 1784.

—Lucy and William Pride, June 16, 1782.

Gray, Anne and Charles Thomes, Sept. 1, 1782.

—James and Susanna Thomes, Jan. 2, 1791.

—Martha and Ephraim Crockit, Jan 5, 1792.

Greeley, John and Elizabeth Thomson, Sept. 1773.

Green, Benjamin and Sarah Lombard, Sept. 29, 1774.

—Isaac and Susanna Rowe, Nov. 15, 1801.

—Jonathan and Rebecca Young, Sept 18, 1796.

—Joseph and Hannah Conant, Mar. 8, 1749.

—Josiah and Eunice Newcomb, Aug. 26, ~~both of Portland. March 10, 1799.~~

Green, Rebecca, and Elijah Evans. ~~1790.~~

—John and Mary Stuart, July 3, 1770.

—Salome, and Ebenezer Shaw, Mar. 4, ~~1~~793.

Greenlaw, John, and Lucy Whitney, March 27, 1788.

Hall, Abraham, and Elizabeth Sanborn, April 18, 1790.

—Dorothy, and John Woodard, Oct. 6, 1791.

—Isaac, and Anna Whitney, May 19, 1793.

—John and Naoma York, Feb. 1, 1769.

—Sarah, and David Sanborn, Dec. 9, 1765.

Hamblen, Abigail, and Stephen Lary, Feb. 12, 1789.

—Almory, and Sally Clark, Oct. 8, 1797. 1799.

MARRIAGES.

—Content, and James Miller, March 1, 1780.
—Content, and Nathaniel Frost, Jr., April 4, 1802.
—Dilla, and Stephen Edwards, Oct. 4, 1798.
—Ebenezer, Jr., and Betty McCorson, Jan. 23, 1799.
—Enoch, and Happy Whitney, June 6, 1802.
—Esther, and Nathaniel Frost, Jr., Feb. 16, 1796.
—George, and Sarah Rich, m. Dec. 20, 1773.
—Gershom, and Lydia Freeman, Sept. 12, 1802.
—Hannah, and Jeremiah Jones, Aug. 26, 1798.
—Joseph, and Hannah Whitney, October, 1755.
—Joseph, and Polly Frost, Dec. 18, 1788.
—Rachel, and Tappin Sawyer, April 12, 1801.
—Rebecca, and Samuel Frost, April 5, 1792.
—Sarah, and Edmund Phinney, Jr., March 26, 1780.
—Sarah, and Joshua Crockit, Nov. 29, 1787.
—Sarah, and Robert Mayo, Jan. 17, 1796.
—Sarah, and Nathaniel Rand, Oct. 18, 1798.
—Susanna, and John Sawyer, Jr., of Standish, Jan. 22, 1797.
—Temperance, and Richard Dresser, April, 1796.
—Timothy, and Anna Harding, Sept. 14, 1769.
Hambleton, Esther, and Joseph Roberts, Nov. 28, 1777.
Hanscom, Aaron, and Rebecca Akers, May 11, 1780.
—Catharine, and Ezra Hanson, August 3, 1788.
—Eunice, and Elisha Sanborn, Dec. 22,
—Hannah, and Joseph Swett, April 27, 1783.

MARRIAGES.

Haskell, Abigail, and David Plummer, July 2, 1799.
—Jacob, and Mary Whitmore, Dec. 29, 1785.
—John and Rebecca Bangs, April 25, 1801.
—Jonathan, and Martha Phinney, Sept. 19, 1793.
—Josiah, and Abigail Wallace, May 15, 1786.
—Mark, and Elizabeth Maxfield, of Falmouth, Sept. 17, 1793.
—Rachel, and David Grant, of Falmouth, Nov. 14, 1802.
—Samuel, and Lydia Plumer, March 17, 1799.
—William and Katherine Weston, Feb. 11, 1773.
Hatch, Asa, and Rebecca Crocket, May 6, 1783.
—Asa, and Jane McIntosh, Dec. 9, 1792.
—Betsy' and Reuben Cobb, April 5, 1801.
—Captain Ebenezer, and Elizabeth McLellan, Feb. 7, 1802.
Hatherton, John, and Hannah Shaw of Standish, Jan. 19, 1791.
Haynes, Hannah, and John Stuart, 3d of Scarboro, April 28, 1796.
—Jerusha, of Buxton, and John Lamb, Aug. 17, 1786.
Hicks, Elizabeth, and Herman Merrick Brown of Freeport, Dec. 20, 1802.
—Lemuel, and Susanna Frost, Nov. 5, 1778.
Higgins, Apphia, and Ithiel Blake, July 13, 1769.
—Mary, and Daniel Lowell, March 18, 1799.
—Matthew, and Dorcas Plumer, June 11, 1797.
Hodgdon, Elizabeth. and Benjamin Donnell. Oct., 1755.
—Joseph and Mary Snow, Feb. 24, 1789.
Holbrook, Mrs. Jane, and John Butler, Jan. 25, 1787.
—Nancy, and Mark Dresser, Aug. 9, 1789.

MARRIAGES.

—Joseph, and Polly Bacon, June 3, 1798.
—Moses, and Phebe Crockit, April 23, 1781.
—Sarah, and Ebenezer Cobb, Jan. 8, 1792.
Hanson, Ezra, and Catharine Hanscom, Aug. 3, 1788.
—Hannah, and Joseph Libby, April 4, 1782.
—William and Metilda Elder, Dec. 8, 1785.
Hardaway, Lois, and John Perkins, May 25, 1769.
Harding, Anna, and Timothy Hamblen, Sept. 14, 1769.
—Barnabas, and Mehitable Jordan, April 19, 1798.
—Content, and Daniel Meserve of Scarboro, Dec. 11, 1796.
—Elkanah, and Hannah Brown, March 14, 1802.
—Hannah, and James Lewis, Sept. 24, 1793.
—Jesse and Elizabeth Alden, March 27, 1777.
—Lois, and James Grant, Nov. 11, 1784.
—Lucy, and Elias Fogg, Sept. 29, 1799.
—Martha, and Jeremiah Tole, Jan. 20, **1791.**
—Nicholas, and Miriam Bacon, June 14, 1789.
—Priscilla, and John Lombard, Jr., Aug. 13, 1780.
—Capt. Samuel and Eunice Huston, Aug. 5, 1790.
—Zephaniah, and Mary Davis, November, 1759.
Hardy, William, and Hannah Parker, Nov. 16, 1791.
Harmon, Doiminicus, of Scarboro, and Susanna Freeman, April 3, 1788.
—Joshua, and Deborah Dunn, Jan. 28, 1790.
—Josiah, of Scarboro, and Rebecca Freeman, Oct. 27, 1785.
—Rufus, of Standish, and Eunice Sawyer March 14, 1798.

MARRIAGES.

Holmes, William, and Emme Marriner, Jan. 9, 1792.

Hooper, Abigail, and John Chase, of Limington, Jan. 13, 1897.

Hopkins, Benjamin, and Hannah Jordan, July 7, 1789.

—Charles, and Martha Bacon, March 7, 1793.

—Josiah, and Sarah Rackliff of Standish, Nov. 23, 1790.

Horr, Philip, of Waterford, and Sarah Cates, Dec. 17, 1786.

How, Daniel, and Abigail Murphy of Standish, Aug. 6, 1789.

Howel, Patience, and Alexander Ross, March 8, 1789.

Hubbard, Rebecca, and Archelaus Lewis, March 21, 1779.

Hunt, Ephraim, and Abigail Cates, Oct. 6, 1769.

—Francis and Nancy Merrill, March 1, 1796.

—Mary, and John Crockit, Dec. 15, 1796.

—Susanna, and Solomon Lombard, Jr., June 17, 1796.

Huston, Anne, and Stephen Phinney, Sept. 22, 1788.

—Elizabeth, and Reuben Elder, Feb. 4, 1787.

—Eunice, and Capt. Samuel Harding, Aug. 5, 1790.

—Rebecca, and William McLellan, Dec. 8. 1762.

—Rebecca, and William Dyer, Oct. 11, 1792.

—Simon, and Elizabeth Ross Whitman, March 22, 1801.

Huzzy, Fanny, and Jeremiah Rolf of Buxton, March 30, 1786.

Irish, Abigail, and Reuben Libby, Jr., Sept. 11, 1794.

—Amy, and Samuel Burnell, Sept. 18, 1791.

—Betty, and John Skillings, Jr., Oct. 3, 1802.

—Isaac, and Anna Flood, Sept. 28, 1786.

—James, and Mary Gorham Phinney. May, ~~1806~~.

MARRIAGES.

—James, Jr., and Rebecca Chadbourne, Sept. 2, 1798.
—Joel, and Elizabeth Cates, May 16, 1779.
—Martha, and Samuel Larrabee, Feb. 3, 1803.
—Mary, and Timothy Bacon, Feb. 19, 1789.
—Mehitabel, and Joseph Smith, Sept. 4, 1796.
—Obediah, and Mary Dean, Jan. 7, 1790.
—Patience, and John Davis, April 16, 1789.
—Samuel, and Martha Blake, July, 1792.
—Sarah, and Joshua Young, June 13, 1779.
—Stephen, and Anna Bangs, April 1, 1779.
—Susanna, and Ebenezer Morton, Jr., Dec. 7, 1780.
—William, and Mary McCullister, July 18, 1765.
Jacobs, Lois, and George Scott, April 3, 1774.
Jenkins, Samuel, Jr., and Lydia Dyer, Oct. 1, 1780.
—Samuel, Jr., and Thankful Snow, Jan. 23, 1794.
Johnson, David, and Jenny Whitney, June 16, 1785.
—Ephraim, and Sally Titcomb, Dec. 15, 1791.
—Jasper, and Rebecca Ross, Dec. 23, 1784.
Jones, Ephraim, and Marcy Phinney, March 21, 1779.
Jones, Jeremiah, and Hannah Hamblen, Aug. 26, 1798.
—Lydia, and Jeremiah Ran, April 14, 1791.
—Stephen, and Sarah Paine, Sept. 12, 1802.
Jordan, Elizabeth, and Benjamin Rowe, both of Phillips Gore, Feb. 26, 1792.
—Elizabeth, and Walter Libby of Scarboro, April 17, 1800.

MARRIAGES.

—Hannah, and Benjamin Hopkins, July 7, 1789.
—Mehitable, and Barnabas Harding, April 19, 1798.
—Roger, and Margaret Crisp, Nov. 25, 1779.
Kilborn, Susanna, and Silas ? Newcomb, July, 1748.
Kilburn, Thomas, and Mehitable Rider, April, 1748.
Kimball, Abigail, and Moses Whitney, Jan. 22, 1792.
—Caleb, and Abigail Skillings, Feb. 17, 1774.
—Martha, and William Davis, June 5, 1796.
—Nathan of Buxton, and Rebecca Parker, Nov. 23, 1788.
—Polly, and Solomon Young, Dec. 4, 1796.
—Rufus, and Lucy Fly, June 17, 1787.
Knight, George, of Windham, and Rebecca Davis, March 14, 1787.
—John, and Mercy Gragg, June 22, 1784.
—Nabby, and Joseph Lakin, Nov. 28, 1798.
—Nathaniel, and Hannah McKinney, Sept. 19, 1782.
—Nathaniel, and Sarah Webb, Feb. 24, 1787.
—Nathaniel, and Susanna Roberts, Jan. 10, 1799.
—Phebe, and John Libby, March 12, 1789.
—Robert of Otisfield, and Christian Gammon, Dec. 22, 1796.
Lakeman, Josiah, and Esther Cobb, Dec. 24, 1783.
Lakin, Joseph, and Nabby Knight, Nov. 28, 1798.
Lamb, John and Jerusha Haynes of Buxton, Aug. 17, 1786.
Larrabee, Nancy, and Samuel Dearing, both of Scarboro, June 8, 1794.
—Samuel, of Limington, and Martha Irish, Feb. 3, 1803.
—Thomas of Durham, and Anna Parker, March 1, 1798.

MARRIAGES.

—William of Scarboro, and Tabitha Whitmore, July 19, 1802.
Lary, Dennis, and Patience Wooster, May, 1761.
—Samuel, of Falmouth, and Elizabeth Wise, Dec. 25, 1796.
—Stephen, and Abigail Hamblen, Feb. 12, 1789.
Leavit, William, of Buxton, and Mary Cobb, Jan. 10, 1796.
Legrow, Margaret, and Samuel Tobin, both of Windham, April 2, 1789.
Lewis, Abijah Peco, and Rebecca Melcher, March 1756.
—Archelaus, and Rebecca Hubbard, March 21, 1779.
—Daniel D., and Olly Dyer, May 13, 1798.
—George Jr., and Ruth Lincoln, Feb. 3, 1780.
—Hannah, and John Darling, Oct. 14, 1785.
—James, and Hannah Harding, Sept. 24, 1793.
—Lothrop, and Tabitha Longfellow, Jan. 20, 1794.
—Sally, and Ebenezer Peabody, March 9, 1792.
Libby, Abigail, and Enos Newcomb, Jan. 16, 1797.
—Betty, and Paul Lombard, Aug. 15, 1791.
—Dorcas, and George Waterhouse, Nov. 23, 1775.
—Joab, and Susanna Lombard, Sept. 21, 1769.
—John, and Phebe Knight, March 12, 1789.
—Joseph, and Hannah Hanson, April 4, 1782.
—Joseph, and Mercy Whitney, June 24, 1801.
—Lemuel, of Scarboro, and Patience Whitmore, June 11, 1795.
—Mehitable, and Timothy Plummer, of Scarboro, Feb. 20, 1800.
—Reuben, Jr., and Abigail Irish, Sept. 11, 1794.

MARRIAGES.

—Richard, and Sarah Ross, Nov. 16, 1788.
—Sarah, and Thomas Blake, of Falmouth. Dec. 16, 1790.
—Susanna, and Jedediah Lombard, Oct. 20, 1784.
—Susanna, and Jedediah Dorset, May 12, 1797.
—Walter, of Scarboro, and Elizabeth Jordan, April 17, 1800.
—William, Jr., and Anna Bolton, March 30, 1797.
Lincoln, Ruth, and George Lewis, Jr., Feb. 3, 1780.
Linskit, Esther, and James Low, Feb. 19, 1762.
Lombard, Bethshua and Elisha Morton of Standish, Feb. 18, 1796.
—Butler, and Jemima Clay, Aug. 9 1787.
—Dorcas, and Jeremiah Fogg, Dec. 21, 1794.
—Ebenezer, and Jenny Freeman, Nov. 12, 1794.
—Ephraim, and Polly Perkins, Nov. 20, 1794.
—Hannah, and Ebenezer Murch, Jr., Nov. 30, 1786.
—James, and Bethiah Smith, Dec. 13, 1792.
—Jedediah, and Susanna Libby, Oct. 20, 1784.
—John, Jr., and Priscilla Harding, Aug. 13, 1780.
—John, and Elizabeth Sawyer, Jan. 13, 1785.
—Joseph, and Fanny Silly, May 12, 1788.
—Luther, and Mary Plummer, Jan. 10, 1793.
—Lydia, and Joseph Morton, Nov. 22, 1789.
—Lydia, and Abraham Nason, Feb. 14, 1793.
—Martha, with Edmund Flood, Aug. 10, 1788.
—Paul, and Betty Libby, Aug. 15, 1791.
—Phebe, and Benjamin Blake, Jr., Oct. 20, 1785.

MARRIAGES.

—Polly, and Nelson Fogg, of Scarboro, June 3, 1790.
—Salome, and Austin Alden, Nov. 25, 1756.
—Sarah, and Benjamin Green, Sept. 29, 1774.
—Sarah and Samuel Thoms, Dec. 23, 1779.
—Solomon, Jr., and Lydia——, married June 15, 1759.
—Solomon, Jr., and Susanna Hunt, June 17, 1796.
—Susanna, and Wentworth Stuart, Feb. 4, 1753.
—Susanna, and Joab Libbe, Sept. 21, 1769.
—Susanna, and Christopher Dunn, Feb. 3, 1782.
Longfellow, Abigail, and Captain Samuel Stephenson, Oct. 13, 1801.
—Tabitha, and Lothrop Lewis, Jan. 20, 1794.
Lord, Elizabeth, of North Yarmouth, and Lot Nason, July 3, 1797.
—Nahum, and Charlotte Waterhouse, July 11, 1802.
Lothrop, Hannah, and Richard Edwards, July 4, 1765.
—Thomas, and Betty Mosher, April 14, 1799.
Loveit, Samuel, and Sarah Phinney, Jan., 1756.
Low, James, and Esther Linsket, Feb. 19, 1762.
Lowell, Daniel, Jr., of Standish, and Mercy Higgins, March 18, 1799.
—Jonathan Moulton, of Flints Town and Rachel Morton, Dec. 11, 1783.
—Mary, and Nathaniel Gammon, Nov. 20, 1777.
Ludlow, Lucy and Thomas Francis, (negros), Sept. 30, 1792.
Lukeman, William, and Hannah Doane, December, 1754.
Lummus, Samuel, and Margaret Elder, May 31, 1801.

MARRIAGES.

Mann, Daniel, and Hannah Phinney, August 22, 1792.

—Nancy, and Eli Phinney, Jan. 27, 1799.

March, Abigail, and Moses Quinby, both of Falmouth, April 28, 1789.

Marriner, Emme and William Holmes, Jan. 9, 1792.

Mars, Elizabeth, of Scarboro, and Samuel Coolbroth, of Buxton, Sept. 21, 1788.

Marston, David, and Deborah Young, Feb. 27, 1789.

—John, of North Yarmouth, and Olly Ross, Sept. 13, 1795.

Martin, Bryan, and Anna Morton, Feb. 4, 1798.

—John, and Hannah Swett, Nov. 5, 1794.

Master, Susanna, and Timothy Gates, both of Bridgton, Dec. 4, 1777.

Maxfield, Anna, and David Watson, Nov. 25, 1789.

—Elizabeth, and Mark Haskel, Sept. 17, 1793.

—William, and Susanna Webb, December, 1753.

Mayberry, John, and Elizabeth Webb, March 20, 1789.

Mayo, Robert, and Sarah Hamblen, Jan. 17, 1796.

McCaslin, Lydia, and William Elder, March 4, 1790.

McCausland, Lydia, of Windham, and Nathaniel Winslow of Falmouth Jan. 23, 1794.

McCollif, Polly, and Samuel Snow, March 26, 1798.

McCollister, Elizabeth, and Gershom Davis, Dec. 26, 1779.

—James, and Mary Flood, Jan. 31, 1782.

McCorson, Betty, and Ebenezer Hamblen, Jr., Jan. 23, 1799.

McCullister, James, and Deliverance Rich, Oct. 6, 1765.

—Mary, and William Irish, July 18, 1765.

McDaniel, Charles, and Priscilla Davis, January, 1762.

MARRIAGES.

McDonald, Abner, and Elizabeth Choat, June 28, 1801.
—Meribah, and Cornelius Bramhall, Feb. 28, 1788.
—Pelatiah, and Dorcas Stuart, August 6, 1787.
—Samuel Melcher, of Standish, and Anna Whitten, Dec. 25, 1794.
—Simon Davis and Betty Brown, July 16, 1800.
—Nancy, and Joseph Foss, Nov. 27, 1792.
McDugle, David, and Anna Elder, Dec. 20, 1786.
McIntosh, Catharine, and Dennis Mulroy of Limington, Oct. 2, 1796.
—James, and Peggy Patrick, March 13, 1798.
—Jane, and Asa Hatch, Dec. 9, 1792.
—Polly, and Benjamin Patrick, March 27, 1796.
—Sophia, and Dudley Whitmore, Nov. 24, 1796.
McKenney, Molly, and Timothy Stuart, July 19, 1772.
McKenzee, Hugh, and Sarah Dyer, of Cape Elizabeth, Oct. 29, 1767.
McKinney, Hannah, and Nathaniel Knight, Sept. 19, 1782.
McLellan, Abigail, and James McLellan, Aug. 26, 1756.
—Abigail, and Enoch Edwards, June 16, 1799.
—Alexander, and Chloe Davis, Feb. 9, 1803.
—Carey, and Eunice Elder, Jan. 1, 1767.
—Eleanor, and Elijah Elder, Aug. 19, 1798.
—Elizabeth, and Capt. Ebenezer Hatch, Feb. 7, 1802.
—James, and Abigail McLellan, Aug. 26, 1756.
—James, of Pepperellboro, and Rebecca McLellan, June 25, 1786.
—James, and Louisa Fogg, Dec. 5, 1802.
—Jenny, and Samuel Barker of Windham, Dec. 16, 1798.

MARRIAGES.

—Joseph, and Mary McLellan, Sept. 1756.

—Margaret, and John Miller, April 15, 1781.

—Margaret, and John Clemmons, Feb. 6, 1789.

—Martha, and Samuel Edwards, July 8, 1792.

—Mary, and Joseph McLellan, Sept., 1756.

—Nancy, and Samuel Staples, April 28, 1794.

—Rebecca, and James McLellan of Pepperellboro, June 25, 1786.

—William, and Rebecca Houston, Dec. 8, 1762.

McQuilla, John, and Abigail Cook, May 4, 1784.

—John, and Elizabeth Brown, Oct. 13, 1796.

—John and Olive Edwards, Sept. 20, 1798.

Melcher, Rebecca, and Abijah Peco Lewis, March, 1756.

Melvins, John, and Abigail Sawyer, January, 1773.

Merrill, Daniel, Jr., and Rhoda Roberts, June 27, 1802.

—John, and Lydia Chamberlain, April 21, 1799.

—Nancy, and Francis Hunt, March 1, 1796.

Meserve, Clement, and Mary Wooster, Sept. 19, 1757.

—Daniel, of Scarboro, and Content Harding, Dec. 11, 1796.

—George, of Scarboro, and Dorcas Weeks, Dec. 8, 1791.

—Hannah, and Timothy Crocker, December, 1754.

—John, and Mary Yaton, March, 1757.

—John, and Sarah Strout, Jan. 28, 1762.

—Margaret, and William Westcot, February, 1757.

Miller, James, and Content Hamblen, March 1, 1780.

—John, and Margaret McLellan, April 15, 1781.

MARRIAGES.

Milliken, Sally, and James Warren, both of Scarboro, May 25, 1794.

Moody, Daniel, and Mary Sawyer,—— 1797.

—Eunice, and Benjamin Carsley, Sept. 23, 1799.

—Joseph, of Buxton, and Tenty Crockit, August 1, 1802.

—Joshua, and Zuby Nickerson, June 22, 1783.

More, Lydia, of Buxton, and David Whitney, June 29, 1785.

Morrel, Anne, of Falmouth, and Joseph Elder, of Windham, May 1, 1788.

Morris, John Wright, and Betty Elder, Oct. 4, 1798.

Morss, Daniel, and Eunice Rays, both of Otisfield, July 4, 1792.

Morton, Abigail, and Ephraim Ryle, Nov. 6, 1792.

—Abraham, and Miriam Roberts, Jan. 25, 1803.

—Anna, and Phineas Whitney, Oct. 19, 1769.

—Anna, and Bryan Martin, Feb. 4, 1798.

—Ebenezer, Jr., and Susanna Irish, Dec. 7, 1780.

—Elisha, of Standish, and Bathshua Lombard, Feb. 18, 1796.

—Hannah, and Edmund Wescot, May 16, 1793.

—Joseph, and Lydia Lombard, Nov. 22, 1789.

—Rachel, and Jonathan Noulton Lowell, of Flintstown, Dec. 11, 1783.

—Rachel, and Thomas Thomes, Nov. 6, 1787.

—Solomon, and Elizabeth Roberts, Sept. 30, 1798.

—Thankful, and Enos Newcomb, Jan. 23, 1783.

—Thomas, and Betty Frost, Aug. 23, 1787.

Mosher, Abigail, and James Phinney, Jr., July 17, 1791.

—Betty, and Thomas Lothrop, April 14, 1799.

MARRIAGES.

—Hannah Bracket, and Moses Akers, December, 1753.
—James, and Abigail Frost, December, 1758.
—Jenny, and Isaac Carsley, June 18, 1797.
—Katharine, and Joseph Weston, September, 1755.
Mosher, Nathaniel, and Eunice Elder, Nov. 15, 1795.
—Susanna, and Joseph Rounds, Nov. 5, 1778.
Moulton, Daniel, Jr., and Deborah Dyer, Nov. 25, 1790.
Mulroy, Dennis, of Limington, and Catharine McIntosh, Oct. 2, 1796.
Murch, Ann, and Jeremiah Murch, Oct. 29, 1788.
—Daniel, and Mary Simpson, Jan. 21, 1768.
—Deborah, and James Whitney, Aug. 15, 1785.
—Ebenezer, Jr., and Hannah Lombard, Nov. 30, 1786.
—Elizabeth. and Elisha Cobb, Nov., 1760.
—Elizabeth, and Samuel Murch, Jr., May 6, 1798.
—George, and Hannah Roberts, March 24, 1791.
—Isaac, and Mary Murray, Sept. 12, 1790.
—Jeremiah, and Ann Murch, Oct. 29, 1788.
—John, Jr., and Martha Foot, Oct. 8, 1772.
—Martha and Josedech Sanborn, Sept. 22, 1796.
—Mary, and Benjamin Skillings of North Yarmouth, July 10, 1794.
—Molly, and John Silly, Dec. 15, 1786.
—Samuel, Jr., and Elizabeth Murch, May, 6, 1798.
—Simeon, and Rachel Paine, Jan. 27, 1791.
—Susanna, and Joshua Newcomb of Buxton, March 26, 1789.
—Walter, and Jerusha Brown, Nov., 1758.

MARRIAGES.

Murphy, Abigail, of Standish, and Daniel How, Aug. 6, 1789.
Murray, Anthony, and Betsy Preston, Feb. 27, 1789.
—Mary, and Isaac Murch, Sept. 12, 1790.
Mussey, Daniel, and Mary Gilk.y, Dec. 7, 1775.
Mussey, Theodar, and Dolly Sanborn, of Standish, July 7, 1791.
Myrick, Dorcas, and Myrick Paine, May 12, 1791.
Nason, Abraham, and Lydia Lombard, Feb. 14, 1793.
—David, and Martha Vineton, Feb. 24, 1791.
—Eleanor, and Nehemiah Wescot, April 10, 1796.
—Lot, and Elizabeth Lord, of North Yarmouth, July 3, 1797.
—William, and Betsy Burnal, Sept. 8, 1791.
Newbegin, Eunice, and John Akers, Nov. 6, 1783.
—John, and Mary Thomes, Feb. 28, 1786.
Newcomb, Enos, and Thankful Morton, Jan. 23, 1783.
—Enos, and Abigail Libby, Jan. 16, 1797.
—Eunice, and Josiah Green, Aug. 26, 1790.
—Joshua, of Buxton, and Susanna March, Nov. 26, 1789.
—Silas, and Susanna Kilborn, July, 1748.
Nickerson, Zuby, and Joshua Moody, June 22, 1783.
—Warren, of Penobscot, and Anner Alden, Nov. 22, 1785.
Page, Caleb, of Conway, and Nancy Crockit, Dec., 1797.
Paine, Hannah, and Isaac Whitney, Aug. 29, 1765.
—Hannah, and Luther Crocker, Oct. 1, 1801.
—Mary, and Ebenezer Davis, Feb. 18, 1790.
—Myrick, and Dorcas Myrick, of Standish, May 12, 1791.

MARRIAGES.

—Rachel, and Simeon Murch, Jan. 27, 1791.

—Sarah, and Stephen Jones, Sept. 12, 1802.

—Thankful, and James Davis, March 21, 1793.

—Thomas, of Standish, and Mary Gooking Whitney, April 26, 1792.

Parker, Anna, and Thomas Larrabee of Durham, March 1, 1798.

—Hannah, and William Hardy, Nov. 16, 1791.

—Hannah, and Moses Parker, Dec. 26, 1802.

—Lydia, and Abner Wescot, Sept. 12, 1793.

—Moses, and Hannah Parker, Dec. 26, 1802.

—Nathan, and Zillah Ward, March 22, 1789.

—Polly, and William Riggs of Portland, Dec. 9, 1792.

—Rebecca, and Nathan Kimball of Buxton, Nov. 23, 1788.

—Sarah, and Samuel Ficket of Cape Elizabeth, July 6, 1794.

Parsons, Jonathan, and Mehitable Bangs, March 25, 1790.

Patrick, Benjamin, and Polly McIntosh, March 27, 1796.

—Peggy, and James McIntosh, March 13, 1798.

Peabody, Ebenezer, and Sally Lewis, March 9, 1792.

—Lucy, and Varnum Beverly, Jan. 28, 1791.

Penfield, Sally, and Ezra Ficket, Dec. 15, 1796.

Perkins, Esther, and James Cates, Sept. 20. 1768.

—John, and Lois Hardaway, May 25, 1769.

—Polly, and Ephraim Lombard, Nov. 20, 1794.

Philbrick, Gideon, and Eunice West, June 3, 1793.

MARRIAGES.

Phinney, Edmund, Jr., and Sarah Hamblen, March 26, 1780.
—Edmund, Esq., and Sarah Stevens, Nov. 21, 1796.
—Eli, and Mercy Mann, Jan. 27, 1799.
—Eunice, and Ithiel Blake, Sept. 9,1802.
—Hannah, and Daniel Mann, Aug. 22, 1792.
—James, Jr., and Abigail Mosher, July 17, 1791.
—John, Jr., and Rebecca Sawyer, Jan. 24, 1755.
—John. Jr., and Susanna Stone, Feb. 16, 1786.
—Joseph, and Susanna Crockit, June 18, 1780.
—Marcy, and Ephraim Jones, March 21, 1779.
—Martha and Jonathan Haskell, Sept. 19, 1793.
—Mary, Gorham, and James Irish, May, 1756.
—Nathaniel, and Mary Bangs, April 30, 1792.
—Patience, and Ebenezer Carsley, Nov. 25, 1766.
—Sarah, and Samuel Loveit, Jan. 1756.
—Stephen, and Anne Huston, Sept. 22, 1788.
Pierce, John, and Mercy Thorne, July 9, 1768.
Plummer, David, and Abigail Haskel, July 2, 1799.
—Dorcas, and Matthew Higgins, June 11, 1797.
—Lydia, and Samuel Haskel, March 17, 1799.
—Mary, and Luther Lombard, Jan. 10, 1793.
—Sally, and Joshua Adams, June 17, 1792.
—Timothy, of Scarboro, and Mehitable Libby, Feb. 20, 1800.
Poland, John, and Fear Brown, April 26, 1791.
Pote, Hannah, and William Proctor, Jan. 11, 1778.
—Samuel, and Priscilla Douty, Oct., 1779.

MARRIAGES.

Pray, James, and Loriana Webb, Sept. 10, 1790.
Prentiss, Lydia, and Joel Watson, Jan. —, 1798.
—Polly, and Ebenezer Freeman, Feb. 3, 1799.
—Samuel, and Rebecca Cook, Nov. 29, 1787.
Preston, Betsey and Anthony Murray, Feb. 27, 1789.
Pride, William, and Lucy Grant, June 16, 1782.
Prince and Chloe, negroes, Sept, 29, 1799.
Proctor, William, and Hannah Pote, Jan. 11, 1778.
Purrington, Eleanor, and Walter Ross, Sept. 21, 1800.
Quinby, Benjamin, and Eleanor Starbird, May 6, 1779.
—Moses, and Abigail March, both of Falmouth, April 28, 1789.
Rackliff, Sarah, of Standish, and Josiah Hopkins, Nov. 23, 1790.
—Pelina, and Benjamin Frost, Nov. 27, 1792.
Rand, Jeremiah, Jr., and Lydia Jones, April 14, 1791.
—Nathaniel, and Sarah Hamblen, Oct. 18, 1798.
—Philemon, of Scarboro, and Patience Carsley, March 20, 1796.
Rays, Eunice, and Daniel Morss, both of Otisfield, July 4, 1792.
Rich, Amos, and Eunice Woodman, of New Gloucester, June 4, 1781.
—Barnabas, and Lydia Brown, June 28, 1779.
—Deliverence, and James McCullister, Oct. 6, 1765.
—Ezekiel, and Sarah Stevens, Nov. 21, 1765.
—Martha, and Jonathan Sawyer, Oct. —, 1763.
—Samuel, and Betty Cates, Jan. 23, 1799.
—Sarah, and George Hamblen, Dec. 20, 1773.
Rider, Mehitable, and Thomas Kilburn, April, 1748.

MARRIAGES.

Rideout, William, of North Yarmouth, and Rachel Thomes, Sept. 18, 1792.
Riggs, William, of Portland, and Polly Parker, Dec. 9, 1792.
—William, and Polly Burnel, April 13, 1794.
Roberts, Dorcas, and John Roberts of Scarboro, July 22, 1802.
—Elizabeth, and Solomon Morton, Sept. 30, 1798.
—Hannah, and George Murch, March 24, 1791.
—Jane, and John Whitmore, Oct. 4, 1792.
—John, of Scarboro, and Dorcas Roberts, July 22, 1802.
—Joseph, and Esther Hambleton, Nov. 28, 1777.
—Joseph, 3d, and Olly Ford, Oct. 21, 1793.
—Joseph, Jr., and Sally Strout, Dec. 16, 1801.
—Katharine, of Falmouth and John Flood, Jan. 13, 1791.
—Lucy, and Philip Seiver, July 26, 1789.
—Lydia, and Morrison Flood, June 17, 1793.
—Miriam, and Abraham Morton, Jan. 25, 1803.
—Molly, and James Sturges, Nov. 6, 1792.
—Rhoda, and Daniel Merrill, Jr., June 27, 1802.
—Susanna, and Nathaniel Knight, Jan. 10, 1799.
Rogers, John, and Hannah Whitney, Nov. 12, 1786.
Rolf, Jeremiah, of Buxton, and Fanny Huzzey, March 30, 1786.
Ross, Alexander, and Patience Howel, March 8, 1789.
—Anne, and William Thomas, Nov. 29, 1798.
—Elizabeth, and Jotham Whitney, April 1, 1792.
—Mary, and William Burton, April 26, 1781.
—Olly, and John Marston, of North Yarmouth, Sept. 13, 1795.
—Rebecca, and Jasper Johnson,, Dec. 23, 1784.

MARRIAGES.

—Sarah, and Richard Libby, Nov. 16, 1788.

—Walter, and Eleanor Purrington, Sept. 21, 1800.

Rounds, Joseph, and Susanna Mosher, Nov. 5, 1778.

—Samuel of Narraganset, No. 1, and Dorcas Edwards, of Wells, Feb. 15, 1768.

Rowe, Benjamin, and Elizabeth Jordan, Feb. 26, 1792. Both of Phillips Gore.

—Noah, and Mary Strout of Flints Town, March 23, 1785.

—Susanna, and Isaac Green, Nov. 15, 1801.

Royal, Priscilla, and James Sinklar, April 4, 1793.

Ryle, Ephraim, and Abigail Morton, Nov. 6, 1792.

Sam, James, and Sarah Abraham, July 29, 1749.

Sanborn, David, and Sarah Hall, Dec. 9, 1765.

—Dolly, of Standish, and Theodore Mussey, July 7, 1791.

Drusilla, and Enoch Crockit, Sept. 1801.

—Eunice, and Rufus Harmon of Standish, March 14, 1798.

—Elizabeth, and Abraham Hall, April 18, 1790.

—Jesedeck, and Martha Murch, Sept. 22, 1796.

—Sarah, and James Crockit, Dec. 25, 1796.

—Simeon, and Hannah Ward, Jan. 9, 1783.

Sawyer, Abigail, and John Melvins, January, 1773.

—Elizabeth, and John Lombard, Jan. 13, 1785.

—Elisha, and Eunice Hanscomb, Dec. 22, 1799.

—John, of Phillips Gore, and Hannah Edwards, Oct. 4, 1792.

—John, Jr., of Standish, and Susanna Hamblen, Jan. 22, 1797.

—Jonathan, and Martha Rich, October, 1763.

MARRIAGES.

Sawyer, Katharine, and Joseph Weymouth, Nov. 3, 1768.
—Mary, and Daniel Moody, —— 3. 1797.
—Nathan, of Falmouth, and Tabitha Skilling, March 17, 1796.
—Rebecca, and John Phinney, Jr., Jan. 24, 1755.
—Rhoda, and Stephen Trip, April 12, 1765.
—Sarah, and Abner Trip, May 12, 1767.
—Sarah, and Benjamin Stevens, Oct. 27, 1793.
—Tappin, and Rachel Hamblen, April 12, 1801.
—Zachariah, and Susanna Skilling, May 13, 1784.
Sceiver, Lucy, and Pelatiah Crockit, July 18, 1802.
Seiver, Philip, and Lucy Roberts, July 26, 1789.
Scott, George, and Lois Jacobs, April 3, 1774.
Shaw, Caleb, and Abigail Whitney, March 10, 1796.
—Ebenezer, and Salome Green, March 4, 1793.
—Hannah, of Standish, and Wentworth Stuart, Nov. 4, 1790.
—Hannah, of Standish, and John Hatherton, Jan. 19, 1791.
—Jonathan, and Polly Blake, 1800.
—Josiah, and Tabitha Watson, May 5, 1797.
—William of Falmouth, and Eunice Gorham, March 31, 1799.
Silla, Isaac, and Rebecca Crockit, Dec. 20, 1798.
Silly, Elizabeth, and Benjamin Skillings, Aug. 5, 1784.
—Fanny, and Joseph Lombard, May 12, 1788.
—John, and Molly Murch, Dec. 15, 1786.
Simpson, Mary, and Daniel Murch, Jan. 21, 1768.
Sinkler, Elizabeth, and Nathaniel Stevens, Jan. 9, 1766.
—James, and Priscilla Royal, April 4, 1793.

MARRIAGES.

Sinclear, Mary, and Joseph Cates, Jan. 13, 1774.

Skillings, Abigail, and Caleb Kimball, Feb. 17, 1774.

—Anne and Benjamin Cates. Aug. 18, 1774.

—Benjamin, and Elizabeth Silly, Aug. 5, 1784.

—Benjamin, of North Yarmouth, and Mary Murch, July 10, 1794.

—Elizabeth and Edmund Brown, Aug. 6, 1797.

—Isaac, and Susanna Watson, Jan. 8, 1766.

—John, Jr., and Betty Irish, Oct. 3, 1802.

—Mary, and Samuel Davis, Jr., Nov. 11, 1784.

—Susanna, and Zachariah Sawyer, May 13, 1784.

—Tabitha, and Nathan Sawyer of Falmouth, March 17, 1796.

Small, James, of Gray, and Rebecca Gilkey, April 4, 1787.

Smalley, George, of Raming Town, and Lydia Strout, March 10, 1784.

—Hannah, and Joseph Stuart, Sept. 30, 1779.

Smith, Bethiah, and James Lombard, Dec. 13, 1792.

Joseph, and Mehitable Irish, Sept. 4, 1796.

Snow, Bersheba, and Nathaniel Edwards, Sept. 29, 1783.

—Elizabeth, and Solomon Cook, Feb. 23, 1781.

—Gideon, and Joanna Edwards, Dec. 28, 1788.

—Hannah, and Samuel Whitney, Aug. 24, 1798.

—Jenny, and Michael Filbrick, Jr., of Standish, Sept. 4, 1788.

—Lydia, and Joseph Young, 3d. Nov. 7, 1793.

—Mary, and Joseph Hodgdon, Feb. 24, 1789.

—Samuel, and Polly McCollif, March 26, 1798.

Thankful, and Samuel Jenkins, Jr., Jan. 23, 1794.

MARRIAGES. [26]

Spurs, Mary, and David Thurston, both of Otisfield, Dec. 24, 1789.
Staples, Samuel, and Nancy McLellan, April 28, 1794.
Starbird, Eleanor, and Benjamin Quinby, May 6, 1779.
Stevens, Benjamin, and Sarah Sawyer, at Philips Gore, Oct. 27, 1793.
—Catharine, and Barnabas Bangs, Jr., Nov. 20, 1777.
—Catherine, and Ebenezer Storer. June 17, 1800.
—Frederic, and Betty Gilkey, March 3, 1801.
—Jane, and Jonathan Emory, of Buxton, Dec. 30, 1801.
—Jonathan, of Portland, and Eliza Cross, Jan. 25, 1795.
—Lucy, and Enoch Waite, May 15, 1788.
—Mehitable, and Joseph Whitney, Oct. 13, 1765.
—Nathaniel, and Elizabeth Sinklor, Jan. 9, 1766.
—Nathaniel, Jr., and Anna Stuart, Nov. 17, 1791.
—Sarah, and Ezekiel Rich, Nov. 21, 1765.
—Sarah, and Edmund Phinney, Esq., Nov. 21, 1796.
Stephenson, Capt. Samuel, and Abigail Longfellow, Oct. 13, 1801.
Stinchfield, John, and Mehitable Winship, Dec. 1759.
Stone, Abigail, and Daniel Whitney, Dec. 7, 1780.
—Susanna, and John Phinney, Jr., Feb. 16, 1786.
Storer, Ebenezer, and Catherine Stevenson, June 16, 1800.
Stuart, Elisha, and Eunice Freeman, Nov. 27, 1764.
—Ellis, and Jess Brown, Dec. 14, 1786.
—Eunice, and William Nason Edgcomb, of Limington, Sept. 13, 1792.
—John, and Jerusha Whittum, Feb. 1761.
—Levi, Jr., of Cape Elizabeth, and Rebecca Strout, Dec. 7, 1786.
—Lydia, and George Smalley, of Raming Town, March 10, 1784.

MARRIAGES.

—Mary, of Flints Town, and Noah Rowe, March 23, 1785.
—Rebecca, and Levi Strout, Jr., of Cape Elizabeth, Dec. 7, 1786.
—Sally, and Joseph Roberts, Jr., Dec. 16, 1801.
—Sarah, and John Meserve, Jan. 28, 1762.
—Susanna, and Daniel Grant, Jan. 11, 1787.
Stuart, Anna, and Nathaniel Stevens, Jr., Nov. 17, 1791.
—Dorcas, and Pelatiah McDonald, Aug. 6, 1787.
—John 3d, of Scarboro, and Hannah Haynes, April 28, 1796.
—Joseph, and Hannah Smally, Sept. 30, 1779.
Stuart, Mary, and John Green, July 3, 1770.
—Susanna, and William Wood, March 4, 1779.
—Susanna, and Francis Brooks, of North Yarmouth, Jan. 4, 1786.
—Timothy, and Molly McKenney, July 19, 1772.
—Wentworth, born Oct. 20, 1731, and Susanna Lombard, born Aug. 14, 1734, were married Sept. 4, 1753.
—Wentworth, and Hannah Shaw of Standish, Nov. 4, 1790.
Sturges, Hannah, and William File, Jr., Dec. 30, 1784.
—James, and Molly Roberts, Nov. 6, 1792.
—Temperance, and George File, Oct. 10, 1789.
Swett, Hannah, and John Martin, Nov. 5, 1794.
—Joseph, and Hannah Hanscom, April 27, 1783.
—Samuel, of Windham, and Sarah Webster, Nov. 2, 1794.
Thomas, John, and Meriam Crocket, Jan. 17, 1796.
—William, and Anne Ross, Nov. 29, 1798.

MARRIAGES.

Thomes, Betty, and Joseph Brown, of Windham, Nov. 5, 1801.
—Charles, and Anne Gray, Sept. 1, 1782.
—Comfort, and Andrew Cates, Oct. 6, 1785.
—Esther, and Samuel File, Sept. 28, 1780.
—Mary, and John Newbegin, Feb. 28, 1786.
—Patience, and Coleman Watson, Sept.
—Rachel, and William Rideout, of North ~~8, 1774.~~
Yarmouth, Sept. 18, 1792.
—Sarah, and Moses Baker, of Sommersworth, Feb. 25, 1800.
—Susanna, and James Gray, Jan. 2. 1791.
—Thomas, and Rachel Morton, Nov. 6, 1787.
Thoms, George, and Lydia Brown, April 6, 1780.
—Mary, and William Elder, Feb., 1777.
—Samuel, and Sarah Lombard, Dec. 23, 1779.
Thompson, Sally, and William Crockit, Nov. 21, 1802.
Thomson, Elizabeth, and John Greely, Sept., 1773.
Thorne, Mercy, and John Pierce, July 9, 1768.
Thurston, David, and Mary Spurs, both of Otisfield, Dec. 24, 1789.
Titcomb, Sally, and Ephraim Johnson, Dec. 15, 1791.
Tobin, Matthew, and Sarah Crockit, Feb. 6, 1780.
—Samuel, and Margaret Legrow, both of Windham, April 2, 1789.
Tole, Jeremiah, and Martha Harding, Jan. 20, 1791.
Trip, Abner, and Sarah Sawyer, May 12, 1767.
—Stephen, and Rhoda Sawyer, April 12, 1765.
Tryon, Simeon, and Mercy Cook, Feb. 16, 1802.
Tyler, James, and Frances Gorham, Dec. 11, 1796.

MARRIAGES.

Vineton, Martha, and David Nason, Feb. 24, 1791.
Waite, Enoch, and Lucy Stevens, May 15, 1788.
Walker, Jabez, and Sarah Atwood, June 1748.
—Mary and Isaac Whitney, Jan. 1, 1784.
Wallace, Abigail, and Josiah Haskell, May 15, 1786.
Ward—Hannah, and Simeon Sanborn, Ja—n. 9, 1783.
Ward, Zillah, and Nathan Parker, Mar. 22, 1789.
Warren, James, and Sally Milliken, both of Scarboro, May 25, 1794.
Waterhouse, Charlotte, and Nahum Lord, July 11, 1802.
—George, and Dorcas Libby, Nov. 23, 1775.
—Joseph, of Falmouth, and Esther Fogg, Sept. 13, 1795.
—Joseph, and Lydia Wescot, May 2, 1802.
Watson, Coleman and Patience Thomes, Sept. 8, 1774.
—Coleman, and Elizabeth Frost, July 25, 1802.
—Daniel, and Anna Maxfield, Nov. 25, 1789.
—James, and Mary Davis, June 30, 1785.
—James, and Mary Carsley, Feb. 23, 1792.
—Joel, and Lydia Prentiss, January. 1798.
—John, and Tabitha Whitney, Dec. 5, 1765.
—Martha, and David Davis, June 12, 1788.
—Sally, and David Cobb, Dec. 9, 1802.
—Susanna and Isaac Skillings, Jan. 8, 1766.
—Tabitha, and Josiah Shaw, May 5, 1797.
Watts, David, and Sarah Davis, Dec. 9, 1779.
—David, and Mary Cresy, Oct. 14, 1784.
Webb, Anna, and William Bolton, Jan. 5, 1786.
—Elizabeth, and John Mayberry, March 20, 1789.

MARRIAGES.

--Josiah, and Rebecca Elder, both of Windham, May 15, 1788.
—Loriana, and James Pray, Sept. 10, 1790.
—Samuel, and Polly Wheeler, April 19, 1789.
—Sarah, and Nathaniel Knight, Feb. 24, 1787.
—Seth, and Hannah Winship, December, 1759.
—Susanna, and William Maxfield, December, 1753.
Webster, Nathaniel, and Jane Frost, October 13, 1799.
—Sarah, and Samuel Swett of Windham, Nov. 2, 1794.
Weeks, Dorcas, and George Meserve, Dec. 8, 1791.
—Mary, and Joseph Burnel, Jan. 7, 1790.
Wescot, Abner, and Lydia Parker, Sept. 12, 1793.
—Dorcas, and Samuel Whitney, Oct. 23, 1800.
—Edmund, and Hannah Morton, May 16, 1793.
—Lydia, and Joseph Waterhouse, May 2, 1802.
—Nehemiah and Eleanor Nason, April 10, 1796.
—William, and Margaret Meserve. February, 1757.
West, Eunice, and Gideon Philbrick, June 3, 1793.
Westerman, Suky Camel, and William Smith Whitaker, July 10, 1791.
Weston, Joseph, and Katharine Mosher, September, 1755.
—Katharine, and William Haskel, February 11, 1773.
Weymouth, Joseph, and Katharine Sawyer, Nov. 3, 1768.
Wheeler, Polly, and Samuel Webb, April 19, 1789.
Whitaker, William Smith, and Suky Camel Westerman, July 10, 1791.

MARRIAGES.

Whitmore, Dorcas, and James Chadbourn, Jan. 4, 1789.
—Dudly, and Sophia McIntosh, Nov. 24, 1796.
—Elizabeth Ross, and Simon Huston, Mar. 22, 1801.
—John, and Jane Roberts, Oct. 4, 1792.
—Lydia, and Uriel Whitney, Dec. 16, 1784.
—Mary, and Jacob Haskell, Dec. 29, 1785.
—Patience, and Lemuel Libby of Scarboro, June 11, 1795.
—Samuel, and Mary Whitney, Oct., 1764
—Tabitha, and William Larrabee of Scarboro, July 19, 1802.
Whitney, Abigail, and Caleb Shaw, Mar. 10, 1796.
—Agigail, and Joseph Davis, Sept. —, 1799.
—Alma, and Isaac Hall, May 19, 1793.
—Asa, and Phebe Davis, July 14, 1785.
—Betsy, and James Cates, Dec. 10, 1797.
—Daniel, and Abigail Stone, Dec. 7, 1780.
—David, and Hannah Brown, Feb., 1754.
—David, and Lydia Moore of Buxton, June 29, 1785.
—Elias, and Polly Fowler, Dec. 14, 1788.
—Hannah, and Joseph Hamblen, Oct. —, 1755.
—Hannah, and Joseph Brown, Dec. 13, 1768.
—Hannah, and John Rogers, Nov. 12, 1786.
—Happy, and Enoch Hamblen, June 6, 1802.
—Hephzibah, and Nathan Freeman, Oct. 15, 1766.
—Isaac, and Hannah Paine, Aug. 29, 1765.
—Isaac, and Mary Walker, Jan. 1, 1784.
—James, and Deborah Murch, Aug. 15, 1785.
—Jenny, and David Johnson, June 16, 1785.
—Joanna, and Caleb Chase, Dec. 31, 1769.
—Joseph, and Mehitable Stevens, Oct. 3, 1765.

MARRIAGES.

—Joseph, Jr., and Mary Freeman, Aug. 2, 1801.
—Jotham, and Elizabeth Ross, April 1, 1792.
—Lucy, and John Greelaw, March 27, 1788.
—Lydia, and John Burnell, July 3, 1766.
—Mary, and Samuel, Crockit, June 10, 1763.
—Mary, and Samuel Whitmore, Oct., 1764.
—Mary Gooking, and Thomas Paine of Standish, April 26, 1792.
—Mercy, and Joseph Libby, June 24, 1801.
—Micah, and Hannah Cobb, Nov. 29, 1779.
—Moses, and Abigail Kimball, Jan. 22, 1792.
—Phineas, and Anna Morton, Oct. 19, 1769.
—Priscilla, and David Young, of Little Falls, Dec. 15, 1796.
—Samuel, and Hannah Snow, Aug. 24, 1798.
—Samuel, and Dorcas Wescot, Oct. 23, 1800.
—Sarah, and Sheba Dyer, July 16, 1797.
—Tabitha, and John Watson, Dec. 5, 1765.
—Uriel, and Lydia Whitmore, Dec. 16, 1784.
—William, and Hannah Bangs, Oct. 11, 1792.
Whitten, Anna, and Samuel Melsher McDonald, of Standish, Dec. 25, **1794.**
Whittum, Jerusha, and John Strout, Feb., 1761.
Wing, Nathan, of Limington, and Love Frost, Dec. 25, 1791.
Winship, Hannah, and Seth Webb, Dec. 1759.
—Mehitable, and John Stinchfield, Dec. 1759.
—Mehitable, and Samuel Dole, both of Windham, Nov. 8, 1787.
Winslow, Nathaniel, of Falmouth, and Lydia McCausland, of Windham, Jan. 23, 1794.

MARRIAGES.

Wise, Elizabeth, and Samuel Lary, of Falmouth, Dec. 25, 1796.

—Joseph, and Abigail Edwards, May 21, 1801.

Wood, Charles, and Sarah Davis, Sept. 17, 1786.

—Hannah, and Nathaniel Blake, March 7, 1793.

—Molly, and Heman Bangs, Jan. 1, 1770.

—William, and Susanna Stuart, March 4, 1779.

—William, Jr., and Polly Dyer, Nov. 25, 1790.

—William and Mercy Bean, Dec. 15, 1796.

Woodard, John, and Dorothy Hall, Oct. 6, 1791.

Woodman, Eunice, of New Gloucester, and Amos Rich, June 4, 1781.

Wooster, Mary, and Clement Meserve, Sept. 19, 1757.

—Patience, and Dennis Lary, May, 1761.

—Thomas, and Susanna Edwards, Sept. 11, 1800.

Yaton, Mary, and John Meserve, March, 1757.

York, Mary, and Reuben Cookson, Feb. 1, 1769.

—Naoma, and John Hall, Feb. 1, 1769.

Young. David, of Little Falls, and Priscilla Whitney, Dec. 15, 1796.

—Deborah, and David L. Marston, Feb. 27, 1789.

—Joseph 3d, and Lydia Snow, Nov. 7, 1796.

—Joshua, and Sarah Irish, June 13, 1779.

—Rebecca, and Jonathan Green, Sept. 18, 1796.

—Solomon, and Polly Kimball, Dec. 4, 1796.

BIRTHS OF CHILDREN.

From the earliest town records of Gorham, Me.

Adams, of Benjamin and Miriam,
—Benjamin Watson, Portland, March 9, 1778.
Adams, of Joshua and Hannah,
—Lucy, June 25, 1778.
—Joseph Crosby, Aug. 10, 1780.
—Isaac, twin with Benjamin, May 25, 1783.
—James, June 27, 1787.
—Hannah, May 2, 1790.
Adams, of William and Susanna,
—Joseph, Sept. 21, 1774.
Akers, Dorcas, Feb. 16, 1779.
Akers, of John and Eunice,
—Hannah, Sept. 13, 1785.
—Thomas, Feb. 9, 1787.
—Mary, Oct. 2, 1789.
—Benjamin, May 13, 1791.
—Moses, Feb. 26, 1792. Died aged 22 months.
—John, Oct. 5, 1798.
—Nancy, March 2, 1800.
—William, April 20, 1802.
Akers, of Moses and Hannah,
—Jenny Mosher, Aug. 13, 1756.
—Daniel Mosher, Aug. 17, 1760.
—John Aug. 25, 1763.
—Hannah Baker, April 25, 1766.
—Rebecca, Oct. 12, 1768.
—Susanna Baker, Oct. 17, 1775.
Alden, Austin, (born, Marshfield, March 25, 1729, and Salome (Lombard), born, Truro, June 10, 1736),
—Elizabeth, Oct. 3, 1757.
—Josiah, March 31, 1760.
—Humphrey, Jan. 21, 1763.
—Anner, April 14, 1765.
—Hezekiah, July 15, 1767. Died Nov. 27, 1768.

BIRTHS OF CHILDREN.

Alden, of Josiah and Sarah,
—Austin, Nov. 3, 1784.
—Salome, Nov. 12, 1786.
—Charles, Jan. 20, 1789.
—Hannah, Jan. 20, 1791.
—Nancy, Feb. 13, 1793.
—Gardner, Jan. 13, 1795.
—Lucy, April 9, 1797.
Babb, of Zebulon and Lydia,
—Thomas, Feb. 5, 1800.
—Mary Ann, Dec. 1, 1801.
Bacon, of Josiah and Lucy,
—Affia, Aug. 31, 1789.
—Rebecca, Aug. 31, 1791.
—Fanny, April 2, 1794.
—Miriam, March 2, 1796.
—Richard, Jan. 20, 1798.
Bacon, of Nathaniel and Affia,
—Josiah, Scarboro, Sept. 24, 1766.
—Martha, Gorham, May 15, 1769.
Bacon, of Nathaniel, Jr., and Betty,
—Thomas, April 21, 1783.
—Polly, Sept. 5, 1784.
—Nathaniel, March 18, 1786.
—Martha, March 24, 1790.
Bacon, of Timothy and Mary,
—Stephen, May 19, 1789.
—Sarah, Jan. 12, 1791.
—James, Jan. 11, 1793.
—Timothy, Dec. 31, 1794.
—Martha, Dec. 5, 1796.
—Nancy, Jan. 6, 1799.
Bacon, of Timothy and Susanna,
—Miriam, July 4, 1812.
—Ebenezer H., Dec. 27, 1813.
—Athise, Jan. 30, 1816.
—Adaline, Feb. 21, 1822.
—Fanny H., Jan. 24, 1824.
Baker, of Daniel and Betsy,
—Ira, Sept. 23, 1796.
—Sally C., May 4, 1800.
—John C., Sept. 12, 1804.
—Jacob C., June 19, 1808.
—Betsy C., Aug. 1, 1813.

BIRTHS OF CHILDREN.

Bangs, of Barnabas and Lornhamah,
—James, Sept. 14, 1752.
—Barnabas, Dec. 1, 1754.
—Thomas, April 17, 1757.
—Anne, March 14, 1760.
—Sarah, July 21, 1762.
—Ebenezer, Oct. 22, 1765.
—Mehitable, Oct. 22, 1768.
—Benajmin, Aug. 6, 1771.
Bangs, of Barnabas, Jr., and Katharine,
—Sarah, June 5, 1778.
—Susanna, May 8, 1780.
—George, Aug. 22, 1782.
—Ruth, August, 1786.
Bangs, of Barnabas, Jr., and Betty, his second wife,
—Susanna, May 19, 1790.
—Anna, May 16, 1793.
—Katharine, Dec. 27, 1795.
—Mary, June 20, 1798.
Bangs, of Benjamin and Elizabeth,
—John, July 6, 1794.
—Benjamin, July 6, 1794.
—Sophia, Feb. 3, 1796.
Bangs, of Herman and Molly,
—Joseph, Dec. 7, 1770.
—Mary, Oct. 1, 1772.
—Hannah, April 19, 1775.
—Nathan, March 9, 1777.
—Herman, May 9, 1782.
Bangs, of James and Deborah,
—Edmund, Oct. 21, 1775.
—Thomas, July 1, 1777.
—John, Dec. 11, 1778.
—James, Sept. 30, 1780.
—Hannah, March 26, 1782.
—Allen, April 8, 1784.
—Esther, May 26, 1786.
Bangs, of James and Elizabeth, his second wife,
—Robert, Sept. 15, 1790.
—Cyrus, April 26, 1792.
—Solomon, Sept. 22, 1793.
—Joshua, Jan. 19, 1795.
Bangs, of Joseph and Mary,
—Thomas, Jan. 1, 1797.
—Lemuel, May 25, 1800.

BIRTHS OF CHILDREN.

Bangs, of Nathan and Sarah,
—Mary, March 10, 1800.
Bangs, of Thomas and Hannah,
—Mary, Oct. 2, 1778.
—William, Jan. 17, 1781.
—Bethia, May 25, 1783.
—Nancy, Nov. 22, 1787.
—Eunice, April 20, 1790.
—Joseph, March 8, 1793.
Blake, of Benjamin, Jr., and Phebe,
—Jedediah, March 14, 1786.
—Edward, May 11, 1789.
—John, Oct. 13, 1791. Died April 6, 1794.
—John, March 15, 1793.
—Joseph, June 5, 1795.
—William, May 23, 1797.
—Silvanus, Feb. 13, 1800.
Blake, of Ithiel and Affa,
—Affa, July 23, 1770.
—Elizabeth, Dec. 15, 1772.
—Martha, Feb. 19, 1775.
—Mary, Feb. 24, 1778.
—Nathaniel, Oct. 1, 1780.
—Freeman, July 25, 1786.
—Timothy, May 22, 1789.
Blake, of John and Deborah,
—Sally, Boston, Jan. 13, 1782.
—Polly, Gorham, Feb. 18, 1784.
—Daniel, June 20, 1786.
—Samuel, July 31, 1788.
—John, Nov. 10, 1792.
—Thankful, Nov. 16, 1794.
—James, June 7, 1796.
—George, Jan. 10, 1798.
Last four name of mother not given.
Blake, of Joseph and Hannah,
—Adriel, April 5, 1782.
—Phebe, Standish, Dec. 7, 1783.
—Hannah, Standish, Sept. 3, 1785.
—Eunice, Standish, Sept. 8, 1787.
—Lydia, Aug. 21, 1790.
—Lucy, May 9, 1793.
—Charles, Nov. 6, 1800.
—Joseph, April 15, 1803.

BIRTHS OF CHILDREN.

Blake, of Nathaniel and Mary.
—Seth, April 26, 1778.
—Ithiel, March 6, 1780.
—Ruth, June 2, 1781.
—Benjamin, May 31, 1783.
—Elias, Sept. 7, 1785.
—Molly, Dec. 5, 1786.
—Leah, March 23, 1788.
—Ephraim, June 26, 1789.
—Elizabeth, Feb. 7, 1791.
Blanchard, of John and Dorcas.
—William, July 25, 1793.
—John, July 13, 1795
Bolton, of Thomas and Hannah.
—William, Dec. 23, 1782.
—Joshua, Oct. 18, 1784.
—Benjamin, Apr. 1, 1787.
Boothby, of Elias and Abigail.
—Daniel March, Feb. 28, 1794.
Bowman, of Dr. Nathaniel and Sally.
—Samuel Gardner, Oct. 9, 1790.
—Sally, Nov. 19, 1792.
—Joshua, Oct. 24, 1795.
Bracket, of Joseph and Sarah.
—Jerusha. July, 19, 1783.
Bragdon, of Jonathan and Lucy.
—William, July 16, 1778.
—Elizabeth, Aug. 3, 1780.
Briggs, of Abiel and Polly.
—John Perkins, Sept. 4, 1791.
—Lucy Perkins, March 4, 1794.
Brimhall of Sylvanus and Esther.
—Cornelius, April 16, 1768.
—Martha, Aug. 28, 1769.
—Betty, Nov. 4, 1771.
—John Bennet, Sept. 5, 1773.
—Sylvanus, Aug. 5, 1775.
—Polly, Oct. 7, 1779.
—Esther, Aug. 25, 1782.
Brooks, of Francis and Susanna.
—Relief, March 10, 1789.
—Dorcas, April 15, 1795.
—William, Oct. 9, 1797.
—Joseph, July 9, 1799.
Brown, of Abel and Abigail.
—Enoch, March 31, 1800.
—Polly, Dec. 17, 1801.

BIRTHS OF CHILDREN.

Brown, of Benjamin and Sarah.
—Edmund, Sept. 22, 1772.
—Joseph, July 22, 1774.
—Betty, Sept. 24, 1776.
—Isaac Cole, Nov. 25, 1778.
—John, May 20, 1781.
—Nancy, Dec. 20, 1783.
—Hannah, Jan. 20, 1786.
—Polly, July 29, 1788.
—Patience, Aug. 10, 1791.
—Sally, July 23, 1795.
Brown, of Hezekiah and Abiah.
—Betsy, July 9, 1795.
—James Moody, April 24, 1797.
—Eliza, May 26, 1799.
—Mary, Nov. 11, 1801.
Brown, of Joseph and Susanna.
—Simeon, May 9, 1753.
Susanna, July 27, 1756.
Brown, of Joseph and Hannah.
—Timothy, Nov. 3, 1769.
—Sarah, June 19, 1772.
—Susanna, Jan. 15, 1775.
Brown, of Joseph and Hannah.
—Eliza Skilling, North Yarmouth, Jan. 3, 1800.
Brown, of Samuel and Barbara.
—Lydia, Eastham, Nov. 1, 1765.
—Samuel, Eastham, Oct. 27, 1767.
—Joseph, Gorham, Aug. 8, 1770.
—Bethiah, Gorham, Feb. 11, 1775.
—Barbara, Gorham, March 25, 1777.
—Lucy, Gorham, May 10, 1782.
Brown, of Silvanus and Fear.
—Fear, July 10, 1767.
—Hezekiah, May 28, 1771.
—Martha, Aug. 30, 1773.
—Silvanus, March, 1, 1775, died same month.
—Silvanus, July 5, 1776.
—Herman Merrick, Feb. 13, 1778.
Brown, of Simeon and Elizabeth.
—James, July 3, 1777.
—Marcy, Jan. 22, 1779, died Nov., 1784.
—Samuel, Nov. 4, 1782.
—Simeon, Jan. 17, 1885.
—Levi, March, 23, 1787.
—Sally, March 27, 1789.
—Charles, March 1, 1792.
—Solomon, March 5, 1795.
—Polly, Feb. 28 ,1797, died Aug. 1, 1798.

BIRTHS OF CHILDREN.

Burnel, of John and Elizabeth.
—Mary, Dec. 17 ,1763.
—John, Feb. 14, 1766.
—Benjamin, Feb. 27, 1768.
—Samuel, June 17, 1770.
—Elizabeth, Sept. 21, 1772.
—Stephen, April 22, 1775.
—Jonathan, Aug. 14, 1778.
—Nabby, June 11, 1781.
—Sally, Oct., 1784.
Burnell, of John and Lydia.
—Joseph, Falmouth, Nov. 22, 1769.
—Nancy, Boothbay, Jan. 15, 1771.
—Jenny, Boothbay, Jan. 15, 1773.
—Samuel, Gorham, Sept. 22, 1778.
—Sally, Jan. 23, 1785.
—David, Aug. 16, 1787.
—Eunice, March 15, 1790.
Brunnels, Owen and Susanna.
—Molly, Jan. 17, 1775.
Burton, of William and Mary.
—Rebecca, Sept. 25, 1784.
—Sarah, Dec. 3, 1786.
—Elizabeth, Dec. 18, 1791.
—Mary, Jan. 19, 1794.
—Mildred, Jan. 7, 1796.
—William, Jan. 13, 1798.
Canley, of Ebenezer and Patience.
—Dorcas, Aug. 5, 1768.
Carsley, of Isaac and Jenny.
—James, Jan. 28, 1798.
—Louisa, May 13, 1801.
Carsley, of John and Mercy.
—Mary, Feb. 10, 1765.
—John, Aug. 19, 1766.
—Nathan, April 6, 1768.
—Ebenezer, April 9, 1770.
—Bethiah, Feb. 16, 1772, died Feb. 25. 1772.
—Isaac, Feb.17, 1773.
—Sarah, Oct. 12, 1774.
—Benjamin, Dec. 19, 1776.
—Dorcas, Jan. 26, 1780, died at age of 4 months.
—Seth, July 18, 1782.
—Eunice, April 30, 1784.

BIRTHS OF CHILDREN.

Cates, of Andrew and Comfort.
—Benjamin, Dec. 20, 1785.
Cates, of Benjamin and Amy.
—James, Feb. 2, 1775.
—Thomas, Sept. 28, 1776.
—John, June 12, 1779.
—Deborah, March 16, 1781.
—Ebenezer, Oct. 25, 1783.
—Joseph, no date.
Cates, children of Ebenezer and Anna.
—William, Oct. 20, 1794, died March 4, 1796.
—Edmund, Aug. 31, 1796.
—Jedediah, March 1, 1801.
—Phebe, June 4, 1804.
—William, Feb. 25, 1805.
—Lydia, June 4, 1808.
—James, Jan. 19, 1811.
—Henry, June 28, 1813, died Oct. 10, 1829.
Cates, of Joseph and Deborah.
—Andrew, Aug. 1763.
—Ebenezer, Aug. 24, 1768.
Chadbourn, of James and Dorcas.
—Samuel, Falmouth, June 28, 1789.
—Phebe, Gorham, June 14, 1791.
—Charlotte, Sept. 4, 1793.
—James, Jan. 23, 1796.
—Rufus, June 20, 1798.
—Gardner, Oct. 23, 1800, died Sept. 1, 1801.
—Gardner, July 17, 1802.
Chadbourn, of Silas and Abigail.
—Isaac, Jan. 22, 1776.
—Rebecca, April 9, 1780.
—Abigail, March 3, 1782.
—Nahum, April 5, 1784.
—Samuel, April 21, 1786.
—Martha, April 13, 1788.
—Polly, July 31, 1790.
—Betty, July 17, 1793.
—Priscilla, Oct. 25, 1795.
—Nancy, Jan. 1, 1798.
Chase, of Caleb and Joanna (Whitney).
—Mary, Jan. 31, 1771.
—Joseph, Aug. 9, 1772.
—Abigail, Aug. 12, 1774.
—William Hills, April 11, 1776.
—Jacob, Feb. 11, 1778.

BIRTHS OF CHILDREN.

Clark, of Benjamin and Sarah.
—Elizabeth, Raymond, April 24, 1778.
—Benjamin, June 23, 1781.
—James, May 5, 1784.
Clark, of Morris and Sarah.
—John, Stratham, N. H., Nov. 6, 1767.
—Jacob, Epen, N. H., Oct. 20, 1769.
—Joseph, Falmouth, July 3, 1772.
—Mary, Aug. 24, 1777.
—James, Jan. 29, 1781.
Clark, of Moses and Martha.
—Patty, Dec. 16, 1792.
—John Rogers, Feb. 14, 1795.
—Horatio, Feb. 15, 1797.
—Leonard, Sept. 5, 1799, died, Aug. 12, 1804.
—Leonard, Aug. 13, 1805, died, Aug. 22, 1808.
Clark, of Samuel and Elizabeth.
—Samuel, May 25. 1794.
Clemmons, of Jacob and Phebe.
—Eleanor, May 26, 1791.
—Ebenezer, Feb. 13, 1794.
—John, May 11, 1796.
—Hanson, Sept. 18, 1798.
—Elizabeth R., Dec. 20, 1800.
—Phebe, Jan. 24, 1803.
—Simeon C., Feb. 14, 1805.
—Daniel B., June 1, 1808.
—Samuel D. R., Dec. 5, 1810.
—Mary C., March 16, 1813.
Cloutman, of John and Elizabeth.
—Elizabeth, Sept. 7, 1801.
Cloutman, Timothy and Katy.
—Betty, May 3, 1767.
—Nancy, May 7, 1769, died in her 10th year.
—Edward, July 1, 1771.
—Nathan, July 29, 1773.
—Jesse, July 29, 1773.
—John, Feb. 20, 1776.
—Mary, July 13, 1779.
—William, Sept. 16, 1780.
—Thomas, Aug. 20, 1783.
—Solomon, Dec. 4, 1785.
—David, Sept. 16, 1788.

BIRTHS OF CHILDREN.

Cobb, of Andrew and Hannah.
—Nathan, Falmouth, March 3, 1767.
—Ebenezer, Gorham, Oct. 4, 1768.
—Chipman, Gorham, March 22, 1771.
—Mary, July 26, 1772.
Cobb, of Ebenezer and Margaret.
—Thomas Lay Roach, Oct. 24, 1800.
Cobb of Elisha and Elizabeth.
—Elisha, June 10, 1761.
—Mary, Oct. 4, 1762.
—Ezekiel, May 9, 1764.
—Phebe, April 16, 1766.
—Reuben, March 9, 1769.
—William, July 20, 1771.
—Samuel, Oct. 15, 1773.
—Ebenezer, Jan. 22, 1777.
—Elizabeth, July 22, 1779.
Cobb, of Elisha, Jr., and Molly.
—Thankful, Nov. 12, 1791.
—John, Sept. 17, 1793.
—Elisha, Nov. 7, 1795.
Cobb, Ezekiel, Oct. 27, 1788.
Cobb, of Reuben and Betsy.
—Ebenezer, Jan. 8, 1802.
—Richard, April 19, 1803.
Cobb, of William and Nancy.
—Arthur, March 31, 1800.
Coffin, of Isaac and Lydia.
—James, Jan. 13, 1791.
—John, Dec. 22, 1792.
—Molly, May 2, 1795.
Cotton, of Ebenezer and Elizabeth.
—Joseph, Oct. 26, 1789.
—Susanna, March 12, 1791.
—Nathaniel, May 20, 1794.
—Polly, April 30, 1796.
—Lydia, March 20, 1799.
—William, Oct. 12, 1802.
Cotton of John and Rebecca.
—Eunice, Sept. 29, 1770.
—Lorwhama, Aug. 22, 1772.
—William, Oct. 5, 1776.
—Elisha, April 25, 1779.
—John, April 11, 1781.
—Samuel, June 6, 1784.

BIRTHS OF CHILDREN.

Cotton, of William and Elizabeth.
—John, Feb. 16, 1760.
—Sarah, Dec. 4, 1761.
—Ebenezer Cobb, Feb. 18, 1764.
—Susanna, April 17, 1766.
—Mary, June 7, 1768.
—Elizabeth, Aug. 10, 1770.
—William, July 1, 1773.
—Abigail, Aug. 26, 1775.
—Dorcas Cobb, Jan. 11, 1778.
Cresey, of Daniel and Eliza.
—Eliza, July 19, 1800.
Cressey, of John and Deborah (Wadley,)
daughter of Amos, of Boston.
—John, Feb. 22, 1749.
—Josiah, Oct. 26, 1753.
—Elizabeth, April 18, 1757.
—Mary, May 1, 1762.
—Noah, May 6, 1765.
Cresy, of John, Jr., and Susanna.
—Daniel, Sept. 4, 1771.
—Betsy, Jan. 31, 1775.
—Hannah, Buxton, April 22, 1777.
—Sarah, Buxton, April 26, 1779.
—Meriam, Buxton, Dec. 1, 1781.
—John, Buxton, June 17, 1784.
Creasy, of Joseph and Hannah.
—Ebenezer, Pomphret. Windham Co.,
Conn, Jan. 16, 1779.
—Alvey, July 12, 1781.
—John, Aug. 22, 1785.
—Joseph, March 14, 1788.
—Mary, Sept. 6, 1792.
—Sally, March 7, 1796.
—Noah, July 28, 1798.
Crocket, of Andrew and Rebecca.
—Ephraim, Falmouth, Jan. 13, 1766.
—David, Gorham, July 21, 1768.
—Mehitable, July 21, 1771.
—Ebenezer, July 27, 1775.
—Rebecca, Feb. 25, 1779.
Crockit, of James and Sarah.
—Vashti, July 3, 1800.

BIRTHS OF CHILDREN.

Crockit, of John and Betty.
—Nabby, July 1, 1797.
—Charles, July 23, 1799, died Nov. 21, 1800.
—Mary, Jan. 7, 1802.
—Caroline, Feb. 17, 1804.
—Angelina, Feb. 22, 1806.
—Catherine, Feb. 21, 1808.
—Albert, March 18, 1810.
—Eliza, March 8, 1812.
—Martha, April 17, 1814.
—Daniel, Oct. 16, 1816.
—Susan, Nov. 22, 1819.
Crockit, of Jonathan and Anna.
—David, Dec. 7, 1775.
—Sarah, March 21, 1777.
—Deborah, March 21, 1779.
—Mehitable, March 20, 1780.
—Andrew, Jan. 17, 1785.
—Nathaniel, March 10, 1788.
Crockit, of Joshua and Hannah.
—Enoch, July 3, 1771.
—Miriam, Nov. 30, 1773.
—Sarah, Sept. 30, 1775.
—Abigail, Feb. 27, 1778.
—William, July 19, 1781.
—Solomon, Sept. 17, 1784.
Crockit, of Joshua, 3d, and Sarah.
—James, April 24, 1789.
—Joshua, Jan. 14, 1791.
Crockit, of Pelatiah and Mary.
—Susanna, Stratham, N. H., May 4, 1761.
—Phebe, Stratham, N. H., July 4, 1762.
—Rebecca, Gorham, Feb. 26, 1767.
—John, March 7, 1776.
Crocket, of Samuel, Jr., and Tabitha (Hamblen).
—Eunice, June 22, 1771, died same month.
—William, Sept. 19, 1772.
—Nancy, Sept. 18, 1774.
—Susanna, July 31, 1777.
—Content, May, 18, 1779.
—Martha, March 19, 1781.
—Joseph, Oct. 11, 1782.

BIRTHS OF CHILDREN.

Crockett, of Samuel, Jr., and Elizabeth (Pickit), his second wife.
—James, Dec. 14, 1785.
—John, March 11, 1788.
—Samuel, Feb. 20, 1790.
Darling, of John and Anna.
—John, June 6. 1787.
—Robert, May 6, 1789.
—George, Oct. 7, 1791.
—Mary, Oct. 8, 1793.
—Martha, Aug. 4, 1796.
—Sarah, April 17, 1799.
—Mehitabel, Nov. 16, 1801.
—Martha, Sept. 4, 1806.
—Tabitha L., Sept. 3, 1808.
—Abagile P., July 30, 1810.
Davis, of Allen and Martha.
—Polly, Oct. 18, 1792.
—Rhoda, Sept. 9, 1794.
—Charles, Jan. 20, 1797.
—Annah Allen, Feb. 5, 1799.
—Josiah, March 3, 1801.
—Eliza, Jan. 28, 1803.
—Emeline, May 13, 1808.
—Frederick, June 6, 1811.
—Ann L., April, 6, 1813.
Father died May 26, 1818.
Davis, of David and Martha.
—Elijah, Nov. 25, 1788.
Davis, of Ebenezer and Mary.
—Isaac, June 11, 1793.
—Mary, March, 1795.
—William Paine, March 16, 1797.
Davis, of Elijah and Phebe.
—Sarah, Buxton, Sept. 17, 1781.
Davis, of James and Thankful.
—Josiah, Dec. 5, 1793.
—Phebe, Jan. 31, 1795.
Davis, John, Jan. 8, 1780.
Davis, of Jonathan and Molly.
—Stephen, June 30, 1797.
—Daniel, Oct. 18, 1798.
—Elijah, Aug. 5, 1800.
—Harriot, Nov. 12, 1802.

BIRTHS OF CHILDREN.

Davis, of Jonathan and Sarah.
—William, November, 1806.
—Mary, July 25, 1808.
—John Colby, November, 1812.
—Sarah, June, 1815.
—Joseph, Oct. 12, 1817.
Davis, of Joshua and Sarah.
—Hannah, Scarboro, Jan. 25, 1758.
—Joshua, Scarboro, March 1, 1760.
—Sarah, Gorham, Jan. 3, 1762.
—Elizabeth, Gorham, July 6, 1764.
—Mehitable, Gorham, Sept. 20, 1767.
—Joseph, Gorham, Aug. 9, 1769.
—Timothy, Gorham, Oct. 18, 1772.
—Gideon, Gorham, Feb. 8, 1775.
Davis, of Josiah and Thankful.
—James, Sept. 27, 1773.
—Joseph, Aug. 10, 1776.
—Solomon, Feb. 6, 1780.
Davis, of Prince and Sarah.
—Isaac, March 27, 1762.
—David, Oct. 20, 1764.
—Rebecca, July 15, 1766.
—Thomas, May 10, 1768, died June 2, 1769.
—Jonathan, July 10, 1770.
Davis, of Prince, Jr., and Betsy.
—Samuel, Sept. 22, 1797.
—Lewis, Sept. 22, 1797.
Davis, of Samuel and Mary.
—Elizabeth, April 14, 1777.
Davis, of Samuel and Mary.
—Elizabeth, Aug. 5, 1785.
—Sarah, Jan. 26, 1787.
Davis, of Silvanus and Hannah.
—Ebenezer, Gorham, Sept. 4, 1790.
—Sarah Hoff, March 4, 1792.
Davis, of Capt. Silvanus and Catharine:
—Nathan Smith, Feb. 1, 1799.
—Silvanus, March 29, 1801.
Dosset, of Jedidiah and Susanna.
—Salome, June 9, 1797.
—Edmund, April 16, 1799.
—Thomas, March 16, 1802.

BIRTHS OF CHILDREN.

Dunn, of Christopher and Susanna.
—Peter, May 31, 1782.
—Rebecca, April 10, 1789.
—Lydia, no date.
—Richard, Jan. 9, 1792.
—Jeremiah, no date.
—Nathaniel, no date.
—George, no date.
—Joshua, no date.
Dunn, of Nathaniel and Mercy.
—Deborah, Feb. 6, 1771.
—Polly, Oct. 10, 1773.
—Josiah, Feb. 22, 1776.
—Samuel, Mar. 15, 1778.
—Betsy, June 17, 1780.
—Benjamin, no date.
—David, no date.
Dyer, of John, Jr., and Molly.
—Dorcas, Oct. 26, 1790.
—Timothy, Feb. 1, 1793.
—William, Oct. 10, 1795; d. Aug. 8, 1796.
—Mehitable, June 6, 1797.
—Deborah, Jan. 22, 1800; d Nov. 22, 1802.
—Deborah, Feb. 24, 1803.
Dyer, of William and Rebecca.
—Horton, May 10, 1793; d. Mar. 14, 1795.
—Samuel, Feb. 24, 1795.
—Nathan, Mar. 4, 1796.
—Ruth, Nov. 12, 1802.
—Pamelia, April 1, 1804.
—James, Dec. 14, 1805.
—Horton, May 10, 1806.
—Lovina, June 15, 1809.
—William, Nov. 20, 1811.
Edwards, of Joseph and Mary.
—Polly, June 13, 1780.
—Abigail, Buxton, Oct. 28, 1782.
—Cyperon Johnson, Feb. 16, 1785.
—Hepzabah, April 19, 1787.
—Lois, Feb. 7, 1792.
Edwards, of Nathaniel and Sarah.
—George, Aug. 3, 1776.
—John, Oct. 3, 1777.
—Stephen, Sept. 22, 1779.

BIRTHS OF CHILDREN.

Edwards, of Nathaniel and Bathsheba.
—Isaac, March 12, 1787.
—Rachel, July 18, 1789.
—Jacob, Dec. 6, 1790.
—Tabitha, June 11, 1792,
—Sally, May 23, 1793.
—Joshua, Jan. 2, 1795.
—Reuben, Dec. 18, 1796.
—Anna. May 31, 1798.
Edwards, Nathaniel and Bathsheba.
—Nathaniel, May 5. 1800.
—Bathsheba, May 5, 1800.
Edwards, of Richard and Hannah.
—John, April 18. 1766, died in three months.
—Sarah, Sept. 3, 1768, died at the age of 13 years.
—Samuel, Jan. 27, 1770.
—Hannah, June 8, 1772.
—Enoch, Sept. 20, 1774.
—Lydia, June 12, 1777.
—William, Sept. 2, 1779.
—Susanna, April 22, 1782.
—Richard, Feb. 18, 1786.
Edwards, of Samuel and Martha.
—James, June 27, 1793.
—Hannah, July 14, 179-.
—Martha, Feb. 17, 1798.
—Brice, March 25, 180-.
—Charles, March 9, 1802, died.
—Charles, May 9, 1805.
—Mary Ann, Dec. 8, 1807.
—Maria, June 8, 1809.
—Abigail, Aug. 25, 1811.
—Theodore, May 25, 1815.
Elder of Elijah and Eleanor.
—John, Dec. 5, 1798.
Elder, of Isaac and Mary.
—John, Aug. 9, 1783.
Elder, of Samuel and Hannah (Freeman).
—Eunice, Nov. 29. 1774.
—Ruth, Jan. 7, 1776.
—Hannah, Oct. 4, 1777.
—Betty, Oct. 4, 1779.
—Samuel, Sept. 2, 1781.

BIRTHS OF CHILDREN.

Elder, of Samuel and Mary (Graffam), his second wife.
—Peter, Oct. 5, 1787.
—Ruth, March 24, 1789.
—Simon, Dec. 4, 1791.
—Lois, July 13, 1797.
Eldridge, of Daniel and Abigail.
—Ebenezer, March, 26, 1771.
Eldridge, of Daniel and Phebe.
—Sarah, June 15, 1785.
Elwell, of Isaac Battle and Mary.
—David, Standish, May 9, 1797.
—John, Nov. 17, 1798.
—Sally, Aug. 28, 1802.
Elwell, of Jonathan and Sarah.
—George, Oct. 31, 1775.
—Mary, May 2, 1778.
—Mercy, April 16, 1780.
Emerson, of William and Elizabeth.
—William, Bridgton, Dec. 6, 1773.
—Jacob, Bridgton, Feb. 21, 1776.
—Elizabeth, Bridgton, Jan. 18, 1778.
—Abigail, Bridgton, Aug. 4, 1780.
Emery, of James and Mercy.
—Nathaniel, July 15, 1786.
—Joshua, Sept. 9, 1792.
Emory, of John and Sarah.
—Benjamin, May 11, 1778.
Farnham, of Simeon and Elizabeth.
—Simeon, Aug. 9, 1788.
—John, March 5, 1790.
—Elizabeth, Feb. 18, 1792.
—Roxsena, April 7, 1794.
—Charles, May 8, 1796.
—Henry, April 1, 1798.
—Frederick, July 30, 1800.
—Edward, Sept. 4, 1802.
File, of Ebenezer and Molly.
—William Elder, April 8, 1781.
—Ebenezer, June 7, 1783.
—Edward, Feb. 11, 1786.
—Molly, June 7, 1789
—Joanna, March 7, 1792.
—Esther, June 23, 1795.
File, of George and Temperance.
—Temperance, Gorham, June 20, 1791.
—Nabby, May 3, 1794.
—Thpnes, Gorham, Aug. 8, 1796.

BIRTHS OF CHILDREN.

File, of Samuel and Esther.
—Samuel, Aug. 7, 1781.
Files, of William.
—Ebenezer, York, Feb. 24, 1758.
—Samuel, York, Aug. 4, 1759.
—William, Gorham, Aug. 15, 1761.
—Robert, Gorham, Feb. 13, 1764.
—George, Gorham, Feb. 2, 1766.
—Joseph, Gorham, Dec. 13, 1767.
File, of William and Joanna.
—Mary, July 2, 1771.
—Joanna, May 11, 1774.
—Elizabeth, July 29, 1778.
File, of William, Jr., and Hannah.
—Jonathan, Nov. 4, 1785.
—Betsy, April 21, 1788.
—Allen, Feb. 4, 1791.
—Nabby, Dec. 14, 1793.
—Nathaniel, July 12, 1796.
—Hannah, May 18, 1799.
—Sylvanus, Sept. 22, 1803.
Fly, of James and Jerusha.
—Hannah, Nov. 24, 1762.
—Isaac, July 7, 1764.
—Mary, April 5, 1766.
—Lucy, May 7, 1768.
—Elizabeth, Jan. 6, 1771.
—Dorcas, April 5, 1773.
—James, Mar. 26, 1775.
—Sarah, Dec. 7, 1776.
—Susanna, Dec. 5, 1779.
—John, March 8, 1782.
—Eleanor, Dec. 22, 1786.
Fogg, of Jeremiah and Mary.
—George, Jan. 11, 1784.
Fogg, of Jeremiam, Jr., and Dorcas.
—Martha, Sept. 10, 1798.
—Edmund, Aug. 28, 1800.
Mother died May 11, 1801.
Folsom, of Doct. Dudley and Lucretia.
—Caroline, Exeter, Jan. 17, 1796.
—Lucretia Ann. Jan. 15, 1799.
—Harriot, Sept. 19, 1800.
—Martha Olive, Aug. 15, 1802.
—Rufus D., Aug. 16, 1804.
—Charles B., Mar. 18, 1806.

BIRTHS OF CHILDREN.

Foss, of Joseph and Nancy.
—Samuel, Aug. 15, 1793.
—Lucy, Dec. 15, 1795; d. Aug. 15, 1797.
—Joseph, May 9, 1798.
—Simon, Sept. 11, 1800; d. Jan. 20, 1801.
Foster, of Asael and Joanna.
—Joseph, Wenham, Nov. 12, 1771.
—Asael, Bridgton, Oct. 4, 1774.
—Benjamin, Bridgton, Sept. 1, 1775.
—Lucy, Bridgton, Sept. 1, 1775.
Freeman, of Jonathan and Sarah.
—Sarah, Falmouth, May 9, 1761.
—Jenny, July 28, 1763.
—Benjamin, June 18, 1765.
—Rebecca, July 28, 1767.
—Susanna, Oct. 8, 1769.
—Jonathan, Feb. 8, 1773.
—Ebenezer, April 8, 1775.
—Affia, Dec. 6, 1777.
—Joshua, May 4, 1789.
Freeman, of Jonathan, Jr., and Hannah.
—Gardner, Mar. 22, 1799.
—Polly, Aug. 25, 1801.
Freeman, of Nathan and Hezibah.
—Bethiah, March 5, 1768. Died same month.
—Nathaniel, Dec. 4, 1769.
—Samuel, Jan. 2, 1772.
—Elizabeth, Aug. 9, 1773.
By second wife, Lydia.
—Hannah, Aug. 11, 1776.
—Ebenezer, July 12, 1780.
—Nathan, Oct. 31, 1782.
Freeman, of Nathaniel and Mary.
—Jenny, Nov. 5, 1775.
—Mary, Jan. 10, 1778.
—Lydia, Aug. 5, 1780.
—David, Nov. 26, 1782.
—Bethiah, Sept. 12, 1785.
—Hannah, Dec. 25, 1789.
—Betsy, Sept. 4, 1792.
—Eunice, Dec. 26, 1794.
—John, Jan. 31, 1797.
Freeman, of Nathaniel, Jr., and Isabella.
—Nathaniel, Aug. 27, 1794.

BIRTHS OF CHILDREN.

Freeman, of Samuel and Olive.
—John, Jan. 14, 1803.
Frost, of Benjamin and Susanna.
—Samuel, Oct. 3, 1765.
—Betty, Aug. 31, 1767.
—Benjamin, Oct. 31, 1768.
—Nathaniel, March 5, 1770.
Frost, of David and Mary.
—Polley, April 17, 1767.
—John, Dec. 28, 1768.
—David, Feb. 5, 1771.
—Jenny, Feb. 13, 1773.
—Nancy, May 13, 1775.
—Nathaniel, June 24, 1777.
—Benjamin, June 24, 1777. Died July 20, 1779.
—Eunice, Jan. 8, 1780.
—Robert, March 28, 1782.
—Charles, Aug. 6, 1784.
—Peter, April 26, 1788.
—William, Oct. 24, 1790.
Frost, of Enoch and Alice.
—Rufus, Nov. 9, 1781. Died in three weeks.
—Cyrus, May 1, 1784.
—Rebecca, May 26, 1786.
—Polly, Oct. 20, 1788.
—Mason, Dec. 19, 1790.
—Coleman, April 13, 1793.
—Nathaniel Bowman, May 25, 1797.
—Patty, June 29, 1799.
—Cyrus, June 23, 1802.
Frost, children of Nathaniel and Mary.
—Jeremiah, Aug. 31, 1780.
—Elizabeth, Feb. 28, 1782.
—Miriam, Jan. 23, 1785.
Frost, of Peter and Margaret.
—Mary, Nov. 26, 1772.
—Betty, Jan. 6, 1774.
—Benjamin, April 9, 1775.
—Sarah, Nov. 19, 1777.
Frost, of Samuel and Rebecca.
—Susanna, May 15, 1793 .
—Daniel Hamblen, Mar. 13, 1795.
—William, Aug. 19, 1797.
—Benjamin, Freeport, May 8, 1800.
—Nathaniel, Mar. 19, 1803.
—James, Oct. 18, 1808.

BIRTHS OF CHILDREN.

Frost, of William and Abigail.
—George, Feb. 22, 1820.
Gammon, of Benjamin and Betty.
—Hannah, Dec. 3, no date.
—Betty, Aug. 18, no date.
Gammon, of Daniel and Mary.
—Daniel, Apr. 1, 1779.
—Simon, June 13, 1782.
—Hannah, Mar. 17, 1788.
—James, Jan. 8, 1790.
Gammon, of Daniel and Polly, his 2d wife.
—Isaac, Jan. 21, 1792.
—Anna, Mar. 13, 1794.
—Samuel, May 14, 1797.
—Elijah, Jan. 16, 1800.
Gammon, of Jonathan and Lydia.
—Pelina, Cape Elizabeth, Dec. 12, 1788.
Gates, of Stephen and Mary.
—Stephen, Bridgton, Nov. 12, 1774.
—Betty, Bridgton, July 29, 1775.
—Timothy, Bridgton, Aug. 1, 1777.
Gilkey, of Isaac and Caty.
—Samuel, Sept. 22, 1793.
—Joseph, July 26, 1795.
—Charles, July 11, 1797.
—Harriot, Sept. 2, 1799.
Gilkey, of James.
—Joseph, April 27, 1751.
—Rebecca, Nov. 17, 1753.
—James, April 29, 1756
—Samuel, Oct. 21, 1761.
—John, Jan. 23, 1764.
—Isaac, July 14, 1768.
Gilkey, of John and Susanna.
—Ebenezer Bacon, Sept. 14, 1790.
—Sally, Aug. 8, 1792.
—John, Aug. 10, 1794.
Gilkey, of Joseph and Phebe.
—Betty, July 29, 1775.
—Martha, April 23, 1777.
—Sarah, Sept. 27, 1779.
—Phebe, June 3, 1782.
—Samuel, May 25, 1784.
—James, July 4, 1786.
—Mary, June 11, 1788.
—William, May 17, 1790.
—Isaac, May 17, 1790.

BIRTHS OF CHILDREN.

Gorham, of William and Temperance.
—Frances, April 22, 1775.
Gould, of Nathan and Elizabeth (McLellan).
—Elizabeth, Feb. 12, 1799.
—Jane, Feb. 4, 1801, died Aug. 23, 1801.
—Jane, Sept. 20, 1802.
—Edward, Jan. 27, 1805.
—Samuel McLellan, Jan. 24, 1809.
—Margaret McLellan, Oct. 18, 1812, died June 21, 1822.
Gray, of Taylor and Tabitha.
—James, April 20, 1767.
Green, of Benjamin and Sarah.
—Joseph, March 3, 1775.
—Benjamin, May 15, 1777.
—Jedediah, Jan. 30, 1780.
—Hannah, Oct. 4, 1781.
—Hezekiah, Feb. 22, 1784.
Green, of John and Elizabeth (Sharp), daughter of John of Biddeford.
—Jonathan, Aug. 27, 1761.
—Thomas, March 11, 1763.
—Josiah, Dec. 26, 1767.
—Moses, March 5, 1769.
Green, of John and Mary.
—Salome, Feb. 3, 1771.
—Stuart, March 27, 1773.
—Wyer, April 30, 1775.
—John, June 12, 1777.
—Molly, Dec. 15, 1779.
—Rebecca, May 26, 1782.
—Joseph, Aug. 24, 1786.
—Elizabeth, May 6, 1789.
Green, of Jonathan and Joanna.
—Rebecca, Falmouth, July 3, 1780.
—Samuel, Gorham, Aug. 6, 1784.
—John, Gorham, Oct. 2, 1786.
—Hannah, North Yarmouth, Oct. 15, 1791.
Green, of Josiah and Eunice.
—Betsy, New Gloucester, June 10, 1791.
—William, April 4, 1793.
—Abigail, Sept. 30, 1794.
—Sarah, Aug. 29, 1798; d. Nov. 22, 1798.
—John, Sept. 22, 1799.

BIRTHS OF CHILDREN.

Green, of Thomas and Mary.
—Jeremiah, June 16, 1788.
—Polly, Aug. 16, 1792.
—Josiah, Mar. 13, 1795.
Hale, of David and Rachel.
—Rebecca. Bridgton, March 10, 1789.
Hall, of Abraham and Elizabeth.
—Hannah, Sept. 2, 1790.
—Esther, Jan. 12, 1793.
—Achsa, June 15, 1795.
—Dorcas, Jan. 6, 1798.
—Joanna, Feb. 11, 1800.
—Elizabeth, March 23, 1803.
—James, April 9, 1806.
Hall, of Ebenezer and Hannah.
—Abraham, Dec. 29, 1765.
—Bethshuah, Aug. 14, 1768.
—Isaac, May 23, 1770.
—Dorothy, March 9, 1772.
—Israel, March 10, 1774.
—Ebenezer, Sept. 19, 1777.
—Bethshuah, Feb. 21, 1781.
—Daniel, July 29, 1783.
Hall, of Ebenezer, Jr., and Susanna.
—Elijah, Sept. 4, 1800.
Hall, of Isaac and Anna.
—Mehitable, Nov. 6, 1793.
—Mercy, Jan. 31, 1796.
—Mary, Oct. 16, 1798.
—Joseph, June 29, 1801.
—Betty, March 18, 1803.
Hall, of Israel and Abigail.
—John, April 14, 1796.
—Stephen, Jan. 19, 1798.
—Sarah, March 23, 1800.
Hamblen, of Almory and Sarah.
—George, Aug. 22, 1800.
Hamblen, of Daniel.
—Ruth, Jan. 27, 1763.
—Rebecca, March 13, 1765.
—Elizabeth, March 22, 1770.
—Dilla, July 30, 1776.

BIRTHS OF CHILDREN.

Hamblen, of Ebenezer and Deborah.
—Susanna, Aug. 7, 1774.
—Sarah, Aug. 13, 1776.
—Dorcas, Aug. 15, 1778.
—Ebenezer, Sept. 13, 1780.
—Denis, Oct. 19, 1782.
—Betsy, Aug. 12, 1784.
—Lovell, Sept. 4, 1786. Died April 20, 1787.
—Love, March 17, 1788. Died in 5 days.
—Levi, Aug. 13, 1789.
—Temperance, Nov. 6, 1791.
—William, Nov. 6, 1791. Died Nov. 29, 1791.
—William Gorham, Feb. 23, 1794.
—Deborah, March 29, 1796.

Hamblen, of George and Sarah (Rich).
—Almary, Jan. 24, 1775.
—Susanna, Nov. 21, 1776.
—George, April 5, 1779.
—John, May 7, 1781.
—Joseph, Feb. 6, 1783.
—Sarah, May 18, 1785.
—Amos, April 8, 1787.
—Allen, Feb. 27, 1789.
—Solomon, Feb. 24, 1791.
—Patty, May 14, 1793.
—William, Aug. 14, 1796.

Hamblen, of Gershom and Deborah.
—Hannah, Nov. 14, 1775.
—Elizabeth, March 12, 1778.
—Ebenezer, July 9, 1780.
—Samuel, twin with Jacob, May 4, 1783.
—Daniel, Dec. 7, 1785.
—Mary, June 18, 1788.

Hamblen, of Jacob and Elizabeth.
—Content, Jan. 5, 1779.
—Eliphalet, Feb. 17, 1781.
—Mercy, July 8, 1783.
—Joseph, April 25, 1785.
—Martha, May 6, 1787.
—James, May 1, 1789.

Hamblen, of Joseph and Hannah.
—Jacob, Aug. 6, 1756.
—Esther, June 30, 1758.
—Sarah, Dec. 17, 1761.
—Joseph, June 10, 1763.

BIRTHS OF CHILDREN.

Hamblen, of Joseph and Polly.
—Cyrus, Oct. 5, 1789.
—Charles, Sept. 19, 1791.
—Sarah, July 7, 1793.
—Nathaniel, Nov. 8, 1794.
—Mary, Sept. 7, 1796.
—Isaac, Sept. 6, 1798.
—Joseph Frost, Nov. 26, 1800.
Hamblen, of Prince and Bethiah.
—Dorothy, March 25, 1782.
—Nancy, July 20, 1783.
—Joseph, July 4, 1784, d. in 2 days.
—Solomon, April 27, 1784, d. in 2 days.
—Fanny, March 12, 1786.
—Sally, June 17, 1788.
—Katy, Sept. 3, 1791.
—Bethiah, Oct. 22, 1795.
—David, June 13, 1797.
—Denis, April 22, 1799.
—Mary, Dec. 16, 1800.
Hamblen, of Samuel, Jr., and Molly.
—Elijah, April 2, 1779.
—Jonathan, Jan. 3, 1781.
—Rachel, Dec. 25, 1782.
—Temperance, Jan. 11, 1785.
—Samuel, May 13, 1787.
—Stephen Safford, June 11, 1789.
—Polly, Oct. 7, 1791.
—Benjamin, Nov. 29, 1793.
—Temperance, Jan. 30, 1796.
—Sophia, March 13, 1798.
—Rebecca Huston McLellan, Sept. 16, 1800.
Hamblen, of Timothy and Anna.
—Martha, July 17, 1770.
—Esther, July 22, 1772.
—Enoch, June 7, 1773.
—Timothy, Jan. 18, 1775.
—Nicholas, June 29, 1777.
—Gershom, Jan. 22, 1779.
—Anna, Jan. 16, 1783.
—Allen, Dec. 14, 1784.

BIRTHS OF CHILDREN.

Hanscom, of George and Abigail.
—Moses, Jan. 15. 1759.
—Hannah, March 12, 1761.
—John, May 19, 1763.
—Katherine, Aug. 9, 1765.
—Joseph, April 30, 1774.

Hanscom, of George, Jr., and Eunice (Whitney).
—Abigail, Sept. 16, 1776.
—Abigail, Oct. 8, 1778.
—Eunice, Oct. 25, 1780.
—Patience.
—John, June 10, 1784.
—Nancy, May 3, 1786.
—Katherine, July 8, 1788.
—Cyrus, Oct. 8, 1790.
—Lewis, Oct. 26, 1792.
—Matty, Oct. 10, 1794; d. Sept. 22, 1795.
—George, Dec. 7, 1797.
—Merritt, Dec. 27, 1799.

Hanscome, of John and Mary.
—Betsey Hill, Sept. 26, 1795.
—Daniel, June 15, 1799.

Hanscon, of Joseph and Polly.
—Almon, Mar. 18, 1799.
—Miranda, Sept. 14, 1800.

Hanscom, of Moses and Phebe.
—Sally, June 16, 1782.
—Hannah, Sept. 8, 1788.
—Mary, July 23, 1791.

Hanscom, of Nathan and Abigail.
—Molly, February 27, 1778.
—Edmund, September 25, 1779.

Harding, of Barnabas and Mehitable.
—Achsah Hitchcock, Feb. 6, 1799.
—Joseph Davis, Feb. 23, 1801.
—Sally Gray, Jan. 24, 1803.
—Edward Preble, Feb. 6, 1807.

Harding, of David, Jr., and Temperance.
—Thomas, Aug. 25, 1784.
—Betsey, Nov. 14, 1786.
—Temperance, Dec. 8, 1788.
—Robert, Sept. 16, 1791.
—Stephen, Oct. 25, 1793.
—David, May 27, 1796.
—Charles, June 26, 1798.
—Amelia, Mar. 19, 1801.

BIRTHS OF CHILDREN.

Harding, of Jesse and Elizabeth.
—Elizabeth, Jan. 17, 1778.
—Jesse, Sept. 21, 1779; d. December, 1781.
—Samuel, July 14, 1781.
—Austin, May 31, 1784, twin with
—Jesse, Hampden on Penobscot.
—Eunice, Hampden, Oct. 3, 1788.
Harding, of John, Jr., and Abigail.
—Nicholas, Jan. 3, 1779.
—Elizabeth, March 30, 1781.
—John, Feb. 15, 1783.
—Abigail, March 8, 1785.
—Seth, July 23, 1787, died Nov. 2, 1881.
—Anna, Dec. 10, 1789.
—William, Nov. 28, 1792, died June 28, 1797.
—Solomon, Dec, 28, 1794, died Aug., 1796.
—Joseph, June 17, 1797.
—Hannah, June 22, 1800.
Harding, Lucinda, Nov. 26, 1800.
Harding, of Nicholas and Miriam.
—Alexander, Jan. 12, 1790.
—Edward, Jan. 28, 1792.
—Polly, Aug. 31, 1794.
—Peggy, Dec. 17, 1797.
Harding, of Samuel and Martha.
—Hannah, Sept. 28, 1775.
—Rebecca, July 5, 1777, died Oct. ,1777.
Harding, of Seth and Elizabeth.
—Samuel, July 15, 1754.
—Abigail, July 14, 1756.
—Martha, July, 14, 1759.
—Seth, Feb. 3, 1763.
Harding, of Simon and Elizabeth.
—Noah, Nov. 27, 1777.
Harding, of Zephaniah and Mary (Davis).
—Priscilla. Dec. 16, 1760.
—Thankful, Jan. 14, 1763.
—Nicholas, Feb. 28, 1765.
—Barnabas, July 5, 1767.
—John, Dec. 16. 1769.
By Lucy, his second wife.
—Lucy, Oct. 5, 1774.
—Content, April 24, 1776.
—Elizabeth, Feb, 4, 1778.
—Zephaniah, Feb. 7, 1780.
—Samuel, Dec. 16, 1783.
—Joseph, Dec. 18, 1785.

BIRTHS OF CHILDREN.

Harding, of Zephaniah and Lucy.
—Lucy, Oct. 5, 1774.
—Content, April 24, 1776.
—Elizabeth, Feb. 4, 1778.
—Zephaniah, Feb. 7, 1780.
—Samuel, Dec. 16, 1783.
—Joseph, Dec. 18, 1785.
Harris, of Stephen and Sarah.
—Mary, Feb. 25, 1786.
—William, March, 17, 1788.
—Levi, May 27, 1790.
—John, Oct. 15, 1792.
—Rebecca, May 3, 1795.
—Owen, July 15, 1797.
—Nathan, Aug. 3, 1800.
Haskell, of Jacob and Mary.
—Samuel, Oct. 3, 1786.
—Eunice, Oct. 7, 1788.
—Jacob, Oct. 13, 1790.
—Williamn, Feb. 28, 1793.
—Sally, May 18, 1795.
—Joel, June 8, 1797.
—Eliza, May 13, 1799.
Haskell, of John and Abigail.
—Jonathan, March 24, 1765.
—Mary Parsons, April 10, 1767.
—Thomas, May 7, 1769.
—Reuben, March 24, 1771.
—Abigail, June 18, 1773.
—Rebecca, Aug. 4, 1775, died Dec. 20, 1776.
—Samuel, Sept. 12, 1777.
Haskell, of John, Jr., and Mary.
—Anna, Feb. 23, 1782.
Haskell, of Josiah and Abigail.
—Josiah, Nov. 8, 1786.
Haskel, of William and Katharine.
—Susanna, Jan. 22, 1775.
Hatch, of Asa and Rebecca.
—Nathaniel, Nov. 30, 1783.
—Stephen, May 10, 1786.
Hatch, of Joseph and Sarah.
—Ezekiel, Nov. 16, 1754.
—Asa, Jan. 30, 1757.
—David, April 6, 1759.
—Mary, Aug. 10, 1764.
—Ebenezer, May 13, 1767.
—Elizabeth, Sept. 13, 1770.

BIRTHS OF CHILDREN.

Hatch, of Nathaniel and Elizabeth.
—Betsy, April 14, 1778.
—Hannah, Cape Elizabeth, April 22, 1780.
—Sally, Cape Elizabeth, Jan. 10, 1783.
—Nathaniel, Gorham, Sept. 30, 1789.
Hebberd, of Daniel and Sarah.
—Moses, April 2, 1782.
Hicks, of Lemuel and Mary.
—Elizabeth, April 9, 1774.
—Lemuel, May 9, 1776.
Hicks, of Lemuel and Susanna, his second wife.
—Hannah, March 4, 1781.
—Ephraim, March, 23, 1783.
—Nathaniel, Sept. 27, 1784.
—Isaac, April 15, 1786.
—Abigail, April 25, 1789.
Higgins, of Joseph and Mercy.
—Joseph, Eastham, Aug. 16,1776.
—Mercy, Gorham, Aug. 5, 1778.
—Isaac, Dec. 16, 1780.
—Barnabas, Jan. 28, 1783.
—Dorcas, May 12, 1785.
—Mary, July 25, 1787.
—Enoch, Freeman, July 25, 1789.
—Abigail Freeman, Sept. 23, 1791.
—Saul Cook, May 11, 1794.
Hine, of Richard and Abiah.
—Josiah, April 29, 1776.
—Prudence, Oct. 19, 1778.
—Holingsworth, Aug. 12, 1781.
—Abby, April 27, 1784.
—Mary, April 15, 1787.
—Chipman, Feb. 20, 1791.
Hodsdon, of Jeremiah and Abigail.
—Mary, Aug. 2, 1762.
—James, Jan. 17. 1765.
—Joseph, Jan. 20, 1768.
—Mehltabel, July 22, 1770.
—Sarah, Sept. 19, 1772.
—Elizabeth, Aug .1, 1774.
—Jeremiah, Sept. 9, 1776.
—Ebenezer, May 17, 1781.

BIRTHS OF CHILDREN.

Holbrook, of Isaac Doane (b. Wellfleet, Feb. 14, 1751) and Lucy.
—Isaiah, Eastham, Nov. 1, 1773.
—Martha, Eastham, May 4, 1778.
—Hepzibah, Gorham, Jan. 15, 1780.
—Lucy, Gorham, Jan. 11, 1782; died next month.
—Isaac Doane, Aug. 15, 1783.
—Lucy, June 13, 1785.

Hopkins, of Constant and Elizabeth.
—Barnabas, Jan. 12, 1778.
—Constant, Feb. 7, 1780.
—Hannah, April 23, 1781.
—Elizabeth, Aug. 6, 1783.
—Phebe, May 12, 1785.

Horton, of John and Elizabeth.
—Charles, March 3, 1796.
—Ruth, Oct. 31, 1797.

Hunt, of Ephraim and Abigail.
—Lydia, Apr. 2, 1770; d. Sept. 16, 1771.
—Lydia, Oct. 9, 1771; d. Feb. 23, 1773.
—Francis, June 3, 1773.
—Daniel, July 28, 1775.
—Susanna, June 12, 1777.
—Betty, Apr. 9, 1779.
—Ephraim, Apr. 9, 1781; d. Nov. 8, 1782.
—Abigail, Sept. 18, 1782.
—John, Jan. 5, 1786.
—Nancy, June 7, 1788.
—Polly, Oct. 1, 1790.
—Katherine, Sept. 3, 1792.

Hunt, of Francis and Nancy.
—Francis, July 29, 1796.
—Elias, June 3, 1798.
—Eliza, Sept. 9, 1800.

Hunt, of Ichabod and Mary.
—William, Mar. 25, 1781.
—James, Mar. 11, 1783.
—Archelaus, Sept. 12, 1785.
—Mary, Mar. 18, 1788.
—Ichabod, Dec. 25, 1790.
—Eunice, May 12, 1793.
—Enoch, Nov. 13, 1795.
—Ephraim, May 3, 1798.

BIRTHS OF CHILDREN.

Hunt, of Capt. Oliver and Sarah.
—Oliver, Providence, Oct. 9, 1780.
—John, Providence, Dec. 19, 1785.
—William, Gorham, May 19, 1792.
—Hannah, Mar. 31, 1794.
—Nabby, May 12, 1796.
—Charles Bonapart, Jan. 31, 1800.
Huston, of Simon and Elizabeth.
—David, Falmouth, Sept. 9, 1762; d. Apr. 8, 1782.
—Elizabeth, Mar. 1, 1764.
—Eunice, Oct. 28, 1765.
—Ann, Dec. 26, 1767.
—Simon, Oct. 1, 1769; d. July 3, 1773.
—Mary, Feb. 28, 1771.
—William, Nov. 20, 1772.
—Rebecca, Dec. 25, 1774.
—Lydia, Nov. 21, 1776.
—Simon, April 17, 1779.
Huzzey, of James and Mehitable.
—James, Pleasant River, Sept. 14, 1768.
Irish, of Benjamin and Jenny.
—Elisha, Dec. 6, 1791.
—Abigail, Nov. 12, 1793.
—Thomas, Mar. 23, 1796; d. Oct. 18, 1799.
—Dolly, Feb. 22, 1798; d. Nov. 26, 1799.
—Thomas, June 1, 1800.
—Isaac, Aug. 16, 1802.
Irish, of Isaac and Anna.
—Benjamin, Feb. 12, 1787.
—Betty, April 16, 1789.
—Jacob, Jan. 20, 1791; d. January, 1799.
—Patty, March, 1795; d. in 15 days.
—Morris, June 4, 1798.
—Patty, Aug. 19, 1800.
—Isaac, Sept. 5, 1807.
—Martha, Oct. 16, 1809.
Irish, of James and Mary (Gorham).
—Stephen, Mar. 24, 1757.
—William, Mar. 12, 1759.
—Martha, Aug. 28, 1761.
—Ebenezer, April 5, 1764.
—Obediah, July 17, 1766.
—Mary, June 24, 1768.
—Patience, Jan. 31, 1771.
—Samuel, April 8, 1773.
—James, Aug. 18, 1776.

BIRTHS OF CHILDREN.

Irish, of James, Jr., and Mary.
—Abijah, Nov. 13, 1779; d. Mar. 16, 1784.
—Elizabeth, June 22, 1782; d. Aug. 6, 1782.
—Elizabeth, Oct. 17, 1783.
—Chloe, Sept. 28, 1786.
—Jacob, Aug. 16, 1789; d. October, 1790.
Irish, of James, Jr., and Rebecca.
—Sophronia, Sept. 5, 1799.
—Mary Gorham, July 3, 1801.
—Isaac, Nov. 29, 1803.
—Abigail, Aug. 15, 1806.
—Martha, July 13, 1808.
—Adoline, Sept. 26, 1810.
—Francis, Sept. 22, 1812.
—Marshal, Sept. 9, 1814.
—James, June 9, 1816.
—Elizabeth, July 29, 1819.
—James H., Mar. 11, 1823.
—Thadeus P., Nov. 25, 1824.
Irish, of John and Sarah.
—Abigail, Dec. 24, 1749.
—John, Aug. 12, 1751.
—Molly, June 15, 1753.
—James, Feb. 18, 1755.
—Sarah, July 8, 1757.
—Elizabeth, June 11, 1760.
Irish, of John Jr., and Eleanor.
—Rebecca, July 8, 1776.
—Jacob, May 10, 1778.
—Abigail, Oct. 14, 1779.
Irish, of Stephen and Anna.
—Mehitable, Feb. 28, 1780.
—Martha, Dec. 4, 1782. -
—Patience, March 4, 1784.
—Mercy, July 5, 1786.
—Daniel, Sept. 15, 1789.
—Dorcas, April 10, 1791.
—Anna, Dec. 5, 1793.
—Loriama, Dec. 1, 1798.
Irish, of Stephen and Martha.
—Ebenezer, March 22, 1803.

BIRTHS OF CHILDREN.

Irish of Thomas Thomes and Deliverance.
—Susanna, Oct. 22, 1760.
—Isaac, March 7, 1763.
—Benjamin, June 20, 1766.
—Jacob, Sept. 14. 1768.
—Amy, April 3, 1770.
—Abigail, May 6, 1773.
—Gemaliel, Oct. 15, 1776. Died in six days.
—Deliverance, May 20, 1779.
—Mary, Dec. 1, 1780.
—Elizabeth, May 1, 1784.

Irish, of William and Mary.
—Thomas, May 17, 1766.
—Edmund, Oct. 2, 1768.
—Margery, April 12, 1771.
—Dorcas, Sept. 2, 1773.
—Miriam, Aug. 20, 1777.
—Sylvanus, Feb. 22, 1780.

Jenkins, of Capt. Josiah and Prudence. Married Jan. 23, 1777.
—Sarah Eleanor, June 14, 1780.
—Mary, April 9, 1783. Died same day.
—Mary Chipman, March 22, 1785.
—Aurelia, Aug. 21, 1787.
—Nancy, June 3, 1791.
—Josiah, May 5, 1794.
—Katharine, March 27, 1796.

Jenkins, of Samuel Jr., and Lydia.
—Rebecca, July 24, 1781.
—Lydia, Nov. 3, 1783.
—Hannah, May 7, 1785.
—Joseph, June 13, 1788.

Jewett, of Rev. Caleb and Betsy.
—Jonathan, Oct. 3, 1784.
—Martha, Dec. 17, 1785.
—Caleb, Aug. 26, 1787.
—Betsy, Dec. 12, 1789.

Johnson, of David and Jenny.
—Amos, Sept. 15, 1786.

Johnson, of John and Eleanor.
—Susannah, Oct. 4, 1785.
—Zebulon, July 1, 1787.
—Eunice, July 26, 1789.
—John, Feb. 8, 1792.
—Rebecca, Nov. 10, 1794.
—David, Aug. 31, 1797.

BIRTHS OF CHILDREN.

Johnson, of Matthew and Hannah.
—Thomas, Oct. 5, 1790.
—Hannah, Nov. 23, 1793.
—William, Jan. 15, 1798.
—John, May 8, 1800.
Johnson, of Robert and Mary.
—Robert, March 14, 1791.
Johnson, of Stephen and Susanna.
—Aaron, Aug. 16, 1776.
Jones, of Ephraim and Mercy.
—Stephen, April 24, 1780.
—Martha, June 10, 1782, died Feb. 10, 1801.
—Susanna, Jan. 23, 1793.
Jones of Henry and Lydia.
—Jeremiah, Scarboro, Sept. 9, 1756.
—Ephraim, Aug. 10, 1758.
—Joseph. July 12, 1761.
—Lydia, Feb. 4, 1772.
Jones, of Jeremiah and Elizabeth.
—Jeremiah, Feb. 18, 1778.
Jones, of Joseph and Deborah.
—Henry, Oct. 29, 1786.
—Moses, Dec. 30, 1788.
—Samuel, Aug. 31, 1790.
—John, March 1, 1793.
—Hannah, Feb. 19, 1795.
Jones, of William and Hannah.
—Sally, Scarboro, Oct. 22, 1789.
—Wealthy, Scarboro, Sept. 11, 1793.
—Hiram, May 5, 1797.
—John. Nov. 16. 1798.
—Sarah, Sept. 9, 1781.
Jordan, of Joseph and Mary.
—Hannah, July 9, 1778.
—William, April 2, 1780.
—Mary, Scarboro, June, 14, 1776.
Jordan, of Moses and Mary.
—Nancy, Mar. 5, 1775.
—Keziah, May 27, 1777.
—Mary, April 20, 1779.
—Rhoda, June 22, 1782.
Kimball, of Caleb and Abigail (Skilling).
—Polly, July 22, 1774.
—Martha, July 8, 1778.
—Eleazar, April 3, 1781.

BIRTHS OF CHILDREN.

Knights, of John and Mary.
—Hannah, Dec. 7, 1784.
Knight, of Capt. Joseph and Lydia.
—Lydia, Falmouth, Apr. 4, 1761.
—Phebe, Windham, July 30, 1763.
—Nathaniel, Gorham, Oct. 9, 1765.
—Daniel, Sept. 7, 1768.
—Joseph, Feb. 19, 1771; d. Nov. 15, 1778.
—Nabby, June 1, 1773.
—Joseph, Oct. 22, 1775.
—Samuel, Mar. 5, 1778.
—Morris, July 30, 1780.
—Wentrop, Oct. 17, 1782.
—Benjamin, Nov. 23, 1785; d. Feb. 15, 1788.
Knight, of Joseph and Mary.
—Mirian, Jan. 9, 1798.
—Charlotte, Nov. 29, 1801.
Lakeman, of Josiah and Esther.
—Solomon, Jan. 18, 1785.
—Polly, Oct. 13, 1787.
—Betsey, Jan. 19, 1790.
Lakeman, of William and Hannah.
—Mary, June 5, 1756.
—Hannah, Mar. 25, 1758.
—Josiah Harding, Mar. 6, 1762.
Lamb, of John and Hannah.
—James, Aug. 24, 1774.
—Richard, Mar. 17, 1777.
—Robert, May 26, 1779.
Lamson, of John and Elizabeth.
—Nancy, no date; d. Sept. 18, 1798.
—William, May 2, 1799; d. Oct. 7, 1800.
—William, Sept. 23, 1802.
Larcy, of Dennis and Patience.
—Stephen, Feb. 14, 1763.
Lary, of Stephen and Abigail.
—Patience, Dec. 12, 1790. Died 1796.
—John, Feb. 20, 1795.
—James, July 31, 1798.
—Stephen, June 10, 1801.

BIRTHS OF CHILDREN.

Lewis, of James and Hannah.
—Samuel Harding Brown, Aug. 25, 1794.
—Desire Parker, May 12, 1796.
—George, July 16, 1798.
—Timothy Merritt, July 16, 1800. Died May 12, 1802.
—James, Oct. 14, 1802.
—Elijah P., Dec. 29, 1804. Died June 19, 1831.
—John, Feb. 24, 1807.
—Martha, March 24, 1809.
—Josiah, April 26, 1811.
—James, Jan. 12, 1814. Died same year.
—Samuel, April 1, 1816.
Libbee, of Reuben and Abigail.
—Isaac, June 27, 1776.
—Mary, July 30, 1779.
—Elizabeth, Oct. 15, 1781.
—John, Jan. 22, 1784.
—Benjamin, May 5, 1786.
Libby, Allison, April 6, 1755.
—Sarah, wife of Allison, Dec. 12, 1760.
Their children were:
—Sarah, Scarboro, Sept. 14, 1781.
—Olive, March 5, 1783. Died June, 1786.
—Ephraim, Scarboro, Oct. 30, 1784.
—Allison, March, 1787.
—Thomas, Jan. 22, 1789.
—Abigail, Feb. 24, 1791.
—Hugh, May 26, 1793.
—Henry, July 15, 1795.
—Joseph, Sept. 11, 1797.
—James, Jan. 20, 1800.
—Briant, Feb. 22, 1802.
Libby, of Benjamin and Phebe.
—Solomon, Scarboro, Nov. 10, 1789.
—Anna, Scarboro, Sept. 27, 1791.
—Pelina, Dec. 17, 1793.
—Benjamin, Sept. 27, 1795.
—Elisha, May 30, 1797. Died in eight months.
—Jordan, Feb. 28, 1799.
—Hannah, Aug. 5, 1801.
Libby, of Hanson and Abigail.
—Polly, Nov. 5, 1791.
—John Jay, May 28, 1793.
—Anna Hanson, April 29, 1795.

BIRTHS OF CHILDREN.

Libby, of Joab and Susanna.
—John, June 13, 1770.
—Jonathan, Oct. 9, 1772.
—Susanna, Jan. 3, 1777.
Libby, of John and Phebe.
—Hannah, Sept. 22, 1789.
—Lydia, Aug. 11, 1791.
—Satira, April 2, 1793.
—Tyng, Dec. 8, 1787.
—Samuel, May 23, 1800.
Libby, of Joseph and Mary.
—Mary, March 28, 1761.
—John, March 10, 1764.
—William, Dec. 22, 1769.
—Sarah.
—Charlotte, Sept. 25, 1776.
—Joseph, June 13, 1780.
—Mary, Nov. 12, 1783.
Libby, of Joseph and Mercy.
—Roxana, Nov. 15, 1801.
—Harriet, July 10, 1804, died same year.
—Stephen, May 27, 1807.
—Ansel, Nov. 22, 1809.
—Edmund, March, 14, 1812.
—William B., Nov. 7, 1814.
—Daniel, July 15, 1818.
Libby of Simeon and Abigail.
—Rebecca, Oct. 4, 1787.
—Olley, March 19, 1789.
—Daniel, March 18, 1791.
—Abigail, June 28, 1793.
—Samuel, April 21, 1797.
—Ai, Nov. 21, 1799.
Lombard, of Butler and Jemima.
—Molly, Dec. 4, 1787.
—Anner, Sept. 25, 1789.
Lombard, of Calvin and Martha.
—Polly, Aug. 4, 1768.
—Martha, Dec, 4, 1769.
—Luther, Jan. 24, 1771.
—Dorcas, April 7, 1772.
—Rachel, Aug, 5, 1773.
—Wentworth. Oct. 1776.
—Hezekiah, Feb. 12, 1779.
—Salome, Oct. 18, 1780.

BIRTHS OF CHILDREN.

Lombard, of Ebenezer and Jenny.
—Tabitha, Aug. 15, 1795.
—Mary, Feb. 7, 1797.
—Lydia, Jan. 16, 1799.
—Eunice, June 20, 1801.
—Jane, July 24, 1803.
—Alfred, M., July 29, 1805.
—Harriet, July 31, 1807.
—Ann, Oct. 31, 1809.
—Benjamin, Feb. 11, 1812.
—James L., March 2, 1814.
—David F., May 12, 1816.
—Simon H., Nov. 4, 1818.
Lombard, of Ephraim and Polly.
—James Hadaway, Aug. 17, 1795, died aged 9 months.
—Lucy, Dec. 2, 1796.
—Solomon, Feb. 23, 1798.
—Eliza, Feb. 21, 1800.
—Susanna, Jan. 31, 1802, died in a few days.
—Bethiah, July 18, 1803.
—Polly, July 18, 1803.
Lombard, of James and Bithiah.
—Polly, July 6, 1793.
—Richard, Mar. 20, 1795.
—James, Dec. 2, 1796.
—Hannah, Oct. 16, 1798; d. Feb. 16, 1815.
—Peter, Mar. 4, 1801.
—Sukey, Apr. 11, 1803.
—Samuel, May 11, 1807.
Lombard, of Jedediah, Jr., and Lydia.
—Marcy, April 27, 1786.
—Nathaniel, July 24, 1788.
—Betsy, Aug. 13, 1796.
Lombard, of John and Elizabeth
—Hannah, Sept. 8, 1785.
—Lydia, Twin with
—Martha, June 24, 1787.
—Abraham, Feb. 2, 1790.
Lombard, of John, Jr., and Priscilla.
—Joseph, Mar. 15, 1781.
—Polly, Feb. 11, 1784.
—John, Aug. 26, 1786.
—Samuel, May 14, 1789.
—James, Aug. 17, 1791.

BIRTHS OF CHILDREN.

Lombard, of Joseph and Fanny.
—Anna, Oct. 6, 1788.
Lombard, of Nathaniel, Jr., and Ruth.
—Abigail, April 20, 1784.
—Nathaniel, Jan. 8, 1786.
Lombard, of Richard and Lydia.
—John, Aug. 11, 1764.
—Paul, June 30, 1766.
—Joseph, Dec. 24, 1768.
—Lydia, March 16, 1770.
—Ebenezer, Jan. 3, 1773.
—Bathshuah, Dec. 3, 1776.
—Richard, June 3, 1782.
—Simon, Aug. 11, 1784.
—Sarah, June 28, 1789.
Lombard, of Solomon, Jr., and Lydia.
—Richard, May 19, 1761.
—Susanna, June 15, 1762.
—Hannah, Jan. 23, 1764.
—Solomon, Oct. 23, 1766, died.
—James, Oct. 19, 1768.
—Lydia, Oct. 25, 1771.
—Peter, Nov. 9, 1772, died same month.
—Ephraim, Jan. 18, 1773.
—Solomon, April 21, 1775.
—Mary, May 10, 1777.
—Samuel, Oct. 18, 1779.
Lombard, of Solomon, Jr., and Susanna.
—Daniel, Dec. 28, 1796, died Nov. 18, 1799.
—Ephraim, Oct. 11, 1798.
Longfellow, of Stephen, Jr., and Patience.
—Tabitha, Oct. 9, 1774.
—Stephen, March 23, 1776.
—Abigail, Jan. 18, 1779.
—Ann, Nov. 26, 1781.
—Katy, Aug. 20, 1786.
—Samuel, July 30, 1789.
Lothrop, of Thomas and Betsey.
—Caroline, Sept. 16, 1799.
—Ebenezer, Dec. 27, 1800.
Lummus, of Samuel and Margaret.
—Eliza, Sept. 27, 1801.
—Sally, ——, died May 2, 1803.
Mann, of Daniel and Hannah.
—Edmund, Jan. 12, 1793.
—Hannah, March 2, 1795.

BIRTHS OF CHILDREN.

Manson, of William and Rachel.
—Mark, Kittery, Feb. 24. 1772.
—William, Gorham, Dec. 4, 1773.
—Samuel, Nov. 8, 1775.
—John, Jan. 12, 1778.
—Jenny, Feb. 5, 1780.
—Benjamin, May 17, 1782.
—Anner, May 8, 1784.
Marks, of William and Mary.
—Rbecca, Penobscot, April 27, 1768.
—William, Penobscot, Aug. 7, 1769.
—John, Penobscot, Oct. 3, 1771.
—Adonijah, Penobscot, June 22, 1773.
—Joseph, Penobscot, Aug. 17. 1775.
—Stephen, Falmouth, Jan. 15, 1778.
—Ebenezer, Gorham, April 30, 1779.
—Benjamin, March 18, 1781.
—Betsy, April 21, 1783.
Mariner, of John and Betsy.
—William, Sept. 30, 1796.
Martin, of Bryan and Anna.
—Hannah, May 22, 1798.
McCollistor, of James and Deliverance (Rich).
—Lemuel, Aug. 28. 1767.
—Amos, June 16, 1769.
—James, Oct. 11, 1771.
—Mary, Jan. 1, 1774.
—Patience, Feb. 26, 1777.
—Betty, Oct. 17, 1779.
McCollistor, of James and Mary (Flood), his second wife.
—Benjamin, Jan. 10, 1783.
—Hannah, Sept. 17, 1784.
—Rebecca, April 4, 1786.
—Mary, Feb. 16, 1789.
—Nabby, Feb. 13, 1792.
—Isaac, Jan. 13, 1794.
—Daniel, Jan. 26, 1796.
McCorson, of James and Mary.
—Joseph, July 6, 1798.
—Sarah, Sept. 7, 1800.
McDonald, of Abner and Polly.
—William, March 13, 1782.
—Dorcas, April 26, 1785.
—Sally, Sept. 16, 1787.
—Enoch, Sept. 11, 1790.

BIRTHS OF CHILDREN.

McDonald, of Abner and Elizabeth Clark.
—Charles, Jan. 29, 1802.

McDonald, of Charles and Priscilla.
—Maribah, Nov. 21, 1763.
—Susanna, Aug. 21, 1766.
—Nancy, Aug. 10, 1769.
—Simon Davis, Aug. 19, 1773.
—Jacob, Nov. 14, 1775.
—Charles, May 16, 1777.
—Joseph, Nov. 23, 1779.
—Mary, Jan. 26, 1782.
—Elizabeth, Nov. 24, 1785.

McDonald, of Pelatiah and Katherine.
—William, Fort Putnam, Hudson River, April 3, 1779.
—Eleanor, Gorham, June 14, 1785.

McDonald, of Robert and Mary.
—Samuel Meleher, Jan. 28, 1771.
—John, April 16, 1773.
—Robert, May 3, 1775.
—Abner, Jan. 14, 1778.
—Miriam, Jan. 21, 1782.
—Benoni, Jan. 28, 1785.

McDonald, of Simon Davis and Betty.
—Joseph Brown, Sept. 19, 1800.

McDougal, of David and Phebe.
—Anna, Dec. 11, 1794.
—Thomas, Oct. 2, 1795.
—William, March 1, 1797.
—Thomas, Oct. 2, 1799.
—David, Dec. 27, 1802.
—James, April 13, 1805.
—Mary, April 22, 1807.
—Hannah, Feb. 9, 1809.

McLellan, of Alexander and Margaret.
—Jenny, Jan. 16, 1766. Died January, 1776.
—James, Jan. 4, 1768. Died January, 1776.
—Isaac, Sept. 15, 1769.
—William, May 7, 1771.
—Nelly, Dec 18, 1772.
—Alexander, Dec. 20, 1774.
—James, May 15, 1777.
—Jenny, Dec. 20, 1778.

BIRTHS OF CHILDREN.

McLellan, of Cary and Eunice.
—Mary, Aug. 2, 1767.
—Eunice, Aug. 13, 1769. Died July 24, 1773.
—Nancy, March 17, 1772. Died Nov. 28, 1773.
—Nancy, Feb. 13, 1774.
—Cary, March 16, 1776.
—Eunice, June 16, 1778.
—Alexander, Feb. 28, 1780.
—William, May 14, 1782.
—Samuel, Aug. 12, 1784.
McLellan, Cary and Mary.
—David, Cape Elizabeth, June 21, 1786.
—Sally, Cape Elizabeth, Jan. 22, 1788.
—Betsy, Cape Elizabeth, Nov. 7, 1789.
—Thomas, Gorham, Nov. 14, 1791.
McLellan, of James and Abigail.
—Sarah, May 28, 1757.
—William, Falmouth, July 7, 1759.
—Brice, Dec. 21, 1761.
—Elizabeth, April 18, 1764.
—Rebecca, Oct. 8, 1766.
—George, Mar. 14, 1769.
—Martha, Nov. 6, 1774.
—James, Dec. 30, 1776.
—Abigail, Aug. 1, 1779.
McLellan, of Thomas and Jane.
—Hugh, April 1, 1779.
—Elizabeth, Jan. 6, 1781.
—Robert, Sept. 30, 1782.
—Polly, Sept. 14, 1785.
—Benjamin, July 6, 1787.
—Jenny, Nov. 1, 1789.
—Mary Ann, Aug. 1, 1791.
—Thomas, Mar. 19, 1794.
—John, Oct. 19, 1795.
McLellan of William, Jr., and Jenny.
—Elkanah, May 22, 1783.
—Sarah, Aug. 8, 1785.
McLellan, of William 3d and Sally.
—Irene, Oct. 8, 1796.
—Harriet, May 15, 1798.
McQuillin, of John and Abigail.
—John, Apr. 9, 1784.
—Rebecca, Feb. 7, 1787.
—William, May 28, 1790.
—Peggy, Feb. 13, 1794.

BIRTHS OF CHILDREN.

McQuillin, of John and Olive, his 3d wife.
—Elizabeth Bowen, Feb. 13, 1799.
—Hannah, Apr. 6, 1800.
—Samuel, Jan. 22, 1802.
—Hugh McLellan, July 18, 1803.
Melvin, of John and Abigail.
—Polly, July 15, 1774.
—Abigail, ——25, 1776.
—Sally, May 25, 1784.
—Benjamin, Feb. 6, 1786.
—Jenny, July 25, 1788.
—Alice, Jan. 16, 1791.
—Patty, Nov. 8, 1792.
Miller, of Jno, and Margaret.
—Polly, Jan. 15, 1782; d. July 1, 1786.
—John, Mar. 4, 1784; d. June, 1786.
—Samuel, May 7, 1786.
Morris, of John and Betsy.
—Hannah, Sept. 14, 1799.
—Samuel, Aug. 10, 1801.
Morton, of Capt. Briant and Lucy his 2d wife.
—Jerusha, Sept. 10, 1772.
—John, Feb. 11, 1775.
Morton, of Ebenezer and Sarah.
—Mary, Mar. 6, 1760.
—Martha, May 17, 1762.
—Joseph, Feb. 9, 1765.
—Mathias, Aug. 31, 1767.
—Elisha, Jan. 25, 1770.
—Ebenezer, July 15, 1771.
—Josiah, July 14, 1773.
—Daniel, Nov. 11, 1776.
Morton, of Jabez and Lucy.
—Isaac, Aug. 18, 1767.
—Anna, Jan. 28, 1770.
—Hannah, July 17, 1772.
—Sarah, Dec. 28, 1774.
—Stephen, July 17, 1777.
—Reuben, May 12, 1780.
—Eunice, Nov. 23, 1782.
—Lucy, Apr. 28, 1785.

BIRTHS OF CHILDREN.

Morton, of James and Susanna.
—Hannah, Aug. 12, 1778.
—Thomas, April 7, 1780.
—Anna, March 30, 1781.
—Mary, July 15, 1783.
—Elliot, Dec. 13, 1789.
—James, Jan. 29, 1792.
—Betsy, Jan. 29, 1794.
—Wealthy, Aug. 13, 1795.
—Major, March 22, 1797.
—Micah, June 5, 1798.
—Randal, Aug. 16, 1800.
Morton, of Thomas and Rachel.
—James, June — 1753.
Morton, of Thomas and Betsy.
—Samuel, May 25, 1790.
—Benjamin, Jan. 14, 1792.
—Nathaniel, Jan. 11, 1794.
—Hannah, Jan. 2, 1796.
—Edmund, Oct. 11, 1797.
—Thomas, March 18, 1799.
—Paul, March 5, 1801.
Mosher, of James and Abigail.
—Susanna, June 17, 1759.
—Nathaniel, Oct. 21, 1762, died Oct. 21 1768.
—James, April 25, 1767.
—Nathaniel, May 5, 1769.
—Abigail, Sept. 1, 1771.
—Benjamin, Jan. 30, 1774.
—Jenny, Oct. 4, 1776.
—Betsy, March 11, 1780.
—Nancy, Nov. 18, 1782.
—Daniel, Jan. 14, 1785.
Mosher, of James, Jr., and Betsy.
—Samuel Frost, April 28, 1795.
—Abigail, April, 24, 1797.
—George, July 28, 1800.
—William, May 28, 1802.
—Esther Frost, Jan. 26, 1803.
—James M., Sept. 5, 1806.
—Elizabeth, Nov. 28, 1808.
—John, Sept. 3, 1810.
—Catherine, June 4, 1812.
—Thomas, Aug. 1, 1814.
—Samuel, March 4, 1819.

BIRTHS OF CHILDREN.

Mosher, of Nathaniel and Eunice.
—Samuel Elder, Nov. 10, 1797.
—James, Jan. 21, 1800.
—Nathaniel, July 30, 1803.
Murch, of Ebenezer and Margery.
—Joseph, Aug. 28, 1764.
—Jeremiah, Feb. 8, 1766.
—Isaac, Nov. 23, 1767.
—John, Sept. 14, 1769.
—Lydia, Aug. 23, 1771.
—Moses, June 29, 1773.
—Aaron, March 8, 1777.
—Sally, Nov. 23, 1778.
—Betty, May 2, 1781.
—Ebenezer, Nov. 11, 1785.
Murch, of Ebenezer, Jr., and Hannah.
—Lydia, July 9, 1787.
—Lucy Perkins, Jan. 16, 1791.
—Hannah, Feb. 28, 1793.
—Susanna, Feb. 6, 1795.
—Deborah, Jan. 20, 1797.
—Solomon Lombard, Nov. 30, 1798.
—Rachel Grant, June 27, 1800.
Murch, of James and Jenny.
—Rebecca, Oct. 20, 1786.
—Edmund, Feb. 13, 1788.
—William, Nov. 13, 1789.
Murch, of Jeremiah and Ann.
—George, July 15. 1789.
—John, Sept. 3. 1790.
—Samuel, July 2, 1796.
Murch, of John and Anna.
—Molly, May 7, 1761.
—William, June 29, 1763.
—Eunice, April 18, 1765.
—George, Feb. 8, 1767.
—Samuel, Nov. 29, 1769.
—Tabitha, April 17. 1773.
—Martha, July 27, 1777.
Murch, of John, Jr., and Martha.
—Samuel, April 24, 1773.
—Thomas, Sept. 9, 1775.
—Mathias, Aug. 23, 1779.
Murch, of John, Jr., and Polly.
—Isaac, Oct. 7. 1802.

BIRTHS OF CHILDREN.

Murch, of Samuel and Deborah.
—Ebenezer, Dec. 30, 1760.
—Deborah, Sept. 25, 1763.
—Mary, July 25, 1769.
—Elizabeth, Dec. 12, 1773.
Murch, of Samuel, Jr., and Elizabth.
—Thomas, Nov. 27, 1801.
—Eliza, Aug. 11, 1799.
Murch, of Simeon and Rachel.
—Rebecca, Gorham, Nov. 11, 1791.
—Josiah, Buxton, July 11, 1793.
—Esther, 25-mile Pond, Sept. 18, 1795.
—Ephraim, 25-mile Pond, Sept. 4, 1798.
Murch, of Walter and Jerusha.
—James, Aug. 29, 1760.
—Sarah, Dec. 4, 1762.
—Benjamin, January, 1765.
—Susanna Sept. 12, 1766.
—Simeon, Feb. 24, 1769.
—Zebulon, March 19, 1771.
—Affia, April 12, 1773.
—Joanna, Sept. 27, 1775.
—Ephraim, Feb. 1, 1778.
—Edmund, Jan. 27, 1780.
Murch, of Zebulon and Molly.
—Molly, Aug. 2, 1798.
—Thomas, March 18, 1800.
—Benjamin, Feb. 2, 1802.
Murrey of Anthony and Abiel.
—Anthony, in ——, Dec. 28, 1767.
—Mary, in ——, Dec. 5, 1769.
—Miriam, Gorham, June 16, 1772.
—James, Gorham, Oct. 27, 1775.
—Thomas, Gorham, March 29, 1778.
—Arnold, Gorham, Dec. 8, 1780.
Nason of Ephraim and Eleanor.
—Eunice, Cape Elizabeth, June 4, 1785.
—Richard, Gorham, no date.
—Abigail, Gorham, no date.
—Eleanor, Gorham, no date.
—Ephraim, Gorham, no date.
—Fanny, Gorham, no date.
—Eleanor, Gorham, no date.

BIRTHS OF CHILDREN.

Nason of Uriah and Abigail.
—Abraham, Nov. 22, 1765.
—William, Feb. 1, 1770.
—Samuel, no date.
—Lot, no date.
—Margaret, no date.
—Abigail, no date.
—Joseph, no date.
Nason, of William and Betsy.
—John, March 29, 1792.
—Samuel, Sept. 15, 1793.
—Lot, June 4, 1795. Died Sept. 30, 1798.
—Betty, April 4, 1797.
—Daniel, May 7, 1799.
—Thomas, Feb. 16, 1801.
Nason, of William and Martha.
—James, Oct. 8, 1793.
—Samuel, Dec. 13, 1798.
Newcomb, of Enos and Thankful.
—Deborah, March 10, 1784.
—Rachel, May 31, 1786.
—David, April 30, 1788.
—Hannah, May 14, 1790.
—Samuel, April 16, 1792.
—Thankful, June 23, 1794.
Newcomb, of Enos and Abigail, his second wife.
—Gardner, Feb. 15, 1798.
—Eunice, Nov. 19, 1799.
—Hanson, July 8, 1802.
—Sarah, Sept. 17, 1804.
—William, Aug. 15, 1806.
Nickerson, of Warren and Anner (Alden), daughter of Austin.
—Nathan, Orrington, Aug. 25, 1786. Died aged 9 years.
—Alden, Orrington, Nov. 18, 1787.
—Salome, Orrington, July 28, 1789.
—Daniel, Orrington, July 22, 1791.
—Betty, Orrington, Oct. 14, 1793.
—Nathan, Orrington, Aug. 9, 1795. Died in a few days.
—Huldah, Orrington, July 24, 1796.
—Jerusha Mudge, Orrington, Oct. 4, 1798.

BIRTHS OF CHILDREN.

Noyes, of Moses and Abigail.
—Thomas, Nov. 5, 1769.
—Eunice, April 21, 1772.
—Moses, Nov. 15, 1774.
—John, Oct. 27, 1777.
—Nathaniel, April 3, 1780.
Noyes, of Nathaniel and Abigail.
—Nathaniel, July 19, 1787.
—Charlotte Wood, twin with
—Lucinda Prichard, Jan. 17, 1789.
Paine, of John and Anna.
—Jonathan, date not given, died young.
—Jonathan, date not given, died young.
—Elisha, July 18, 1777, died young.
—Thomas, July 2, 1784.
—Leonard, April 9, 1786.
Paine, of John and Hannah.
—Abner, June 4, 1799.
Paine, of Richard and Thankful.
—Phebe, Jan. 7, 1771.
—Richard, July 17, 1773.
By Elizabeth (Partrick,) his second wife.
—Thomas, Nov. 23, 1774.
—Joseph, Feb. 21, 1777.
—James, April 21, 1779.
—Thankful, Jan. 27, 1782.
—David, May 20, 1784.
Paine, of Thomas and Anna.
—Joseph, no date.
—Nancy, no date.
—Pegge, no date.
—William, no date.
Paine, of William and Sarah.
—Mary, Oct. 23, 1767.
—William, Dec. 29, 1770.
—Thankful, Nov. 26, 1773.
—Samuel, Nov. 10, 1775.
—Sarah, Oct. 22, 1779.
—Hannah, April 21, 1781.
—John, Sept. 1, 1783.
Paine, of William, Jr., and Hannah.
—Eliza, Oct. 19, 1799.
—James, no date.
—Charles, April 10, 1806.
Patch, of Nehemiah and Peggy.
—Sally, Sept. 2, 1799.

BIRTHS OF CHILDREN.

Partrick, of Charles and Mehitable.
—David, Sept. 1, 1776.
—Charles, Jan. 8, 1779.
—James, Aug. 19, 1780.
—Thomas, Nov. 15, 1782.
—Eleanor, Dec. 31, 1784.
—Stephen, Feb. 15, 1787.
—Nancy, Dec. 29, 1798, died July 4, 1801.
Partrick, of David and Betsey.
—Stephen, Feb. 7, 1804.
—Clement, July 5, 1808.
—Charles, Feb. 28, 1811.
—David, May 26, 1818.
—Elizabeth, July 3, 1827.
Peabody, of Ebenezer and Sally.
—Kendal Osgood, Dec. 20, 1792.
—Charles, June 20, 1814.
—Hannah P., Sept. 10, 1815.
—Elizabeth H., Aug. 5, 1818.
—Louisa, March 1, 1821.
Perkins, of John and Lois (Harding).
—Lucy, Feb. 16, 1770.
—Mary, Nov. 10, 1774.
  1802.
—Sarah, Sept. 29, 1803.
—Ann, Sept. 8, 1805.
—Patience, Nov. 20, 1807.
—Elizabeth, March 14, 1810. Died next year.
—Benjamin, March 29, 1812.
—Ebenezer, Sept. 3, 1794.
—Louisa, Aug. 10, 1796.
—Caroline, July 9, 1798.
Peabody, of Jonathan and Mary.
—Phebe, Bridgton, May 17, 1776.
Penfield, of Nathan and Molly.
—Benjamin, Sept. 10, 1801. Died Aug. 31,
Phinney, of Coleman and Margaret.
—Rebecca, April 10, 1794.
—Margaret, June 25, 1796.
—Annie, Aug. 15, 1798.
Phinney, of Decker and Hannah.
—Hannah, June 28, 1774. Died Aug. 4, 1795.
—Eli, April 9, 1777. Died Aug. 31, 1800.
—Martha, June 30, 1779. Died Aug. 4, 1799.
—Patience, May 2, 1782.
—James, April 12, 1785.
—Stephen, May 4, 1788.
—Betty, April 9, 1793.

BIRTHS OF CHILDREN.

Phinney, of Edmund and Betty.
—Decker, Nov. 17, 1752.
—Sarah, Jan. 3, 1754.
—Joseph, March 14, 1757.
—Betty, April 1, 1759.
—Edmund, Nov. 30, 1760.
—Stephen, March 10, 1763.
—James, Sept. 2, 1768.
—Nathaniel, Aug. 19, 1771.
Phinney, of Edmund, Jr., and Sarah.
—Clement, Aug 16, 1780.
—John, Nov. 26, 1783.
—Betsy, May 1, 1787.
—Joseph, Oct. 18, 1789.
Phinney, of Eli and Mercy.
—Patty, Sept. 17, 1799.
Phinney, of James, Jr., and Abigail.
—Eliza, Sept. 24, 1795, died Oct. 19, 1800.
—Eliza, Aug. 26, 1801.
—James, Aug. 31, 1803.
Phinney, of John, Jr., and Rebecca.
—Sarah, Nov. 21, 1755.
—Rebecca, Aug. 18, 1757.
—Ebenezer, Dec. 14, 1759.
—John, April 11, 1762.
—Martha, April 29, 1764.
—Abigail, May 16, 1766.
—Coleman, Dec. 13, 1770.
Phinney, of Joseph and Susanna.
—Mary, March 17, 1781.
—Eunice, Oct. 29, 1783.
—Hannah, July 25, 1787.
—Nathaniel, July 25, 1790.
—Rebecca, April 14, 1794.
—Phebe, April 20, 1797, died Sept. 24, 1799.
—Patience, Oct. 26, 1799.
Phinney, of Stephen and Anna.
—Betty, June 5, 1789.
—David, Dec. 15, 1792.
—Love, Nov. 12, 1796.
Plaisted, of Andrew and Molly.
—Betsy, Scarboro, Dec. 20, 1787.
—Sarah, Scarboro, July 1, 1788.
—Joseph, Scarboro, March, 9, 1790.
—Andrew, Sept. 18, 1792.
—Polly, Oct. 30, 1795.
—Major, March 17, 1798.

BIRTHS OF CHILDREN.

Plummer, of Aaron and Lydia.
—Sarah, Scarboro, March 9, 1771.
—Mary, Scarboro, Sept. 12, 1772.
—Dorcas, Scarboro, April 18, 1774.
—David, Scarboro, Oct. 4, 1776.
—Lydia, Scarboro, Oct. 23, 1778.
—Elizabeth, Scarboro, Nov. 6, 1780.
—Aaron, Gorham, June 9, 1784.
—Martha, Gorham, July, 9, 1786.
—Abigail, Gorham, Sept. 14, 1788.
Poland, of John and Fear.
—Moses, June 11, 1791.
—Silvanus, Jan. 2, 1793.
—Arvada, Hartford, May 9, 1795.
—Dorcas, June 19, 1798.
—Zoe, in the woods, July 19, 1800.
—John, in the woods, May 5, 1803.
Pote, of Samuel and Priscilla.
—Betty, July 31, 1780.
Pote, of Thomas and Sarah.
—Judith, May 16, 1762.
—Elisha, July 25, 1764.
—Dorathy, Oct. 29, 1766.
—James, Aug. 7, 1768.
—Deborah, Nov. 21, 1774.
Prentiss, of Samuel and Dolly.
—Dolly, July 29, 1785, died July 6, 1802.
—Hannah, July 2, 1788.
—Rebecca, Aug. 20, 1790.
—Phebe, Dec. 4, 1791.
—Joanna, Nov. 5, 1793.
—Betsy, Sept. 3, 1795.
—Frances, Nov. 13, 1798.
Pumroy, of John and Elizabeth (Harding,) daughter of Jesse.
—Robert, Hampden, Sept. 2, 1794.
—Anner, Hampden, May 7, 1796.
—John, Hampden, April 28, 1798.
Rand, of Jeremiah and Lydia.
—John Blake, Oct. 10, 1781.
Rand, of Jeremiah, Jr., and Lydia.
—Mary, Nov. 17, 1791.
—Henry, June 30, 1794.
—George, Dec. 11, 1796.
—Sally, April 15, 1799.
Rand, of John B. and Ruth.
—Hannah, Dec. 10, 1799.

BIRTHS OF CHILDREN.

Rich, of Amos and Eunice.
—Moses, June 22, 1783.
—John Woodman, Dec. 25, 1785.
—Sarah, April, 1788.
—Betsy, July 19, 1790.
—Lydia, May 2, 1792.
—Eunice, June 20, 1794.
—Isaac, Oct. 3, 1796.
Rich, of Barnabas and Lydia.
—Martha, June 4, 1781.
—Samuel, Sharon, June 26, 1783.
Rich, children of Ezekiel, son of Lemuel and Elizabeth, born in Truro, Nov. 25, 1738.
and Sarah (Stevens) daughter of Benjamin and Sarah, born in Gorham, Jan. 7, 1744.
—Ezekiel, twin with
—Samuel, June 23, 1766.
—Reuben, Jan. 17, 1769.
—Elizabeth, Jan. 12, 1771.
—Benjamin, March 4, 1773.
—Sarah, April 4, 1775.
—Jerusha, May 17, 1777.
—William, July 9, 1779.
—Mehitabel, July 6, 1781.
—Peter, July 26, 1783.
—Eunice, June 16, 1786.
—Stephen, Philips Gore, Nov. 27, 1789.
Rich, of James and Abigail.
—Robert, Feb. 4, 1776.
—Mary, Feb. 15, 1778.
—Abigail, April 23, 1780.
—Joseph, Ossipee, June 17, 1782.
Rich, of Joel and Elizabeth (Cates).
—John, Sept. 26, 1780.
Rich of Lemuel, Jr., and Molly Colley.
—Lemuel, Jan. 3, 1770.
—Boaz, Feb. 23, 1772.
—Samuel, May 13, 1774.
—Israel, July 25, 1776.
—Mary, Jan. 30, 1779.
—Zeckariah, April 15, 1781.
Rich, of Zephaniah and Sarah.
—Jonathan, March 23, 1771.
—Ebenezer, Sept. 12, 1774.
—Zephaniah, Jan. 30, 1777.
—Samuel Snow, March 27, 1779.
—Ephraim, Aug. 19, 1781.
—Benjamin, Feb. 19, 1784.
—William, April 13, 1786.

BIRTHS OF CHILDREN.

Riggs, of William Tyng and Mary.
—William, twin with
—Susanna, Jan. 31, 1795.
—Hannah, March 21, 1797.
—Jane, Jan. 21, 1799.
Rion, of John Butler and Hannah.
—Sarah, Feb. 27, 1792.
—Mary, June 8, 1794.
—Martha, April 1, 1801.
—Louisa, March, 18, 1803.
Roberts, of Benjamin and Mary.
—Mary, Falmouth, April 30, 1767.
—Benjamin, Falmouth, Aug. 29, 1768.
—John, Falmouth, May 17, 1770.
—Jane, Falmouth, Nov. 13, 1771.
—William, Cape Elizabeth, Oct. 23, 1771.
—Susanna, Gorham, Oct. 5 1776.
—Stephen, Aug. 28, 1778.
—Dorcas, Aug. 27, 1781.
Roberts, of Joseph and Hannah.
—William, Cape Elizabeth, May 26, 1763, died July 16, 1769.
—Lucy, Cape Elizabeth, Dec. 10, 1767.
—Hannah, June 26, 1769.
—Catherine, March 9, 1771.
—Lydia, Sept. 14, 1772.
—Joseph, July 10, 1773.
—Elizabeth, Sept. 16, 1775.
—William, Aug. 22, 1778, died Oct. 5, 1780.
—Eunice April 9, 1780, died Feb. 18, 1784.
—Joshua, March 8, 1783.
—Anna, April, 11, 1785.
—Miriam, June 26, 1787.
Roberts of Joseph, Jr., and Anna.
—Rhoda, Nov. 27, 1782.
—Rachel, July 13, 1785.
—Anna, March 17, 1789.
Ross, of James and Hannah.
—Sarah, Dec. 13, 1766.
—Alexander, Aug. 7, 1769.
—Walter, April, 20, 1771.
—Olley, Oct. 1, 1773.
—John T., May, 1778, died June, 1779.
Sanborn, of Elisha and Eunice.
—Martha, Oct. 11, 1800.
—Mary, April 1, 1803.

BIRTHS OF CHILDREN.

Sanborn, of Joseph and Esther.
—Elisha, Nov. 28, 1777.
—Drusilla, Aug. 7, 1782.
—Samuel Burley, Feb. 25, 1793.
Sawyer, David, March 13, 1764.
Sawyer, of Joel and Elizabeth.
—Eunice, Feb. 19, 1775.
—Polly, May 22, 1778.
—Betsy, July 22, 1783.
—Dorcas, March 29, 1786.
Sawyer, of Jonathan and Martha.
—Elizabeth, March 12, 1765.
—Martha, June 5, 1767.
—John, May 8, 1769.
—David, March 27, 1771.
—Barnabas, March 25, 1773.
—Sarah, Feb. 25, 1775.
—Mary, April 13, 1778.
—Deliverance, April 15, 1780.
—Jonathan, July 16, 1782.
—Eunice, April 20, 1785.
—Samuel, June 7, 1787.
Sawyer, of Zeckariah and Susanna.
—Levi, May 13, 1786.
Shaw, of Josiah and Tabitha.
—James, June 10, 1797.
—John, Nov. 29, 1798.
—Samuel, Aug. 29, 1800.
—Leonard, Jan. 14, 1805.
—Josiah, Dec. 3, 1807.
—William, Sept. 10, 1811.
—Franklin, Oct. 11, 1814.
—Maria, June 19, 1816.
Silly, of John and Molly.
—Rebecca, Feb. 22, 1788.
—David, July 15, 1789.
Silly, of William and Anna.
—Mary, Sept. 23, 1765.
—Anna, twin with
—Fanny, April 19, 1768.
—William, March 27, 1770.
—Peter, twin with
—Hannah, April 19, 1772.
—Simon, June 13, 1774.
Simpson, of Alexander and Mary.
—Alexander, Oct. 12, 1792. Died 1797.
—Amos, Oct. 12, 1792.
—John, Sept. 23, 1794.
—Fanny, May 23, 1796.
—Elizabeth, Dec. 16, 1798.

BIRTHS OF CHILDREN.

Skillings, of Benjamin and Mary.
—Deliverance, Oct. 15, 1741.
—Susanna, twin with
—Isaac, Jan. 22, 1744.
—John, Falmouth, March 2, 1746.
—Thomas, Falmouth, May 8, 1748.
—Abigail, March 30, 1753.
—Anna, May 2, 1755.
—Martha, March 2, 1760.
—Benjamin, April 2, 1763.
Skillings, of Benjamin and El'zabeth.
—Mary, Nov. 15, 1787.
—Anna, Nov. 7, 1789.
—Isaac, Nov. 12, 1791.
—William, March 12, 1794.
—Frances, May 12, 1797.
—Abigail, Sept. 4, 1799.
—Nathaniel, Jan. 2c, 1802
Skillings, of Isaac and Susanna
—Mary, Jan. 13, 1767.
—Elizabeth, July 16, 1768.
—Tabitha, Nov. 23, 1770.
—Susanna, Nov. 13, 1772.
—Daniel, March 5, 1775.
—John, January 15, 1777.
—Joseph, Jan. 2, 1779.
Skilling, of Thomas and Mary.
—Benjamin, Oct. 12, 1782.
—John, Aug. 2, 1784.
—Isaac, May 24, 1786.
—Thomas, April 12, 1788.
—Mehitable, June 19, 1791.
—Betsy, Nov. 15, 1793.
—Polly, Sept. 2, 1796.
—Caleb, Dec. 3, 1798.
—Molly Dec. 15, 1802.
Smith, William, Jan. 13, 1784.
Snow, of Benjamin and Ba'hsheba.
—Ruth, Sept. 8. 1774.
—Anna, Dec. 27, 1777.
Standish, of Ellis and Mary.
—Jane, Oct. 24, 1797.
—Mary, Sept. 16, 1799.
Staples, of Samuel and Nancy.
—Samuel, Mar. 25, 1795.
—William, Apr. 26, 1797.
—Stephen, June 13, 1800.

BIRTHS OF CHILDREN.

Stevens, of Benj. and Sarah.
—Nathaniel, Falmouth, Dec. 12, 1741.
—Sarah, Gorham, Jan. 7, 1744.
—Mehitable, July 15, 1750.
—Abigail, April 27, 1753.
—Catharine, Aug. 5, 1757.
—Benjamin, May 9, 1763.
—Joseph, Mar. 14, 1764.
—Samuel, April 14, 1766.
Stevens, of Benjamin and Amy
—Harry, Dec. 17, 1784.
—John, Dec. 11, 1786.
—Charlotte, Nov. 5, 1788.
—Amy, June 4, 1790.
Stevens, of Joseph and Joanna.
—Polly, June 22, 1787.
—Benjamin Rackley, Feb. 23, 1789.
—Ebenezer, June 8, 1792.
Stevens, of Nathaniel and Elizabeth
—Lucy, Dec. 17, 1766.
—Robert, Jan. 17, 1769.
—Nathaniel, Jan. 17, 1772.
—Frederick, May 3, 1774.
—Hezekiah, Nov. 3, 1776.
—Polly, Oct., 1779, d. June, 1780.
—John, July 7, 1781.
Stevens, of Nathaniel, Jr., and Anna.
—Mehitable, Jan. 9, 1792.
—Nathaniel, Feb. 18, 1795.
—Hezekiah, July 25, 1797.
Stevens, of Samuel and Ellis.
—Sarah, Nov. 1, 1792.
—Anna, Aug. 8, 1794.
—Samuel Gott, Sept. 10, 1796.
Stone, of Jonathan and Damaris.
—Jonathan, Oct. 26, 1783.
—William, Aug. 22, 1785.
—Damaris, Oct. 17, 1787.
—Solomon, Aug. 1, 1789.
—Archelaus, Oct. 18, 1791.
—Anna, Nov. 26, 1793.
—Miriam, Dec. 6, 1795.
—Eunice, Apr. 25, 1797.
Strout, of Elisha and Eunice.
—Simeon, Nov. 24, 1765.
—Susanna, July 28, 1767.
—Eunice, July 26, 1770.
—Dorcas, March 1, 1773.
—Elisha, Apr. 13, 1775.
—Solomon, Apr. 13, 1777.

BIRTHS OF CHILDREN.

Strout, of George and Rebecca.
—Lydia, Sept. 6, 1763.
—Samuel, April 13, 1768.
—Rebecca, Feb. 13, 1770.
—Ellis, Jan. 19, 1771.
—Sally, April 29, 1775.
—George, April 9, 1780.

Stuart, of Joseph and Hannah.
—Joseph, July 1, 1780.
—Hannah, Mar. 5, 1782.
—Elizabeth, Feb. 13, 1784.
—Samuel, April 16, 1786.
—Susanna, June, 1788.
—Wentworth, Sept. 26, 1790.
—Achsah, June 8, 1793.
—Solomon, April 22, 1796.
—Josiah Alden, April 20, 1798.

Stuart, of Wentworth and Susanna.
—Mary, January 20, 1754.
—Susanna, May 21, 1757; d. Jan. 4 ,1759.
—Joseph, April 3, 1759.
—Solomon Lombard, Feb. 13, 1762; d. Dec. 29, 1763.
—Sarah Purrenton, June 28, 1764.
—Dorcas, June 8, 1766.
—Susanna, April 1, 1768.
—Wentworth, August 17, 1770.
—Solomon Lombard, February 24, 1773.
—Anna, October 31, 1775.

Stubbs, of James and Sarah.
—Huldah, Wellfleet, Aug. 9, 1762.
—Ephraim, Wellfleet, Aug. 17, 1764.
—James, Wellfleet, July 14, 1766.
—Benjamin, Wellfleet, Sept. 26, 1768.
—Moses, Wellfleet, March 8, 1771.
—John, Gorham, Nov. 27, 1774.
—Sarah, Gorham, March 7, 1778.
—Reuben, Gorham, Jan. 10, 1781.

Sturges, of Jonathan and Temperance.
—Hannah, Barnstable, Dec. 9, 1776.
—Temperance, Barnstable, Nov. 5, 1768.
—James, Gorham, Dec. 3, 1770.
—Nathaniel, Sept. 3, 1774.
—Abigail, March 4, 1777.
—David, June 27, 1779.
—Joseph, Jan. 30, 1783.
—Sarah, July 24, 1785.
—Jonathan, Feb. 6, 1788.
—Ebenezer, June 9, 1790.

BIRTHS OF CHILDREN.

Swett, of Captain Joshua and Mary.
—Clark, Falmouth, Dec. 6, 1790.
—David, June 22, 1792.
—Eliza, Jan. 3, 1795.
—John, Feb. 28, 1796.
—Simeon, Oct. 23, 1797.
—Mary, March 8, 1799.
—Hail, June 1, 1800.
Swett, of Josiah and Hannah.
—James, Aug. 21, 1784.
Swett, of Doct. Stephen and Sarah.
—Nathaniel, Oct. 9, 1771.
—Sarah, May 18, 1773.
—Nancy, Feb. 9, 1775.
—William, Dec. 6 1776.
—Hannah, March 7, 1779.
—Stephen, April 11, 1781.
Thacher, of Rev. Josiah and Apphia.
—Peter, July 13, 1769; died Aug. 8, 1769.
—Apphia, Aug. 19, 1770; died Sept. 3.
—Peter, Aug. 15, 1771; died Jan. 2, 1772.
—Apphia, March 23, 1773; died Jan. 30, 1782.
—Peter, July 21, 1774.
—Mary, May 8, 1776; died June 5, 1789.
—Faith, Oct. 30, 1778.
—John, Feb. 18, 1781.
—Apphia, April 7, 1785.
—Josiah, Jan. 21, 1789.
Thomas, of James and Charlotte.
—Peggy, Oct. 4, 1795; died 1798.
—Polly, Nov. 3, 1798.
—Sophia, March 2, 1800.
Thomas, of John and Miriam.
—Hannah, Dec. 15, 1796.
—Susanna, Feb. 22, 1799.
Thomes, Benjamin, July, 1779.
Thomes, of Charles and Anna.
—Comfort, April 19, 1785.
—James, Nov. 27, 1786.
—Susanna, July 3, 1788.
—Mary, Dec. 16, 1790.
—Job, May 19, 1792.
—Hannah, Oct. 12, 1793.
—Martha, June 17, 1795.
—Stephen, April 13, 1797.
—Joseph, Aug. 26, 1800.

BIRTHS OF CHILDREN.

Thomes, of George and Lydia.
—Betty, March 1, 1781.
—Ezra, May 18, 1782.
—Mary, Dec. 20, 1783.
—William, Feb. 13, 1787.
—Amos, Oct. 30, 1788.
—Eunice, Dec. 20, 1790.
—Mehitable, Dec. 7, 1792.
—Lydia, Nov. 22, 1795.
—Nancy, July 3, 1799.
Thomes, of Samuel and Sarah.
—Sarah, Sept. 7, 1781.
—Nathan, Jan. 25, 1784.
Titcomb, George Washington, Oct. 25, 1797.
Towell, of Thomas and Lydia.
—Sarah, Falmouth, Dec. 27, 1752.
Towle, of Jeremiah and Martha.
—Jael, May 22, 1791.
—Theophilus, Feb. 1, 1794.
—Stephen, Dec. 14, 1795.
—Martha, April 25, 1799.
Tufts, of Thomas and Fanny.
—James, Falmouth, March 7, 1771.
—John, Falmouth, Sept. 9, 1772.
—William, Falmouth, March 7, 1774.
—Isaac, Gorham, Dec. 31, 1777.
Vickrey, of David and Sarah.
—David, Dec. 25, 1780.
—Susanna, June 12, 1784.
Ward, of Joseph, Jr., and Hannah.
—Hannah Lummus, Oct. 23, 1801.
Ward, of Nathan and Isabella.
—Joseph, Jan. 3, 1800.
—Simon, Jan. 17, 1802.
Warren, of James and Martha.
—Samuel, July 14, 1775.
—Hugh, Aug. 18, 1777.
—James, Sept. 24, 1780.
—Alexander, Dec. 24, 1783. Died June 13, 1786.
—Martha, Jan. 16, 1787.
—Alexander, May 30, 1789.
Warren, of Nathaniel and Margaret.
—John, Oct. 12, 1786.

BIRTHS OF CHILDREN.

Warren, of Samuel and Sarah.
—James, Dec. 10, 1780.
—Sarah, Feb. 4, 1784.
—Mary, April 19, 1787.
—Samuel, July 16, 1789.
—Sophia, March 6, 1794.
—David, April 22, 1796.
Waterhouse, of George and Dorcas.
—Polly, March 11, 1776.
—Joseph, April 16, 1778.
—George, Nov. 3, 1780.
—Charlotte, Oct. 19, 1783.
—Betsy, July 2, 1786.
—Isaac, Nov. 9, 1789.
—David, June 4, 1793.
—Simon, Aug. 14, 1795.
—Sally, Jan. 12, 1799.
—Sargent, June 6, 1801.
Waterhouse, of Joseph and Elizabeth.
—Olley, Jan. 11, 1793.
—Zebulon, Sept. 14, 1794.
—Benjamin, Oct. 7, 1796.
Waterman, of Malachi and Mary.
—Sarah, July 22, 1785.
—Mary, Nov. 13, 1787.
—Satira, Sept. 25, 1791.
—Ebenezer, Sept. 15, 1795.
—John, June 19, 1798.
Watson, of Coleman Phinney and Patience.
—Mercy, April 27, 1775.
—Stephen Phinney, Dec. 19, 1776.
—Hannah, Sept. 28, 1778.
Watson, of Daniel and Anna.
—Martha, Feb. 10, 1791.
—Hannah White, Dec. 7, 1794.
—Daniel, Oct. 27, 1797.
Watson, of Ebenezer and Anna (Whitney, daughter of Nathan.)
—Stephen, Sept. 8, 1772.
—Joseph, July 1, 1774.
—Samuel, Jan. 31, 1777.
—Elizabeth Sept. 24, 1779.
—Stephen, May 25, 1782.
—William, April 22, 1785.
—John, Jan. 4, 1789.
—Nathan, Sept. 5, 1791.
—Eliphalet, Gray, June 14, 1797.

BIRTHS OF CHILDREN.

Watson, of Edmund and Betsy.
—Susanna, April 18, 1799.
—Polly, Dec. 3, 1801.
—John, Oct. 13, 1803.
—Naham, Dec. 1, 1804.
—Tabitha, July 23, 1807, died 1829.
—George, Feb. 18, 1812.
—Elizabeth, May 2, 1816.
Watson, of Eliphalet and Elizabeth.
—John, Sept. 23, 1741.
—Martha, Dec. 4, 1743.
—Susanna, Feb. 3, 1746.
—Ebenezer, Sept. 28, 1748.
—Coleman Phinney, Dec. 4, 1757.
—Elizabeth, Feb. 11, 1754.
—Mercy, July 12, 1756.
—Eliphalet, March 20, 1759.
—James, Aug. 13, 1761.
—Daniel, Oct. 11, 1763.
Watson, of Eliphalet, Jr., and Zipporah.
—Ebenezer, Sept. 20, 1782.
—Nathan Partridge, Aug. 21, 1788
Watson, of James and Mary.
—Mehitable, Aug. 11, 1786.
Watson, of Joel and Lydia.
—William, Sept. 29, 1798.
Watson, of John and Tabitha(Whitney).
—Mercy, Oct. 15, 1766, died Oct. 18, 1769.
—Martha, April 22, 1769.
—Edmund, Jan. 17, 1772.
—Coleman, Feb. 23, 1774.
—Miriam, Dec. 24, 1776.
—Tabitha, May 16, 1779.
—Molly, April 9, 1781.
—Sally, March 19, 1784.
—Greenleaf Clark, March 14, 1786.
—Desire, Dec. 5, 1788.
Watts, of David and Sarah.
—Samuel, Jan 3, 1782.
—David, Oct. 13, 1785.
—Betsy, Sept. 21, 1787.
Weeks, of Benjamin and Sarah.
—William, Scarboro, Aug. 25, 1790.
—Dorothy Libby, Scarboro, Feb. 25, 1793.
—Loving, June 27, 1797.
—Benjamin, Nov. 1, 1799.

BIRTHS OF CHILDREN.

Weeks, of William and Dorcas.
—Benjamin, Cape Elizabeth, March 17, 1771.
—Mary, Gorham, Sept. 30, 1774.
Wescot, of Edmund and Hannah
—James, Sept. 12, 1793.
—Elmira, Oct. 2, 1795.
—Anna, July 2, 1800.
—Charlotte, May 6, 1802.
Wescot, of Nehemiah and Eleanor.
—John, June, 9, 1797, died March 9, 1798.
—Betty, Jan. 19, 1799.
—John, April 10, 1801.
West, of Desper and Mary.
—Joseph, July 8, 1768.
—Hannah, March 5, 1770.
—Eunice, April 24, 1772.
—Eli, April 12, 1774.
—Sarah, Jan. 17, 1777.
—Lydia, Aug. 29, 1779.
Wescot, of Reuben and Abigail.
—John, April, 25, 1786.
—Reuben, July 18, 1788.
—Peggy, July 15, 1790.
—Sally, Feb. 12, 1792.
—Eleanor, March 21, 1795.
—Polly, Jan. 12, 1797.
—Betsy, Oct. 5, 1798.
Weston, of Joseph and Catherine.
—James, Feb. 22, 1758.
—Joseph, March 27, 1760.
—Zachariah, June 27, 1762.
—Thomas, Dec. 4, 1764.
—Sarah, June 14, 1767.
Weston, of Thomas and Abigail.
—Patience, Dec. 3, 1751. Died Dec. 23, 1784.
—Anna, Oct. 24, 1756.
—Abigail, April 14, 1760.
Whitmore, of Daniel and Anna.
—Rebecca, Dec. 12, 1783.
—Joseph, March 12, 1787.
—Simon, Aug. 12, 1789.
—Mary, March 17, 1792.
—Hill, Aug. 3, 1794.

BIRTHS OF CHILDREN.

Whitmore, of Capt. Samuel and Mary.
—Lydia, Aug. 5, 1765.
—Mary, Aug. 1, 1767.
—Dorcas, March, 1770.
—John, Feb. 21, 1773.
—Patience, Sept. 8, 1775.
—Elizabeth Ross, May 2, 1777.
—Samuel, April 25, 1779.
—Samuel, March 26, 1780.
—Joel, Dec. 15, 1781.
—Sarah, Oct. 31, 1783.
—Joanna, Sept. 10, 1785.
—Eunice, June 25, 1788.
Whitney, of Aaron and Jenny.
—Hannah, July 20, 1766.
—Anna, Oct. 18, 1767.
—Samuel, May 22, 1769, died Aug. 11, 1773.
—Jenny, May 10, 1771.
—Sarah, June 8, 1773.
—Susanna, Feb. 16, 1775.
—Tabitha, twin with
—Miriam, May 16, 1777.
—Betty, May 7, 1780.
Whitney, of Abel and Thankful.
—Joseph, May 1, 1760.
—Lydia, July 28, 1763, died July 1767.
—Betty, July 22, 1765.
—Sarah, twin with
—Nathaniel, June 20, 1769.
—Reuben, July 21, 1771.
—Simeon, Feb. 9, 1774.
—Susanna, April 2, 1776.
—Levy, May 15, 1779.
—Lydia, April 30, 1782.
Whitney, of Amos and Sarah (Payne), daughter of Thomas of York.
—Elias, April 12, 1763.
—Jotham, April 2, 1766.
—Ruth, June 25, 1769.
Whitney, of Asa and Patience.
—Samuel, Aug. 28, 1777.
—Benjamin, Aug. 19, 1779.
—Abigail, March 10, 1781.
—John, April 17, 1783.
—Patience, Dec. 7, 1784.

BIRTHS OF CHILDREN.

Whitney, of Asa and Phebe, his second wife.
—Anna, Jan. 25, 1786.
—Alice, April 9, 1788.
—Mary, Aug. 10, 1790.
—George, June 14, 1792.
—Hannah, Aug. 21, 1794.
—Eunice, April 30, 1796.
Whitney, Daniel and Abigail.
—Reuben, July 20, 1781.
—Betsy, Nov. 10, 1783.
—Nabbe, May 16, 1786.
—Peter, Aug. 14, 1788.
—Olive, Jan. 8, 1791.
—Mary, Dec. 31, 1792.
—Luther, May 6, 1795.
—Damaris, July 31, 1797.
—Miriam, Nov. 14, 1799.
—Happy, Nov. 16, 1802.
Whitney, of David and Hannah.
—Susanna, June 25, 1756.
—Jesse, March 28, 1758.
Whitney, of David and Abigail, his second wife.
—Joshua, Aug. 17, 1761.
Whitney, of David and Rebecca, his third wife.
—Daniel, Nov. 18, 1762.
—Hannah, June 12, 1764.
—Thomas, Oct. 5, 1765.
—Nathan, Sept. 10, 1769.
Whitney, of Isaac and Hannah.
—Barnabas, Aug. 18, 1766.
—Henry, July 24, 1767.
—Timothy, Oct. 10, 1768. Died Sept. 22, 1769.
—Sarah, Dec. 27, 1769. Died Jan. 17, 1770.
—Timothy, Aug. 1, 1771.
Whitney, of James and Deborah.
—Humphrey, April 26, 1786.
Whitney, of John and Elizabeth.
—Mary, Jan. 18, 1766.

BIRTHS OF CHILDREN.

Whitney, of Joseph and Mehitabel.
—Abel, July 24, 1767.
—Mary, July 27, 1769.
—Anna, March 17, 1774.
—Marcy, Oct. 31, 1776.
—Solomon, June 23, 1780.
Whitney, of Joseph and Betty, (Phinney) his second wife.
—Stephen, July 28, 1782.
—Joseph, Oct. 18, 1784.
—Patience, Sept. 25, 1786.
—Sarah, Dec. 3, 1788.
—Hannah, Oct. 16, 1791.
—Betty, Aprl 1, 1794.
—Peggy, Nov. 10, 1796.
—Edmund, Dec. 7, 1799.
Whitney, of Joseph Jr., and Mary.
—Vrania, May 7, 1802.
Whitney, of Micah and Hannah.
—Sally, Jan. 11, 1781.
—William, May 3, 1783.
—Lydia, Feb. 8, 1785.
—Joel, May 7, 1787.
Whitney, of Moses and Mary.
—Mary, Aug. 17, 1764.
—Lucy, Sept. 30, 1768.
—Enoch, April 8, 1773.
—Moses, Aug. 30, 1776.
—Betsey, Nov. 1, 1777.
—Richard, July 20, 1780.
—Susanna, April 9, 1783.
—Samuel, July 2, 1785.
Whitney, of Moses and Abigail, his second wife.
—Sally, Oct. 22, 1793.
Whitney, of Moses and Priscilla.
—Nabby, April 12, 1777.
Whitney, of Phineas and Anna.
—Stephen, Sept. 23, 1771.
—Crosby, Sept. 20, 1773.
—Affia, Jan. 12, 1776.
—Jonathan, Feb. 8, 1778.
Whitney, of Stephen and Martha.
—Mary, Sept. 14, 1781.
—Sarah, Nov. 4, 1783.

BIRTHS OF CHILDREN.

Whitney, of Uriel and Lydia.
—Statira, Dec. 24, 1785. Died same month.
—Mary, Jan. 21, 1787.
—Statira, Dec. 1, 1789. Died Aug 11, 1794.
—Joel, Aug. 7, 1791.
—Bewlah, June 3, 1793.
—Betsy, May 27, 1795.

Whitney, of Zebulon and Joanna.
—Abigail, Jan. 23, 1776.
—Happy, Aug. 11, 1778.
—Matte, Feb. 14, 1781.
—Rufus, April 5, 1784.
—Eli, Aug. 16, 1786.
—Eunice, Aug. 30, 1789.
—Hannah, April 21, 1792.
—Tabitha, Aug. 30, 1795.
—Elmira, July 14, 1798.

Williams, of Jeremiah and Deborah.
—Martha, March 9, 1778.
—Mary, May 24, 1782.
—Peter, Oct. 29, 1783.
—Susanna, Feb. 15, 1785.
—Lydia, Aug. 5, 1787.
—Daniel, Aug. 2, 1789.
—Joseph, April 14, 1791.
—Hannah, March 26, 1793.

Wood, of Charles and Sarah.
—Heman, Dec. 23, 1786.
—Polly, Feb. 28, 1789.
—Relief, Nov. 20, 1791.
—Mehitable, Feb. 10, 1794.
—Hannah, July 15, 1796.
—Charles, Nov. 6, 1798.
—Eliza, Nov. 18, 1802.

Wood, of William and Hannah.
—Charles, Gorham, May 31, 1767.

Wood, of William, Jr., and Polly.
—Levi, July 26, 1791.
—William, Dec. 16, 1792.
—Rachel, Oct. 27, 1794.

Wood, of William, Jr., and Mercy, his second wife.
—Anna, Aug. 16, 1797.
—Olive, Aug. 6, 1799.
—Stephen, Feb. 10, 1803.

BIRTHS OF CHILDREN.

Woodward, of John and Dorothy.
—Samuel, Dec. 1, 1791.
—Ebenezer, Oct. 6, 1793.
—Sally, Oct. 15, 1795.
—Emila, March 23, 1798.
—Eliza, April 18, 1800.
Young, of Joseph, 3d, and Lydia.
—Sally, March 15, 1794.
—Enos, July 20, 1795.
—Affia, Standish, July 17, 1797.
—Anna, Gorham, April 7, 1800.
Young, of Joshua and Sarah.
—Joshua, Wellfleet, Nov. 13, 1775.
—Benjamin, Gorham, July 21, 1780.
Young, of Solomon and Polly.
—Katherine, Nov. 21, 1797.
—Jesse, June 27, 1800.

DEATHS.

The early records of the town mention but few deaths in Gorham, the clerks evidently noting only those of their personal acquaintances. The following list is a compilation from the town and church records, newspaper notices and gravestone inscriptions:

ADAMS—In Portland, June, 1805, Benjamin Adams, late of Gorham.

ALDEN—March 23, 1804, Deacon Austin Alden, aged 75 years.

ALDEN—Sept. 8, 1831, Gardiner Alden.

ALDEN—Nov. 27, 1768, Hezekiah, son of Austin Alden, aged 16 months and 12 days.

ALDEN—Nov. 8, 1834, Josiah Alden.

ALDEN—May 18, 1780, Salome, (Lombard) wife of Austin Alden, in 44th year.

ALDEN—August, 1820, Sarah Alden.

BARON—April 14, 1803, Lydia, wife of Edward Baron and sister of William Gorham, aged 62.

BARON—July, 1769, Nathaniel Baron.

BARON—Jan. 31, 1812, Miriam Baron.

BAILEY—July 14, 1829, Levi Bailey.

BAKER—Aug. 17, 1859, Betsey C., wife of Daniel Baker, aged 83.

BAKER—June 9, 1856, Daniel Baker, aged 90.

BANGS—April 19, 1795, Lornhamah, wife of Barnabas Bangs.

BANGS—Oct. 1, 1829, Mary, wife of Herman, aged 84.

DEATHS.

BANGS—May 7, 1832, Thomas Bangs, aged 36.
BISHOP—June 8, 1830, Ezekiel Bishop.
BLAKE—Feb. 18, 1850, Deborah Blake, aged 96 years.
BLAKE—Feb. 24, 1849, Hannah Blake, aged 90 years.
BLAKE—March 21, 1826, John Blake.
BLAKE—Feb. 28, 1843, Nathaniel Blake, aged 91 years.
BOLTON—Nov. 11, 1812, Rachel Bolton.
BOWMAN—June 8, 1797, Dr. Nathaniel Bowman, killed by the falling of the meeting house steeple, aged 30 years.
BRACKETT—Aug. 30, 1826, Capt. Joshua Brackett, aged 64 years.
BRACKETT—1821, Kerren Happuch Brackett, aged 92 years.
BRACKETT—July 1, 1832, Mehitable Brackett, aged 80 years.
BRIGGS—June 10, 1783, Lucy, wife of Abiel Brackett, aged 19 years.
BROAD—April 28, 1838, Betsy Broad.
BROWN—Jan. 30, 1838, Levi Brown.
BROWN——, 1825, Sarah Brown.
BURNELL—Oct. 29, 1834, Lydia, wife of John Burnell, aged 89 years.
BURNELL—Jan. 13, 1822, John Burnell, aged 80 years.
BURTON—April 11, 1830, Mary, wife of William Burton.
CATES—March 29, 1829, Ebenezer Cates, aged 60.
CATES—March 15, 1810, Joseph A. Cates.
CHADBOURN—Aug. 17, 1817, Abigail, wife of Silas Chadbourn, aged 65.
CHADBOURN—June 15, 1823, Lieut. Silas Chadbourne, an officer in the Revolution, aged 71.
CHAMBERLAIN—Dec. 25, 1855, Benjamin Chamberlain, aged 94.
CHICK—Jan. 1820, Abigail Chick.
CLARK—Nov. 13, 1829, Mrs . Martha Clark, aged 67.
CLARK—Jan. 2, 1824, Moses Clark.

DEATHS.

Clay—Jan 9, 1846, Thomas Clay, aged 96.
CLOUTMAN— Mar. 24, 1832, Mrs. Catherine Cloutman, aged 91.
CLOUTMAN—Sept. 16, 1801, Elizabeth, wife of John Cloutman.
CLOUTMAN—Oct. 22, 1829, Timothy Cloutman, aged 91.
COBB—June 11, 1794, Elisha Cobb.
COBB—Sept. 6, 1798, Elizabeth, wife of Elisha Cobb.
COBB—April 30, 1803, Hannah, wife of Dea. Andrew Cobb, aged 60 years, 10 months, 20 days.
COBB—Aug. 2, 1833, Jedediah Cobb, aged 91.
COBB—Sept. 24, 1839, Capt. Nathaniel Cobb, aged 90.
COBB—May 17, 1830, Olive, wife of Capt. Nathaniel Cobb.
COBB—Sept. 14, 1808, Priscilla, wife of James Cobb, aged 50.
COBB—July 6, 1807, Susanna, wife of Nathaniel Cobb of Barnstable, born Dec. 24, 1718.
COBB—Oct. 18, 1840, Tabitha Cobb.
CODMAN—July 16, 1829, Elizabeth W. S. Codman.
COLE—Sept. 3, 1816, William Cole.
COLLEY—April 2, 1823, John Colley.
CRENY—Nov. 24, 1818, Louis A. Creny, aged 33. z
CRESEY—July 31, 1829, Ebenezer Cresey, aged 76.
CRESEY—July 22, 1832, Joseph Cresey, aged 79.
CROCKIT—Sept. 1798, Elizabeth, wife of Johsua Crockit.
CROCKETT—Dec. 14, 1827, John Crockett, Jr.
CROCKIT—Feb. 18, 1800, old Mr. Joshua Crockit.
CROCKIT—Sept. 25, 1801, Mary, wife of Pelatiah Crockit.
CROCKETT—Oct. 14, 1828, Peter Crockett.
CROCKET—Dec. 19, 1798, Samuel Crocket, aged 82.
CROCKETT—March 8, 1830, Samuel Crockett.

DEATHS.

CROCKITT—June 5, 1825, Solomon Crockitt.
CROSS—May 21, 1821, Lucy Cross.
CROSS—Feb. 15, 1819, Thomas Cross.
DARLING—In Portland, April 29, 1842, Anna, wife of John Darling.
DARLING—April 7, 1832, John Darling, aged 74.
DARLING—Jan. 6, 1817, Sarah Darling.
DAVIS—May 26, 1818, Allen Davis.
DAVIS—Feb. 8, 1824, Josiah Davis.
DAVIS—Nov. 23, 1823, Josiah Davis.
DAVIS—Aug. 10, 1806, Molly, first wife of Jonathan Davis.
DAVIS—Oct. 3, 1825, Polly Davis.
DAVIS—1819, Prince Davis, aged 96.
DAVIS—Aug. 8, 1824, Rhoda Davis.
DECKER—April 30, 1829, George W. Decker.
DYER—Oct. 17, 1812, Hannah, wife of Clark Dyer, and, their child likewise.
DYER—March 14, 1831, Capt. Jonah Dyer, aged 76.
DYER—April 27, 1831, Jonah Dyer, Jr.
DYER—Nov. 10, 1803, Rebecca, wife of William Dyer.
DYER—Sept. 23, 1832, William Dyer, aged 69.
EDWARDS—April 25, 1827, Dolly, wife of James Edwards.
EDWARDS—Jan. 3, 1823, Hannah, wife of Richard Edwards.
EDWARDS—Jan. 4, 1823, Richards Edwards.
ELDEN—Oct. 4, 1837, Gibeon Elden.
ELDER—April 22, 1786, Hannah, wife of Samuel Elder.
ELDER—July 15, 1795, Isaac Elder, aged 57.
ELDER—Dec. 22, 1820, Mary, wife of Simon Elder.
ELDER—Aug. 27, 1829, Mary, wife of Samuel.
ELDER—Jan. 29, 1815, Peter, son of Samuel Elder, aged 28.
ELDER—Sept. 7, 1830, Reuben Elder.

DEATHS.

ELDER—Feb. 10, 1786, Ruth, daughter of Samuel, aged 10.
ELDER—May 10, 1819, Samuel Elder, aged 71.
ELWELL—1827, Nabby Elwell.
FILES—Jan., 1816, Joanna Files.
FILES—March 3, 1833, Robert Files.
FILES—Sept. 20, 1824, Temperance Files.
FILES—March 21, 1823, William Files, aged 95.
FOGG—Oct. 23, 1829, Daniel Fogg.
FOGG—May 11, 1801, Dorcas, wife of Jeremiah Fogg, Jr.
FOGG—May 11, 1801, Martha, wife of Jeremiah Fogg, Jr.
FOLSOM—Nov. 21, 1836, Dudley Folsom.
FOLSOM—Sept. 27, 1837, Lucretia Folsom.
FOSTER—April 25, 1839, Betsy Foster.
FOSTER—1838, William H. Foster.
FREEMAN—Dec. 4, 1832, Enoch Freeman, aged 82.
FREEMAN—Jan. 22, 1805, Isabella, wife of Nathaniel Freeman, aged 30.
FREEMAN—Feb. 27, 1844, Mehitable, wife of Enoch Freeman, aged 84.
FREEMAN—Sept. 7, 1815, Sally, daughter of Enoch, aged 18.
FROST—Oct. 17, 1769, Benjamin Frost, Sen.
FROST—Feb. 14, 1849, Mary Frost, aged 91.
FROST—May, 1838, Col. Nathaniel Frost, aged 89.
FROST—Dec. 25, 1822, Rebecca Frost.
GILKEY—Nov. 27, 1827, Charles Gilkey.
GILKEY—May 19, 1817, Isaac Gilkey.
GORDON—Sept. 26, 1832, Robert Gordon.
GORHAM—April, 1788, Temperance, wife of William Gorham, aged 43.
GORHAM—1840, Temperance Gorham.
GORHAM—July 22, 1804, Hon. William Gorham, aged 61.
GOULD—Oct. 2, 1794, Betsy, wife of Nathaniel Gould.

DEATHS.

GOULD—Feb. 8, 1836, Elizabeth (McLellan) born in Cape Elizabeth Sept. 8, 1773, second wife of Nathaniel. The first wife was Elizabeth, daughter of Rev. Paul Coffin.

GOULD—Nov. 12, 1853, Nathaniel Gould, born in Ipswich, Feb. 3, 1767.

GREEN—Jan. 24, 1794, Joanna, wife of Jonathan Green.

HALL—June 36, 1835, Harriet Hall, aged 32.

HAMBLEN—April 14, 1797, Hannah, wife of Gershom Hamblen of Barnstable, aged 77.

HAMBLEN—June 3, 1774, Jacob Hamblen, aged 72.

HAMBLEN—Oct. 17, 1826, Jacob Hamblen.

HAMBLEN—Feb. 1, 1829, Jonathan, son of Samuel Hamblen, aged 48.

HAMBLEN—June 17, 1763, Joseph Hamblen.

HAMBLEN—Aug. 11, 1833, Mary, wife of Samuel Hamblen.

HAMBLEN—March 7, 1860, Polly Hamblen, aged 93.

HAMBLEN—Dec. 24, 1834, Samuel Hamblen.

HAMBLEN—Sept. 3, 1830, Sarah, wife of George Hamblen, aged 76.

HAMBLEN—At New Portland, June 13, 1805, Timothy Hamblen.

HANSCOM—March, 1832, Daniel Hanscom.

HANSCOM—July 4, 1830, Esther, wife of Humphrey Hanscom.

HANSCOM—May 30, 1820, Mary Hanscom.

HANSCOM—Feb. 20, 1830, Mary, wife of John Hanscom.

HARDING—Oct. 2, 1829, Abigail Harding.

HARDING—Feb. 14, 1861, Anna Harding, aged 93.

HARDING—March 2, 1828, David Harding, aged 97.

HARDING—Jan. 10, 1831, David Harding, Esq., aged 69.

DEATHS.

HARDING—Feb. 4, 1834, David Harding, aged 38.
HARDING—Aug. 27, 1850, Elkanah Harding, aged 91.
HARDING—July 19, 1828, Hannah, wife of Elkanah Harding, aged 50.
HARDING—Jan. 20, 1818, John Harding.
HARDING—Sept. 28, 1824, Lucy Harding.
HARDING—July 8, 1828, Lucy Harding.
HARDING—July, 17, 1828, Mary, wife of Zephaniah Harding.
HARDING—April 14, 1829, Nicholas Harding, aged 50.
HARDING—June 18, 1836, Rebecca Harding.
HARDING—At sea, June 10, 1789, Capt. Samuel Harding.
HARDING—June 4, 1804, Sarah, wife of David Harding.
HARDING—Nov. 2, 1831, Seth Harding.
HARDING—Aug. 28, 1810, Temperance Harding.
HARDING—March 24, 1816, Temperance Harding.
HARRIS—March 3, 1852, Sarah Harris, aged 97.
HARRIS—August 1, 1831, Stephen Harris.
HAWES—Dec. 2, 1806, Joseph, aged 36. (Born Dorchester.)
HAYNES—In 1811, J. Haynes, aged 90.
HAZELTON—In February, 1833, John Hazelton, aged 68.
HORTON—July 7, 1829, John Horton, aged 76.
HIGGINS—Feb. 16, 1895, Capt. Saul C. Higgins, aged 101.
HUNT—April 20, 1833, Capt. Daniel Hunt, aged 58.
HUNT—Sept. 10, 1800, Mary, wife of Ichabod Hunt.
HUSTON—Aug. 10, 1808, Betsy, wife of Simon Huston.
IRISH—Jan. 10, 1794, Jacob, son of Thomas Irish.

DEATHS.

IRISH—Apr. 1, 1816, James Irish, aged 80. He was son of James, who came from Boxfordshire, Eng., about 1710, settled first in Falmouth, and removed to Gorham, 1738.

July 19, 1828, the blowing up of the powder mill, owned by Fowler and Loomis, occasioned the death of William Moses, Noah Babb and James Green, of Standish; Josiah Clark, Jr., and Hanson Irish of Gorham, and Major Means of Windham.

IRISH—May. 13, 1825, Mary Gorham (Phinney,) wife of James Irish, aged 89.

The first white child born in town.

IRISH—Oct. 5, 1831, Rebecca, wife of James, aged 51.

IRISH—Aug. 14, 1832, Thomas Irish, aged 96 years 8 days.

JENKINS—Oct. 20, 1831, Captain Josiah Jenkins.

JEWETT—April 16, 1802, Rev. Caleb Jewett.

JEWETT—May 15, 1833, Elizabeth Jewett..

JEWETT—March 16, 1801, Mrs. Martha Jewett, aged 84.

JOHNSON—June 1805, suddenly, John Johnson.

JOHNSON—April 16, 1830, Mary, wife of Thomas Johnson.

JOHNSON—In Gorham, Jan. 17, 1828, Sampson Johnson of Brownfield.

JONES—April 13, 1802, Lydia, wife of Henry Jones.

JONES—Feb. 7, 1838, Mercy Jones.

KIMBALL—Aug. 9, 1827, Amos Kimball.

KING—June 7, 1847, James King, aged 73.

KING—In Cornish, Oct. 5, 1874, Susanna (Thompson), widow of James King.

KING—Jan. 10, 1804, Mrs. Joanna King, aged 78.

KNIGHT—Drowned at Horse Beef Falls, Sept. 9, 1797, Capt. Joseph Knight, aged 62. A widow and nine children lament their loss.

DEATHS.

KNIGHT—July 14, 1829, Joseph Knight.
LARY—Dec. 1796, Dennis Lary.
LARY—1809, Patience, wife of Dennis Lary, aged 94.
LARY—April 23, 1838, Stephen Lary.
LEWIS—April 6, 1824, Achsa, wife of George Lewis.
LEWIS—May 19, 1815, Desire (Parker), second wife of George Lewis, aged 79.
LEWIS—June 19, 1831, Elijah P., son of Rev. James and Hannah Lewis, aged 26.
LEWIS—July 24, 1819, George Lewis, aged 78.
LEWIS—At Bangor, Oct. 9, 1822, Hon. Lothrop Lewis, aged 58.
LEWIS—Sept. 26, 1807, Margaret, daughter of George Lewis, aged 25.
LEWIS—Sept. 27, 1804, Mary, daughter of George Lewis, aged 25.
LEWIS—Apr.15, 1807, Tabitha, (Longfellow), wife of Lothrop Lewis, aged 33.
LIBBY—Dec. 28 1855, Ann Libby, aged 93.
LIBBY—Nov. 17, 1839, Daniel Libby.
LIBBY—April 17, 1781, Joab Libby.
LIBBY—Feb. 5, 1801, Joseph Libby.
LIBBY—Oct.11, 1831, Mrs. Martha Libby.
LIBBY—Dec. 28, 1810, Pelatiah Libby.
LIBBY—August, 1840, Phebe Libby.
LIBBY—April 19, 1833, Sarah, wife of Richard Libby, aged 79.
LINCOLN—Dec. 15, 1828, Eliza, wife of Samuel Lincoln.
LINCOLN—1828, Sarah F. Lincoln.
LINCOLN—Oct. 26, 1831, Thankful Lincoln.
LITTLE—March 26, 1809, John P. Little, (Lawyer), aged 36.
LOMBARD—Jan. 13, 1880, Charity, wife of Samuel Lombard.
LOMBARD—Sept. 18, 1808, James Lombard.
LOMBARD —Jan. 24, 1820, Jedediah Lombard, aged 92.
LOMBARD—Sept. 18, 1823, Lydia, wife of Richard Lombard, aged 83.

DEATHS.

LOMBARD—July 18, 1803, Polly, wife of Ephraim Lombard.

LOMBARD—Oct. 21, 1825, Col. Richard Lombard, aged 84.

LOMBARD—1781, Hon. Solomon Lombard.

LONGFELLOW—Dec. 7, 1817, Ann Longfellow, aged 36.

LONGFELLOW—July 5, 1804, Catharine, daughter of Stephen Longfellow.

LONGFELLOW—Aug. 12, 1830, Patience, wife of Stephen Longfellow, born Dec. 5, 1745.

LONGFELLOW—Oct. 13, 1818, Col. Samuel Longfellow, aged 29.

LONGFELLOW—May 28, 1824, Hon. Stephen Longfellow, born Aug. 13, 1750.

MANN—Aug. 14, 1795, Hannah, wife of Daniel Mann, aged 21.

MARBLE—Jan. 17, 1830, Anna, wife of Daniel Marble, aged 86.

MARCH—March 29, 1823, Col. James March.

MERRILL—July 11, 1830, Daniel Merrill, aged 85.

MERRILL—June 22, 1830, Dorcas, wife of Daniel Merrill.

MERRILL—Feb. 24, 1828, Joanna, wife of Col. Seward Merrill, aged 30.

McCORSON—In Standish, Oct. 14, 1820, Rev. James McCorson, one of the first Freewill Baptists in Gorham, was born in the old fort on Fort Hill, March 7, 1750. His father was William McCorson (or McCorrison) from England.

McDONALD—Sept. 14, 1828, Sarah McDonald.

McLELLAN—May, 14, 1821, Abigail, wife of Dea. James McLellan.

McLELLAN—Oct. 4, 1779, Capt. Alexander McLellan.

McLELLAN—June 4, 1813, Chloe D., wife of Alexander McLellan.

McLELLAN—Jan. 2, 1787, Elder Hugh McLellan, aged 77.

DEATHS.

McLELLAN—At Havana, of yellow fever, Aug. 21, 1803, Hugh McLellan, aged 24.

McLELLAN—Jan. 15, 1792, Dea. James McLellan.

McLELLAN—Sept. 23, 1812, Rebecca, second wife of Samuel McLellan, aged 25.

McLELLAN—Oct. 13, 1823, Rebecca, wife of William McLellan, aged 81.

McLELLAN—Nov. 23, 1830, Capt. Robert McLellan.

McLELLAN—July 22, 1825, Capt. Samuel McLellan.

McLellan—Sept. 12, 1810, Sarah B., first wife of Samuel McLellan, aged 25.

McLELLAN—Jan. 13, 1829, Thomas McLellan, aged 75.

McQUILLAN—Sept. 19, 1821, Olive McQuillan.

MILLER—Jan. 8, 1812, Jane, wife of Samuel Miller.

MILLER—May 25, 1820, John Miller.

MILLER—March, 20, 1820, Margaret, wife of John Miller, father and mother of Samuel Miller.

MORRIS—March 8, 1821, Ann Louisa Morris.

MOSHER—Oct. 23, 1815, Abigail, wife of James Mosher, aged 74.

MOSHER—Oct. 2, 1834, James Mosher, aged 99 years, 2 months, 8 days.

MOTLEY—Sept. 7, 1855, Ellen Waite Motley, aged 40.

MOTLEY—Feb. 27, 1848, Capt. Robert Motley, aged 75.

MURCH—April 27, 1803, Deborah, wife of Samuel Murch.

MURCH—Nov. 18, 1831, Mrs. Hannah Murch.

MURCH—Oct. 20, 1829, Margery Murch.

MURCH—Dec. 6, 1831, Mary, wife of Matthias Murch, aged 71.

NASON—Mar. 5, 1837, Abigail Nason, aged 98.

NASON—Oct. 14, 1831, Lewis Nason.

NASON—May 13, 1833, Uriah Nason, aged 91.

NEWBEGIN—Dec. 17, 1799, John Newbegin.

DEATHS.

NEWCOMB—Apr. 29, 1796, Thankful, wife of Enos Newcomb.

NOYES—Jan. 15, 1807, Rev. Jeremiah Noyes.

PAINE—Nov. 12, 1831, Mrs. Anna Paine, aged 77.

PAINE—Mar. 13, 1829, Elizabeth Paine, aged 76.

PAINE—June, 1810, Richard Paine.

PAINE—Nov. 2, 1817, Sarah, wife of William Paine.

PAINE—Jan. 20, 1827, William Paine.

PATRICK—Mar. 2, 1841, Betty Patrick, aged 90.

PATRICK—Mar. 15, 1830, Charles Patrick, aged 85 years.

PERKINS—Aug. 6, 1796, John Perkins.

PHINNEY—Mar. 19, 1822, Abigail, daughter of James Phinney, aged 16.

PHINNEY—Oct. 26, 1840, Abigail Phinney.

PHINNEY—January, 1806, Daker Phinney.

PHINNEY—Dec. 15, 1808, Col. Edmund Phinney, aged 85.

PHINNEY—Aug. 19, 1800, Eliza, daughter of James Phinney, aged 5.

PHINNEY—Aug. 6, 1795, Elizabeth, wife of Col. Edmund Phinney, aged 65.

PHINNEY—Mar. 15, 1833, Elizabeth, wife of Benjamin Phinney.

PHINNEY—Oct. 5, 1793, Heman, son of Nathaniel and Mary Phinney, aged 11 months.

PHINNEY—Aug. 23, 1806, James, son of Decker Phinney, aged 22.

PHINNEY—Oct. 18, 1834, James Phinney, aged 93.

PHINNEY—Jan. 13, 1860, James Phinney, aged 93.

PHINNEY—Dec. 29, 1780, Capt. John Phinney, the first settler in the town of Gorham, aged 86.

PHINNEY—May 3, 1815, John Phinney, Jr., aged 83.

PHINNEY—Sept. 22, 1828, Joseph Phinney.

DEATHS.

PHINNEY—Dec. 29, 1836, Lucy, second wife of James Phinney, aged 82.

PHINNEY—Dec. 16, 1784, Martha, wife of Capt. John Phinney, aged 86.

PHINNEY—Sept. 3, 1816, Martha, wife of James Phinney, aged 76.

PHINNEY, June 19, 1796, Deacon Stephen Phinney.

PHINNEY—Nov. 27, 1800, Stephen Phinney, aged 38.

PLAISTED—Nov. 27, 1855, Andrew Plaisted, aged 93.

PRENTISS—Jan. 10, 1815, Samuel Prentiss.

PRENTISS—1802, Sargent Smith, son of Samuel Prentiss, postmaster at Gorham, on his passage from Surinam, aged 20.

PRENTISS—Feb. 23, 1826, William Prentiss.

POMEROY—Sept. 11, 1831, Catherine, wife of Rev. Thadeus Pomeroy.

PURRINTON—June 27, 1758, Deacon Humphrey Purrinton, aged 56.

PURRINTON—Feb. 7, 1836, John Purrinton, aged 39.

PURKIS—June 8, 1828, Martha, wife of Rev. John, aged 35.

RAND—April 28, 1818, Grata Rand,

REYNOLDS—Sept. 4, 1826, Sylvester, son of Solomon, of Southport,, N. Y., aged 29.

RICE—April 26, 1827, Mary, wife of John, aged 36.

RICE—Dec. 4, 1868, Mary D., widow of Joseph Rice, and daughter of Nicholas Harding, in Paris, Me., aged 74.

RICH—March, 1791, old Mr. Lemuel Rich. His wife died the same month.

ROAK—Sept. 7, 1831, Margaret Roak, aged 86.

ROBIE—1832, Harriet Robie.

ROBIE—Feb. 23, 1811, Lydia Brown, wife of Toppan Robie.

ROBIE—Oct. 22, 1838, Deacon Thomas S. Robie.

ROBIE—Jan. 14, 1871, Hon. Toppan Robie, aged 89.

ROBIE—April 23, 1828, Sarah T., wife of Toppan Robie, aged 35 years.

DEATHS.

ROBINSON—Oct. 9, 1830, Samuel Robinson.

ROSS—Oct. 19, 1833, Hannah Ross, aged 98.

ROSS—1780, James Ross.

ROUNDS—Oct. 23, 1835, Samuel Rounds, aged 55.

SAWYER—Oct. 31, 1823, Elizabeth Sawyer.

SCAMMON—Oct. 3, 1825, Polly, wife of Edward.

SHAW—Oct. 15, 1806, Betsy, wife of Enoch Shaw, aged 21.

SMITH—Feb. 15, 1820, Mary Longfellow - (Lewis,) wife of Jacob S. Smith, aged 23.

SMITH—Oct. 23, 1829, Nancy, wife of Steven Smith.

SNOW—Jan. 9, 1832, Dorcas, wife of William Snow, aged 79.

SNOW—March 5, 1837, Jane Snow, aged 102.

SNOW—Jan. 24, 1832, William Snow.

STARBIRD—Oct. 26, 1835, Moses Starbird.

STAPLES—Feb. 22, 1835, Ai Staples.

STAPLES—June 15, 1839, Nancy, wife of Samuel Staples, aged 65.

STAPLES—Feb. 4, 1837, Samuel Staples, aged 71.

STEPHENSON—Dec. 21, 1836, Almira S. Stephenson.

STEPHENSON—Aug. 6, 1824, Neptune Stephenson, colored man of Col. Tynge, aged 44.

STEPHENSON—March, 19, 1831, Capt. Stephen Stephenson, aged about 50.

STONE—Feb. 25, 1836, Damoris Stone.

STONE—April 12, 1834, Jonathan Stone.

STONE—Oct. 7, 1833, Mary Stone.

STONE—June 3, 1830, Moses Stone.

STUART—Jan. 4, 1758, Susannah Stuart, aged 56.

STUART—April 17, 1776, Capt. Wentworth Stuart, of small pox, at siege of Boston.

STURGIS—Dec. 6, 1821, David Sturgis, aged 48.

STURGIS—May 11, 1834, Jonathan Sturgis, aged 91.

DEATHS.

STURGIS—Nov. 26, 1824, Temperance Sturgis.

STURGIS—Sept. 9, 1859, widow, aged 92 .

SWETT—Sept. 3, 1828, Hannah, wife of James Swett.

SWETT—April 20, 1851,Captain Joshua Swett, aged 90.

SWETT—Oct. 15, 1858, Nancy Swett, aged 92.

SWETT—June 2, 1812, Sophia, wife of James Swett.

TIBBETS—Oct. 8, 1831, Mrs. Sarah Tibbets.

THACHER—Dec. 25, 1799, Hon. Josiah Thacher.

THACHER—1807, Josiah Thacher.

THOMAS—June 16, 1818, Ezra Thomas, aged 36.

THOMAS—April 28, 1821, George Thomas, aged 76.

THOMAS—May 13, 1822, Lydia, wife of George Thomas, aged 77.

THOMAS—May 20, 1846, Sarah, wife of Samuel Thomas, aged 83.

THOMAS—March 3, 1798, Samuel Thomas, aged 51.

THOMAS—Nov. 3, 1798, Samuel Thomas, aged 51.

THOMES—Dec. 16, 1790, Thomas Thomes.

THOMES—Dec. 13, 1786, Mary, wife of Thomas Thomes.

TOWNSEND—Sept. 27, 1804, Alanson Townsend, the schoolmaster, late of Hopkinton, Mass., aged 20.

TYLER—Sept. 26, 1822, Daniel Tyler.

TYNG—Oct. 25, 1831, Mrs. Elizabeth Tyng, aged 80.

TYNG—Dec. 10, 1807, of apoplexy, Col. William Tyng.

WALKER—July 15, 1828, Elizabeth, wife of John Walker, aged 59.

WARD—Sept. 6, 1831, John Ward.

WARREN—April 16, 1821, James Warren.

WATTS—Jan. 11, 1784, Sarah, wife of Capt. David Watts, and only daughter of Josiah Davis, aged 20.

WATSON—Jan. 3, 1838, Betsey Watson.

DEATHS.

WATSON—1828, Dea. Eliphalet Watson, aged 98.

WATSON—In Norway, 1814, Eliphalet Watson.

WATSON—Oct. 26, 1834, John Watson, aged 93.

WATSON—Oct. 28, 1829, Tabitha Watson.

WATSON—Sept. 13, 1831 Tabitha, wife of John Watson, aged 86.

WEBB—April 8, 1810, Jonathan Webb. aged 55.

WHITMORE—Nov. 17, 1800, Elisha Whitmore.

WHITMORE—Dec. 12, 1831, Elisha A. Whitmore.

WHITMORE—Dec. 21, 1797, Joseph, son of Elisha whitmore.

WHITMORE—Dec. 21, 1808, Capt. Samuel Whitmore.

WHITMORE—Aug. 28, 1808, Col. Samuel Whitmore, lawyer, aged 28.

WHITNEY—Feb. 14, 1828, Mrs. Betsy Whitney, aged 69.

WHITNEY—May 27, 1828, Damaris S. Whitney.

WHITNEY—Feb. 14, 1828, Elizabeth Whitnyy.

WHITNEY—Sept. 3, 1834, Louisa Whitney.

WHITNEY—July 30, 1831, Mary Whitney, aged 32.

WHITNEY—1804, Nathan Whitney, aged 95.

WILLIAMS—Dec. 4, 1797, Capt. Hart Williams.

WILLIAMS—Dec. 16, 1751, Deborah Williams, aged 93.

WILLIAMS—Sept. 11, 1800, Martha, wife of Capt. Hart Williams.

WISE—Jan. 25, 1799. Elizabeth, widow of Dr. Joseph Wise, and daughter of Moses Pearson, aged 77.

ERRATA.

Transposition of lines have occasioned a few errors, those in publishments and marriages are easily detected as all are entered under the names of both parties.

In "Birth of Children" substitute as follows:

PEABODY, of Ebenezer and Sally.
—Kendal Osgood, Dec. 20, 1792.
—Ebenezer, Sept. 3, 1794.
—Louisa, Aug. 10, 1796.
—Caroline, July 9, 1798.

PERKINS, of John and Lois (Harding).
—Lucy, Feb. 16, 1770.
—Mary, Nov. 10, 1774.

PENFIELD, of Nathan and Molly.
—Benjamin, Sept. 10, 1801. Died Aug. 31, 1802.
—Sarah, Sept. 29, 1803.
—Ann, Sept. 8, 1805.
—Patience, Nov. 20, 1807.
—Elizabeth, March 14, 1810. Died next year.
—Benjamin, March 29, 1812.
—Charles, June 20, 1814.
—Hannah P., Sept. 10, 1815.
—Elizabeth H., Aug. 5, 1818.
—Louisa, March 1, 1821.

www.ingramcontent.com/pod-product-compliance
Lightning Source LLC
Chambersburg PA
CBHW070739160426
43192CB00009B/1504